Homeschooling and Libraries

Homeschooling and Libraries

New Solutions and Opportunities

Edited by VERA GUBNITSKAIA *and*
CAROL SMALLWOOD

Foreword by Lesley S.J. Farmer

McFarland & Company, Inc., Publishers
Jefferson, North Carolina

ISBN (print) 978-1-4766-7490-2
ISBN (ebook) 978-1-4766-3923-9

LIBRARY OF CONGRESS AND BRITISH LIBRARY
CATALOGUING DATA ARE AVAILABLE

Library of Congress Control Number 2020008487

Front cover photograph by George Muresan (Shutterstock)

Printed in the United States of America

*McFarland & Company, Inc., Publishers
Box 611, Jefferson, North Carolina 28640
www.mcfarlandpub.com*

Table of Contents

Foreword

Lesley S.J. Farmer

As a YA librarian in suburban Philadelphia more than thirty years ago, I remember teaching homeschooled youth weekly, collaborating with their teachers and families. Homeschooling is increasingly popular now for a variety of reasons: personal, ideological, physical, and educational. Similarly, the need for librarians to help homeschool families become information and media literate is more important than ever. Thus, this volume fills an important and timely gap. More specifically, this edited collection includes various librarians' voices, which underscores the diverse needs and learning experience of homeschooled youth.

As each homeschool child has a unique background, needs assessments are vital for effective library service. Part I explains why families choose to homeschool and lists several learning opportunities for them, mentioning the library's potential role and relevant resources. The second essay in this part focuses on African American needs for culturally relevant library practices. The third essay uses a system-wide approach to assessing and meeting the library needs of homeschool families.

Homeschooled youth often experience special circumstances, which inform library services. Part II addresses the unique needs of atypical populations. The essay by Sarah M. Sieg and the one by Angiah Davis and Cordelia Riley focus on children with disabilities and learning differences, listing targeted services and relevant resources. Barbara J. Hampton's essay addresses the needs of gifted and talented youth, including support for their families.

Part III focuses on specific library programs; case studies provide a rich lens for analysis. The essay by Sarah Polace, Amy Dreger and Meghan Villhauer, and the one by Leah Flippin, include several types of program ideas, and suggest ways to plan and publicize these programs, including modifications to address the needs of this population; and Holly S. Hebert's essay highlights the social aspects of these programs. The essays by Leslie Paulovich and Casey O'Leary and Ruth Szpunar both provide case studies of specific initiatives for homeschoolers: a homeschool hub and programs to revitalize the homeschool community.

While public libraries tend to serve as the main source for information literacy instruction, other informal educational settings also teach homeschooled youth important information literacy concepts. Part IV showcases other library settings where homeschool families are supported: academic libraries for parenting advice, services and expanded collections; school libraries for socialization; and special resources in various types of libraries.

1

Part V focuses on one important aspect of library services for homeschooled youth: finding resources. Essays in this part describe general strategies for best practices as well as funding sources, strategies for financing, and examples of grant-funded initiatives.

Part VI recognizes that homeschooled youth might become librarians themselves: from a personal narrative to a systematic outreach initiative to recruit librarians within groups of homeschooled learners. Maryann Mori's essay details in-service training of a youth services librarian to gain competency in direct instruction for homeschoolers.

Part VII presents points of view of family and library trustee stakeholders, by collecting and analyzing data from surveys, direct observation, and interaction.

Part VIII, titled "Infinite Possibilities," offers three promising library practices for homeschooled youth: free play, role-playing games, and keeping current on homeschooling issues. Details include case studies of planning, implementation, and modifications.

In sum, librarians need to know their communities and reach out explicitly to homeschooling families. As with other populations, librarians need to assess the needs of homeschooling families and identify ways to provide physical and intellectual access to library resources. Such librarian efforts need to build relationships and address the needs of the entire family. Indeed, libraries, especially public libraries, serve as a social safety net for homeschooling families.

To this end, this book offers varied proven practical insights into providing relevant resources and services to homeschooling families. Not only should librarians consider this population part of the community that they serve, but they should realize the unique support role they can play in educating, informing, and inspiring homeschooling families who have unique needs that are often overlooked by the rest of their communities.

Lesley S.J. Farmer, a professor at California State University (CSU) Long Beach, coordinates the librarianship program and manages CSU's ICT Literacy Project. She chairs CSLA's Committee on Standards Integration and the Research TF. Her research interests include digital citizenship, information literacy, and data analysis. She is the author of Managing the Successful School Library *(ALA, 2017).*

Preface

Parent-led homeschooling is the choice of many families in the United States and other countries. *Homeschooling and Libraries* is a collection of 27 original essays from U.S. practicing academic, public, school, and special librarians, LIS faculty, library administrators, and board members. The contributors provide creative, practical, how-to essays and case studies depicting a variety of specific programs, projects, aspects, and angles of the library role and impact on homeschooling process, families, and students, within the library walls and beyond. Ideas that can serve as a basis, a foundation, to incorporate into an MLIS course, a human resources or an organizational plan, as well as a kick-start to personal career goals planning were also included.

PART I

Assessing Needs

Understanding Homeschoolers

CASEY CUSTER *and* REBECCA RICH-WULFMEYER

The authors of this essay are librarians who homeschool their children. Between them, they have eighteen years of homeschooling experience. In this essay, they bring insight into the values and motivations of homeschoolers, clarify misconceptions, and offer tips for how libraries can serve this community.

Reasons why families choose to homeschool are as varied as the colors of the sea, and yet, there are some common themes of what is important to them. The family unit, learning opportunities, socialization, socio-emotional development, experiences for their children, post-high school opportunities, homeschooling economically, and expert help are some areas of importance. Religion is significant to some homeschoolers. Curricula and homeschooling styles are central to daily life.

The Family Unit

As it is for most parents, the family unit is of great importance to homeschooling families. One reason why some parents choose to educate their own children is to be more involved with and have more control over the details of their children's lives, including their education, and have closer relationships with them. Learning and experiencing life together through studying academics, enjoying literature, volunteering in the community, and traveling build breadth and depth of experiences that help keep family ties close. A few programs that homeschoolers participate in through their local libraries include family yoga, movie nights, pajama story times, and board game meet-ups. While homeschoolers enjoy family events during daytime hours when most other children are at school, evening programs also benefit everyone and encourage extended family or working parents' participation.

Learning Opportunities

Homeschooling affords families time to study academic subjects, but also presents chances to discover so much more. The opportunities for learning outside of the classroom abound for the homeschool family. There are myriad museums to wander, natural areas to adventure, and cities to explore. The school field trip is no longer a once-a-year endeavor. Homeschooling can be a bit of a misnomer—some homeschoolers call themselves "out-schoolers" where some of the academic subjects are done on the way to living life through car-schooling. These learning opportunities, outside of a traditional classroom or even the home classroom, include life skills, socio-emotional development, and entrepreneurial prospects. Homeschoolers want to know what places and events are available in their area, such as:

- museums
- industry tours
- farms
- natural areas
- concerts
- people to show/teach their craft (e.g., woodworking, knitting, cooking)
- fairs
- art shows
- rodeos
- author visits
- cooperatives
- entrepreneurial fairs
- maker spaces/fairs
- theater (e.g., children's plays, musicals).

Homeschoolers want to learn aside from books, curriculum, online classes, and worksheets. In-person, hands-on learning rounds out their education. The library can help in several ways. Library staff can curate lists of local educational, enrichment, and entertainment opportunities to be experienced in and out of the library. For example, for families learning engineering, a list of related events, programs, and places would be valuable. Or course, libraries have early literacy programs, teach technology skills, provide education enrichment activities, and offer general learning support. Below are specific examples of programs of interest to homeschoolers offered by the Austin Public Library, Texas. Note that only some of the programs are marketed specifically to homeschoolers.

- Homeschool Support Group: a monthly meetup event for parents
- Not Back to School Day: a fall event to introduce homeschool families to library services, collections, and programs
- Savvy Shopper: a tween program taught by the Financial Literacy Coalition of Central Texas
- Kids Create: a weekly tween program during which different STEM projects are offered, such as coding with Ozobots
- Beginning Sewing Class for adults and teens: learn a new life skill and express creativity
- Chess Club: for teens and adults
- Board with Books: a board gaming meetup event for youth of all ages
- Youth Art: an exhibition of artworks created by homeschooling, private, and public school students grades K–12.
- College Admissions 101: part of a college planning series.

Homeschoolers are interested in conducting their own programs as well, so making spaces available for homeschoolers to offer their own classes meets a great need. Programs that they might be interested in presenting are similar to ones the library offers, but are nuanced to meet specific learning, cultural, or religious needs. Examples are foreign language story-times, movie watching meet-ups, math clubs, and attachment parenting meetings.

Socialization

Socialization means interacting with other people and learning to behave in socially acceptable ways. Social skills development is tied to other areas of a child's development. Through social interactions children learn skills that will be with them their entire lives.

Socialization is important to homeschoolers. They participate in activities outside of the home and with people other than their family members. Although many homeschoolers learn from their mothers at their kitchen tables, this is not the only activity in their days. Communities offer a variety of rich opportunities that homeschoolers take advantage of. Homeschoolers attend library programs, museum tours, park playdates, movies, concerts, chess clubs, sports leagues, dance classes, geography clubs, birthday parties, marriages, funerals, and holiday celebrations with family, friends, and strangers. Homeschoolers do not just hang around with other homeschoolers. Their social groups include children from private, public, and hybrid schools, too. They also participate in the commonplace activities that take them into the community, like buying groceries, shopping for new clothes at the mall, and checking out books from the library.

Homeschoolers frequently interact with the world as a family unit. In a day, they will socialize with people of both genders, as well as adults, teens, tweens, children, and babies. They learn how to communicate and work with many kinds of people.

It is important to note that some homeschoolers have trouble with social skills, just as some children who attend public and private schools do. Also, some homeschoolers left the school environment because of negative social experiences with students, faculty, staff, and/or administrators at the schools. Through the homeschooling, parents aim to develop and improve social skills and confidence by exposing kids to neutral or positive interactions with adults and children.

Libraries can help these families by providing the same level of acceptance and helpfulness that they offer to other customers. Some traditional library programs can be nuanced for homeschoolers, as well as adjusted to fit homeschoolers' daytime schedules. Some favorites that attract homeschoolers and fit the bill for social activities include book groups, teen advisory boards, movie nights, board game meet-ups, manga, or cosplay events. Teens especially enjoy having the space to meet for study, educational play, video games, and hanging out.

Socio-Emotional Development

Relatedly, being together as a family allows for a daily focus on socio-emotional development. Often near their children, parents can correct behavior immediately and work towards solutions that are constructive versus punitive. Children also learn to interact with adults and peers in a variety of environments. Parents help develop habits now that serve children throughout their lives.

Not only is the library a wonderful place for homeschoolers to gather (and socialize!), but also care taken with library policies and procedures can aid parents, and not just homeschool parents, with socio-emotional development. Self-checkout kiosks invite children to take responsibility for the items they are checking out of the library while learning independence. Libraries can also take advantage of the time homeschooling families have to give. Giving time to volunteer, and to volunteer together as a family meets the needs of the library and family's need for socio-emotional growth. Children's librarians can take care to make themselves available not only to parents' questions, but even the smallest of children's questions and concerns. Scavenger hunts in the library are passive edutainment programs that serve several purposes: they make libraries fun; teach library skills; develop independence by encouraging a child to explore the library on his/her own, tell the desk staff that the puzzle is complete, and ask for a prize. For a young or shy child, these things can be a big deal.

Experiences for Their Children

Taking field trips, traveling, volunteering in the community, trying new foods, learning new life skills, working, and getting involved in new activities are important to many homeschooling families. Experiences reinforce lessons learned in academic subjects, build critical thinking and problem solving skills, develop healthy self-confidence, and contribute to rich life. Art exhibitions and science fairs in the library allow children opportunities to show off their hard work and talents and to experience authentic work of other contributors. Cultural events such as author talks and concerts, while great for all patrons, can be especially marketed towards homeschoolers. Having curated lists of field trip opportunities, field trip programming, or helping homeschoolers create their own group field trips with the help of knowledgeable library staff enrich the lives of homeschoolers.

Post–High School Opportunities

A microcosm of the larger schooled population, homeschoolers also value opportunities post–high school for a college education, a trade education, military experience, or any other choice that fits the needs, wants, and personalities of the children. Because parents are with their children a good deal of time, they can deeply get to know each of them, nourish their individual gifts, and guide them towards adulthood. Libraries can provide space, programs, services, and collections to serve this demographic. For example, they offer print and electronic examination study guides, including those for academic, vocational, and military tests. Homeschoolers use meeting rooms to study and practice for college entrance examinations. Experts offer programs on various topics geared towards the college bound, such as planning for college; selecting a college; writing application essays; applying for financial aid and scholarships; and choosing a major. For example, Boston Public Library's "Beyond High School" webpage directs people to resources related to college, vocational school, and scholarships and financial aid (Boston Public Library, n.d.).

For the college-bound students, providing SAT practice tests, or even having SAT practice tests in a meeting room, is something parents can do and proctor themselves. A library can invite an expert to come in to help parents prepare transcripts. Without a high school counselor to guide parents and teens, the library becomes a place for research in applying for college and financial aid. Librarians and staff can bridge the gap by providing information or hosting classes that point parents and teens in the right direction, especially through databases and other library resources that are often overlooked.

For students on vocational paths, libraries can host career days, give resume help, or provide exam study guides. ASVAB test study materials may be another resource that would interest this group of patrons.

Homeschooling Economically

The costs of homeschooling vary widely based upon the style of homeschooling being used and a family's personal finances. If a family has either a more relaxed or an individualized approach to homeschooling, then obtaining curriculum piecemeal, either used or new, may be their choice. To keep costs lower, homeschoolers purchase used materials at yard sales, thrift stores, swap meets, and used bookstores. Additionally, they borrow materials from libraries and friends. Families who want a more structured or classroom-style learning environment may choose to purchase entire sets of package curricula, which can be costly. A curriculum set could include a teacher's manual, student workbook, tests, special projects, corresponding textbooks and novels, mathematics manipulatives, and other supplemental materials.

Libraries can curate lists offering general tips and suggestions specific to their locales for homeschooling economically. Such tips, which are especially useful to people new to homeschooling, include purchasing materials from used curriculum sales and stores; using free resources online; utilizing free curriculum on the Internet such as the websites Khan Academy and Easy Peasy All-in-One Homeschool (see details below); participating in learning co-ops; buying school supplies at the beginning of the school year or the end of the school year when their prices are discounted; swapping curriculum, books, and games; volunteering with an organization to get a discount; networking to find people willing to mentor one's child in a specific topic; attending programs offered by parks and recreation departments; and using resources offered by libraries.

All library services, collections, programs, and facilities contribute to the homeschooling family's ability to educate economically. Library staff and/or parents can utilize library space to organize curriculum fairs with samples to review and experts to discuss options. Other ideas are:

- curriculum sales
- used book sales
- free magazine exchange
- resource center with "try before you buy" resources
- educational games
- math manipulatives free homeschool curricula catalogs (offer selection of three or more to avoid appearing to recommend or favor one company over another).

Examples/Resources

Easy Peasy All in One Homeschool. 2018. "Complete. All Free Curriculum." https://allinonehomeschool.com/.

Khan Academy. 2018. "You Can Learn Anything." https://www.khanacademy.org/.

Expert Help

Homeschooling one's children is a beautiful, rewarding, and sometimes daunting experience. Parents have many decisions to make and rely upon the advice of experts to guide their decisions. Of the many issues parents have to navigate, some of their concerns include needing to know the legalities of homeschooling in their states; determining academic curricula to use; understanding how to track their children's progress; selecting which extracurricular activities to involve their children in; ensuring that social needs are met; providing opportunities for children to exercise; and facilitating downtime. For religious homeschoolers, it is important that faith-based knowledge and values are imparted. Homeschoolers look to other homeschoolers for guidance through email lists, conferences, Facebook pages, meet-up events, cooperative learning experiences, and other avenues. Other community members are sources of information for homeschoolers, including library employees. Libraries can additionally supply homeschool support groups; knowledgeable and non-judgmental staff; information literacy sessions (tours, technology sessions, basic library skills, outreach, early learning workshops); signs in libraries indicating where homeschool resources are; books published by authors about homeschooling, education, and parenting topics; printed information guides on topics related to homeschooling compiled by library staff, such as getting started in homeschooling, homeschooling groups in your area, homeschooling sports and academic teams, record keeping.

The Religious Spectrum

In the homeschooling community, religious belief is a true spectrum. Many homeschoolers value this variety. For example, in one homeschooling co-op in Austin, Texas, two members are atheist. One of those atheists participates in another co-op that rents facilities from a local church. The other atheist refuses to participate in any activity that takes place in any church. Of the other members, one is Mormon, a few are Jesus-following Christians, and others are agnostic. Yet the value held for true connected relationships among moms, kids, and families tops religious views. The co-op meets weekly for 4–6 hours of time together outside, as well as additional days celebrating birthdays, enjoying smaller meetings, camping, and exploring through field trips.

There are some co-ops that require members to sign statements of faith, as well as co-ops that are staunchly secular, prohibiting any faith-based curriculum or proselytizing. Again, the choices available (to choose one side, another side, or to mix it all up) are an important part of the homeschooling process.

Library workers can remove unproductive stereotyped notions about homeschoolers by getting to know their communities. It is fortunate when one works and lives in an area where people of all religious beliefs place the value of people, friendships, and the core of homeschooling above any religious differences. When community acceptance is not there, libraries and their staff can work on bridging the gaps that may exist in areas where one type of religious belief seems dominant in the homeschool community. The religiously neutral programs and services that libraries offer as a matter of course are helpful. Collections reflecting a variety of points of view are important. And having staff members and volunteers who are tolerant, accepting, understanding, neutral, and non-judgmental, regardless of individual beliefs, is paramount.

Curricula

Homeschoolers are as varied as the people on our planet, and, therefore, the curricula they use or do not use are just as varied. Many homeschoolers use more than one curriculum. Some unschoolers do not use organized curricula. If you have ever been overwhelmed by the amount of books and publishers at a library conference, you can imagine parents' overwhelm at the amount of available curricula for homeschooling. As homeschooling gains popularity, resources for homeschoolers will also continue to expand. Homeschoolers love the choices available to them, and when librarians and staff are cognizant of the choices, they can develop collections, curate resource lists, and point homeschooling patrons in the right direction as part of a readers' advisory and reference interactions. In addition to traditional library offerings of books and databases, libraries can have circulating and non-circulating curricula plus educational aids like math manipulatives, educational games, puzzles, microscopes, and maker kits.

Some Common Homeschool Styles

The type of curricula selected is related to the style of homeschooling practiced. Below is a discussion of nine styles of homeschooling along with associated resources.

Traditional

Traditional homeschoolers typically follow in the "tradition" of the more common government-schooled children in that they may use the school schedule to follow and may replicate at home the same type of curriculum used in public schools. Some companies provide all content areas with full lesson plans and textbooks in one package. The assignments and content emulate what students might also be doing in a traditional public school.

Examples/Resources

Abeka. 2018. "Inspire Learning & Teach Biblical Values with Comprehensive Christian Curriculum." https://www.abeka.com/homeschool/.

Calvert Education. 2018. "Why Calvert." http://www.calverteducation.com/.

My Father's World. n.d. "Inspiring Excellence in Family Education." Accessed August 28, 2018. https://www.mfwbooks.com/.

Oak Meadow. n.d. "Your Trusted Partner in Joyful Learning: Experiential

Education for Curious and Creative Learners." Accessed August 28, 2018. https://www.oakmeadow.com/

Time4Learning. 2018. "Time4Learning and Fun for Everyone: Online Education for Pre-K–12th." https://www.time4learning.com/.

Classical

While there are many Christian classical homeschoolers, secular classical home-schoolers also embrace the kind of education that chases after truth, beauty, and goodness. The trivium is a main component of a classical education that says that children learn in three stages of development (grammar, logic, rhetoric).

Examples/Resources

Classical Conversations. 2018. "Classical Christian Community." https://www.classicalconversations.com/.

Memoria Press. 2018. "Classical Christian Education for All Ages." https://www.memoriapress.com/.

Thomas Jefferson Education. 2012. "Leadership Education." https://www.tjed.org/.

Well-Trained Mind. 2016. "Well Trained Mind." https://welltrainedmind.com/.

Eclectic

Homeschoolers who choose a little of this and a little of that to best fit the interests and needs of their children are often called eclectic or relaxed homeschoolers. They pick curriculum in each of the subjects they choose to study—it may be an online class in literature for one child and a tutor for English for another. Or it may look like one company's math program, a separate company's history line-up, and field-trips all year for biology and nature study. Books, videos, audiobooks, periodicals, databases, music CDs or other resources obtained from the library are integral parts of the eclectic teaching style.

Subject/Content

Within each of the subject areas such as reading, math, science, and history, various companies provide complete content curriculum. When homeschoolers pick and choose their curricula, they consider themselves eclectic—choosing the very best things that fit just right for their individual families.

Examples/Resources

Math

Art of Problem Solving. 2018. "Art of Problem Solving." https://artofproblemsolving.com/.

Math-U–See. 2018. "Math-U–See." https://www.mathusee.com/.

Right Start Mathematics. 2018. "Helping Children Understand, Apply and Enjoy Mathematics." https://rightstartmath.com/.

Saxon Math. 2018. "Saxon Math." https://www.hmhco.com/programs/saxon-math

Singapore Math. 2018. "Singapore Math Inc." http://www.singaporemath.com/.

Teaching Textbooks. n.d. "Teaching Textbooks: The Award Winning Homeschool Math Curriculum." Accessed August 28, 2018. http://www.teachingtextbooks.com/.

Reading

All About Learning Press. 2018. "All About Reading." https://www.allaboutlearningpress.com/all-about-reading/

Barton Reading. 2016. "Barton Reading & Spelling System." https://bartonreading.com/.

Shurley Instructional Materials. 2017. "Shurley Instructional Materials." https://www.shurley.com/.

Science

Apologia Educational Ministries. 2018. "Apologia." https://www.apologia.com.

Time4Learning. 2018. "Time4Learning and Fun for Everyone: Online Education for Pre-K–12th." https://www.time4learning.com/.

History

Bauer, Susan Wise. (multiple dates). *The Story of the World* series. The Well Trained Mind Press.

Beautiful Feet Books. 2018. "Beautiful Feet Books: History Through Literature." http://bfbooks.com/.

The Mystery of History. 2018. "The Mystery of History." https://www.themysteryofhistory.com/.

Languages

Duolingo. n.d. "Learn a Language for Free. Forever." Accessed August 28, 2018. https://www.duolingo.com/.

Guarnera, Anne. n.d. "Language Learning at Home." Accessed August 28, 2018. https://languagelearningathome.com/.

Mango Languages. 2018. "Mango Languages." https://mangolanguages.com/.

Simon & Shuster. 2018. "Pimsleur." https://www.pimsleur.com.

Philosophical

Educational philosophers such as Charlotte Mason, Maria Montessori, Rudolph Steiner, John Taylor Gatto, and John Holt inform the way homeschoolers go about their days of educating and living.

Charlotte Mason was a Christian, forward-thinking educator in Britain at the turn of the 20th century who believed that children are born persons and that all children could and should be educated regardless of class. Her philosophy of education is outlined in her own words through six volumes and her ideas made a comeback in the 1990s with the publication of *For the Children's Sake* by Susan Schaefer Macaulay highly regarded as the starting place for learning about Charlotte Mason and her educational philosophy (Macaulay 1984). While there are Charlotte Mason Schools, a great many homeschoolers study her works and implement her philosophies with their own children. Today, there are a great many resources, blogs, books, conferences, that educate parents in the Charlotte Mason way, and many curricula that incorporate her philosophy.

Examples/Resources

AmblesideOnline. 2018. "AmblesideOnline Curriculum." https://amblesideonline. org/.

Andreola, Karen. 1999. *A Charlotte Mason Companion*. New York: Charlotte Mason Research & Supply.

Charlotte Mason Institute. 2018. "Charlotte Mason's Alveary." http://www.char lottemasoninstitute.org/alveary-membership/.

Macaulay, Susan Shaeffer. 1984. *For the Children's Sake*. Westchester, Illinois: Crossway Books.

While myriad Montessori schools abound, there are many families who take her ideas and use them in their homeschools, especially in the pre-school and early elementary years. Maria Montessori, MD, "was the first woman to receive an MD degree in Italy. She has inspired people around the world, for over 100 years, basing education on observation of children to discover their needs, rather than on a curriculum. She discovered that long periods of concentration on purposeful work involving both the mind and the body (real work, not TV or computers) heals the child mentally and physically" (Montessori 2018). Homeschoolers enjoy Montessori's methods because at the practical sense, much of her philosophy can be incorporated in the home.

Examples/Resources

Montessori: The International Montessori Index. 2018. "Montessori Homeschooling." Accessed August 8, 2018. http://www.montessori.edu/homeschooling.html).

Stephenson, Susan Mayclin. 2013. *Child of the World: Montessori, Global Education for age 3–12+*. Michael Olaf Montessori Company.

_____. 2013. *The Joyful Child: Montessori, Global Education for Birth to Three*. Michael Olaf Montessori Company.

Some homeschoolers enjoy studying Rudolf Steiner and use Waldorf-at-home curriculums to follow the philosophy. According to Christopher Bamford and Eric Utne, "Waldorf Education has its roots in the spiritual-scientific research of the Austrian scientist and thinker Rudolf Steiner (1861–1925). According to Steiner's philosophy, the human being is a threefold being of spirit, soul, and body whose capacities unfold in three developmental stages on the path to adulthood: early childhood, middle childhood, and adolescence" (Bamford and Utne 2018).

Examples/Resources

Dancy, Rahima Baldwin. 2012. *You Are Your Child's First Teacher*. Berkeley, California: Ten Speed Press.

Christopherous Homeschool Resources. 2018. "Waldorf-Inspired Parenting and Education." https://www.christopherushomeschool.com/.

EarthSchooling. 1994. "About Earthschooling." https://earthschooling.info/the bearthinstitute/.

Enki Education. n.d. " Enki Education." Accessed August 27, 2018. http://www. enkieducation.org/index.htm.

Lavender's Blue Homeschool. 2018. "Lavender Blue's Homeschool." https://www. lavendersbluehomeschool.com/.

Nielsen, Melissa. n.d. "Waldorf Essentials." Accessed August 27, 2018. https://www.melisanielsen.com/wehome.

Oak Meadow. n.d. "Your Trusted Partner in Joyful Learning: Experiential Education for Curious and Creative Learners." Accessed August 28, 2018. https://www.oakmeadow.com/.

Road Schooling/World Schooling

Roadschoolers take their curricula on the road, usually for an extended period of time. Traveling families can be eclectic, use unit studies, be classical, or use other styles. Some unschool, using the travel as life-schooling and education for their children and themselves. As space is usually tight, online programs or loaded-up kindles make learning while traveling easier. While traveling, roadschoolers take advantage of their home library's digital resources by being able to access them anywhere; additionally, thoughtful libraries have policies that encourage out of town patrons to take part in their programming and give them the ability to both use and check-out resources. Here are some resources for road schooling/world schooling.

Examples/Resources

Boyink, Michael, and Chrissa Boyink. 2015. *Homeschool Legally While You Travel in the USA.* Kindle.

Lainie and Miro. 2018. "Raising Miro." http://www.raisingmiro.com/about.

Miller, Hannah. n.d. "Edventure Girl." Accessed August 27, 2018. http://www.edventuregirl.com/.

Oxenreider, Tsh. 2017. *At Home in the World: Reflections on Belonging While Wandering the Globe.* Nashville, Tennessee: Thomas Nelson.

Unit Studies

Home educators who use unit studies begin with a subject in mind, and then build the entire curriculum around that subject. For example, if a unit study was being conducted around space, the literature, history, science, art, music, etc., would all have to do with space. Parents can collaborate with librarians in putting together unit studies for their children; finding resources across subjects to fit a unit study theme is both challenging and exciting. Homeschoolers often look for a culminating event that pulls all of the learning together and parents can either use the library for space for such an event or work with the librarians to bring an event that would have broad appeal to the larger community.

Project-Based Homeschooling

Project-based learning is everywhere, and homeschoolers lead the charge in creating the project-based learning environments for their students. Project-based learning is an approach built upon a problem or challenge that the student is interested in. Project-based learning blends the traditional subjects of school with professional behaviors or life skills a student may use as an adult to create a well-rounded authentic experience, often with results that continue to flame interest for years to come. A project can be a personal challenge, community matters, or global humanitarian issue. The emphasis is on the process of problem solving while building life-learner skills. Lori Pickert's book *Project Based Homeschooling: Mentoring Self Directed Learners* is an excellent resource to have in any library's collection.

Examples/Resources

Pickert, Lori. 2012. *Project Based Homeschooling: Mentoring Self-Directed Learners.* CreateSpace Independent Publishing Platform.

Unschooling/Radical Unschooling

No matter the name—unschooling, child-led learning, delight directed learning, self-directed learning—these homeschoolers use life and living to inform their families. Just as an adult might research a topic of interest until it is exhausted, a parent or caregiver allows the child the same freedoms and often helps by pulling books of interest or guiding to appropriate websites. Unschooling families may still take advantage of curriculum when the child shows interest in a certain subject or curiosity. Unschooling families love the library, often taking advantage of programs, meet-ups for socialization, and of course, collections resources. The library is the perfect place for those deep-dive learning sessions that drive both children and parents. The following list includes books and blogs that staff can recommend to patrons who are interested in unschooling.

Examples/Resources

Dodd, Sandra. 2009. *Sandra Dodd's Big Book of Unschooling.* New Mexico: Lulu.com.

Gatto, John Taylor. 2010. *Weapons of Mass Instruction: A Schoolteacher's Journey Through the Dark World of Compulsory Schooling.* Gabriola Island, B.C.: New Society Publishers.

_____. 2012. *Dumbing Us Down: The Hidden Curriculum of Compulsory Schooling.* Gabriola Island, B.C.: New Society Publishers.

Gray, Peter. 2013. *Free to Learn: Why Unleashing the Instinct to Play Will Make Our Children Happier, More Self-Reliant, and Better Students for Life.* New York: Basic Books.

Hewitt, Ben. 2014. *Homegrown: Adventures in Parenting, Unschooling, and Reconnecting with the Natural World.* Boulder, Colorado: Roost Books.

Holt, John. 1991. *Learning All the Time.* Ticknall: Education Now.

_____. 1995. *How Children Fail.* Reading, Massachusetts: Addison Wesley Publishers.

_____. 2009. *Teach Your Own: The John Holt Book of Homeschooling.* Cambridge, Massachusetts: Da Capo Press.

_____. 2017. *How Children Learn.* New York: Da Capo Press.

Llewellen, Grace. 1998. *The Teenage Liberation Handbook: How to Quit School, Get a Real Life and Education.* Eugene, Oregon: Lowry House.

Weldon, Laura Grace. 2015. *Free Range Learning: How Homeschooling Changes Everything.* Prescott, Arizona: HOHM Press.

Conclusion

Homeschoolers are varied in their reasons, educational styles, and curricula used, but they share some values and behaviors. Misconceptions about homeschooling exist and the authors are confident that this essay will help dispel some of them. It is not necessary for homeschoolers to replicate public school at home in order for their children to be well-educated. The authors hope libraries/library workers will use this information to develop or improve programs, services, and collections for homeschoolers. They encourage library workers to get to know the homeschoolers that use their libraries.

Works Cited

Bamford, Christopher, and Eric Utne. n.d. "History of Waldorf Education: A Brief Overview." Accessed August 27, 2018. https://waldorfeducation.org/waldorf_education/rudolf_steiner_waldorf_history.

Boston Public Library. n.d. "Beyond High School." Accessed August 27, 2018. https://www.bpl.org/beyond-high-school.

Montessori: The International Montessori Index. 2018. Accessed August 8, 2018. http://www.montessori.edu/homeschooling.html.

Pickert, Lori. 2012. *Project Based Homeschooling: Mentoring Self-Directed Learners.* CreateSpace Independent Publishing Platform.

African American Parents
and Decision-Making

CLARISSA WEST-WHITE *and* AMANDA WILKERSON

This essay explores, examines and identifies ways in which African American home-schooling parents as decision makers co-construct equitable educational experiences through library services. There is a common appraisal in education which suggests that libraries provide rich educational resources in an accessible manner. While there is no question that libraries are indeed resource rich, there is little information regarding the review of how people of color, specifically African Americans, utilize available resources for the educational benefit of their families, or how they arrive at their decisions not only about homeschooling, but also about curriculum, programming, and library selection. The essay chronicles how five Black families, with accounts of three of them presented in detail, have approached reaching and teaching their children through library sources; it also investigates choices using a framework for decision makers. Through the process of knowledge transfer, this case study, also informed by a phenomenological framework, describes efforts to support homeschool children and provides guiding principles and integrated approaches other homeschoolers can utilize to increase academic success. The significance of this essay lies in the reconceptualization of educational practices that can be replicated both by other homeschool families and professional library staff. This approach also aims to encourage responsible innovation through the development of engaged culturally relevant practices that seek to decrease and eliminate barriers which might contribute to class issues in education.

While challenges persist in collecting precise data on homeschooled students (school-age children ages 5–17 in a grade equivalent to at least kindergarten and not higher than 12th grade who receive instruction at home instead of at a public or private school either all or most of the time), their number continues to increase (Redford, Battle and Bielick 2017). Although Whites (83 percent) continue to constitute the majority of those homeschooled, Blacks comprised 5 percent during the 2011–12 school year. Since 1999, the number of Black children homeschooled increased from 84,000 to 132,000 in 2016 (McQuiggan and Megra 2017). Current trends indicate that the African American homeschool population will continue to grow, spurring questions regarding the decision-making practices used to incorporate public libraries into the planning and design of their curriculum.

Framework for Decision Makers

According to Brighouse et al. (2016), what matters most in people's lives is the creation and distribution of opportunities for them to flourish and possessing the educational goods—knowledge, skills, dispositions, and attitudes—to make life flow (4). Decision makers, therefore, have to supplement the directive "promote flourishing" with a set of intermediate educational aims (e.g., educational goods) they desire (5). For African American homeschooling parents, it is critically important that curricular decisions are aligned not only with their desire to create a brighter, healthier path for their children, but also with providing opportunities for themselves and their children to flourish. Brighouse et al. (2016) propose a four-part procedure for making decisions that explicitly combines values: (i) identify the values in play, (ii) identify the key decisions relevant to those values, (iii) evaluate the options in the light of the pertinent values, and (iv) choose the option with the best expected overall outcome (18–20). Unfortunately, little is known about the decision-making practices of African American homeschooling parents. The long established norm that homeschooling parents turn to their local libraries for assistance drives researchers' inquiry into unmasking whether or not this is true of African American parents who homeschool, and how a library's use influences their decision making.

Libraries as Schools During the Jim Crow Era

As schools failed to serve the needs of African Americans at the close of Reconstruction, African American parents believed public libraries could potentially pick up the slack (Knott 2015, 52). African American homeschooling parents that we interviewed cited echoing sentiments as rationale for withdrawing their children from public education or keeping them home altogether. It is a given that much like most homeschooling parents, African American parents naturally look to public libraries in planning curriculum for their children. A 2003 NCES report showed that the majority of homeschooled families (78 percent) used the public library for sources of curricula or books for their children's home education. This appears in keeping with findings from Scholastic's *Kids and Family Reading Report* (2019) which reported that Black children have fewer books in their homes than white, multi-racial, Asian, or children of other racial backgrounds. Similar to the late 1800s, even when librarians encouraged and supported reading, library use was hampered not only by access and unequal and separate facilities, but also by low literacy skills, an outcome of state and local policies that underfunded public education for African Americans (Knott 2015, 226). The situation was particularly dire for people who could not afford to move to towns with accessible libraries or to enroll in private schools with longer academic years and adequate educational equipment (226). Although African American patrons can now obtain a library card and enjoy its privileges, a number of those interviewed for this study stated that they became card-carrying members of numerous libraries (where permitted) in order to find adequate resources, collections, and programming that intentionally reflected, included and celebrated their culture. In some areas, parents are either not allowed to become members of libraries outside of their zip code or must pay an annual fee to reap the benefits of membership. Like many Southern institutions that implemented Jim Crow practices, public libraries struggled with equitable funding and access. Birthed from a system that maintained separate facilities, libraries were equally complicit in ensuring that African American libraries retained woefully inadequate resources and collections, and maintained collections that kept African Americans in their place. For example, some public libraries would not include books about the "emancipated Negro" or simply banned books that portrayed the races as equal (Knott 2015, 202). Others would not allow African American librarians to work at their facilities and mandated that they staff African American libraries instead. In our current investigation, several parents raised concerns about the lack of African American librarians in the libraries they frequent. Droughts of diversity in librarianship is an ongoing, well documented issue within the profession. Parents explain that this drought forces them to "library hop" to locate diverse programming and robust collections. According to Scholastic's *Kids and Family Reading Report* (2019), the desire for more diverse books is strongest among Black children and their parents, and parents of Black and Hispanic children are most likely to look for diverse book characteristics than other parents. Jim Crow era libraries found other ways to discourage African American patronage, especially during the Great Migration: a stern expression on a white librarian's face, an all-white staff and clients, the request for a Black library user to sit at a table where white users wouldn't sit (Knott 205, 208). Present day portrayals of libraries maintain this facade of whiteness, whether in movies, on television, or in literature; the face of libraries retain a look of homogeneousness that needs restructuring.

Despite concerns, a Pew Research Center survey reveals that African Americans utilize their public libraries more than other ethnic minorities (Horrigan 2016). The telephone survey of 1,601 Americans ages 16 and older conducted from March 7 to April 4, 2016, shows that 52 percent of African Americans surveyed had been to the library within 12 months. Blacks were also more likely to say that libraries should definitely provide more comfortable spaces for working and reading, buy 3-D printers and other high-tech tools, and move books and stacks to provide other kinds of working spaces (Horrigan 2016, 10). The survey also found that library users who take advantage of libraries' computers and internet connections are more likely to be young, black, female, and lower income (Horrigan 2016, 13). Black families are also most likely to look for books that include diverse storylines, characters or settings. They report that locating these diversity-related characteristics is as important as finding books that help their child imagine and understand other people's lives and make their child think and feel; as well as having books that inspire kids to do something good or make them laugh (Scholastic 2019). The Scholastic report also finds that more than 80 percent of both kids and parents across all income levels and children's ages enjoy read-aloud time; however, lower-income families read aloud less frequently than families with incomes of $100,000 or more and are also less likely to have received information on the importance of reading aloud when their children were babies.

The use of technology affords many homeschooling parents and their children access to information, programs, activities, lessons, and apps at varying grade and ability levels, but a recent study highlights the concerns of relying on eBooks and online texts to stimulate children's desire to read. African American homeschooling parents who opt to use online reading apps and eBooks may reduce their child's chatter and collaboration. Munzer et al. (2019) conducted a study of 37 parent-toddler pairs reading a book in 3 formats—enhanced eBooks including sound and animation, basic eBooks without sound and animation, and print—and discovered that parent-toddler pairs verbalized less with eBooks and participated in lower collaboration. In other words, there is no substitution for the printed text. Parents interviewed intuitively made the connection between printed texts and increased engagement during reading time. However, not all best practices can be implemented based on intuition. Research findings may be unknown to African American homeschooling parents, who may not have access to academic journals or time to scour them for sound practices. For this reason, libraries naturally understand the importance of prominently incorporating findings in their planning, but do always feature them in and around the library and on social media. Children's and youth librarians are adept at remaining abreast of the latest research and intentionally devising programming to encourage participation.

The more frequently African American homeschooling parents visit the library, the greater are the chances that they will incorporate the library in their planning and use it to strengthen their teaching skills. Libraries provide a number of print-rich and electronic displays throughout their facilities encouraging families to participate in activities and programs. One interviewee (Personal Communication 2019) stated that she has yet to incorporate the library into her planning and visits the library once a month. This may indicate that she is unaware of the many services her library offers and thus does not see it as a curricular resource. Identifying such patrons will assist libraries in targeting African American homeschooling parents and establishing practical solutions, such as hanging a poster in the children's section that directs homeschooling parents to the children's librarian for more information, or providing a list of specifically curated resources. African American homeschooling parents included in our study who went to the library weekly, tended to see the library as a tool to strengthen their own and their children's skills, and were more aware of programming, activities, and events.

Our Study Participants: Critical Narratives

Let's examine the experiences and perceptions of Black homeschooling families and their usage of public libraries. Our work with families provided us with rich and robust understanding of their educational practices allowing us to share collected critical narratives. While presenting the data, we will discuss our participants' approaches to teaching and homeschooling. To begin, in our study, we found that the practices of Black homeschooling families were informed by reproducing knowledge in digestible bites. Furthermore, through the narratives of our participants, we learned that homeschooling was interconnected with reinforcing educational values which focused on the interviewees' cultural frame.

Sheila's Story: Co-Op and Cultural Cohesion

For Black homeschooling families, homeschooling is a non-traditional educational approach. Moreover, homeschooling classroom experience was not a fluid or linear process. On the contrary, it was a confluence of understanding academic behavior and unpackaging the information to fit the needs of their children. As such, we found that learning was an introspective process tool that appealed to the social, emotional, and cultural underpinnings of the learner. Such is the case with Sheila (all narratives are signed with a pseudonym for privacy).

As a self-described biracial African American and Native American parent, Sheila pointed out key differences in teaching approaches which she felt were suitable for her children. She is the parent of four and the lead educator for three of them with their ages ranging from eight to thirteen. The wide age range meant that Sheila had to find ways to adjust and adapt her instructional processes.

On one hand, she wanted to educate her children alongside the work of educational professionals. Her desire was to create alliances and partnerships with the traditional in-school teachers. On the other hand, she understood that in order to build the academic skills of her children, she could not solely rely on the traditional model of instruction.

Her desire to closely work with her children was also motivated by harsh societal realities. As a mother of Black boys, she was keenly aware of the dehumanizing statistics regarding boys of color, and the unprecedented rise of the school-to-prison pipeline; that was not what she hoped her children would encounter in their educational process. Given the multidimensional factors that could either help or hinder her children's success, she has firmly inserted herself in the middle of their learning. This approach was not easy. Sheila is a hard working mother who provides for her family by offering her artisan skills to a number of county agencies and nonprofits. To foster a sense of cohesion between pedagogical interventions and societal concerns, she organized her teaching approach utilizing a co-op system.

> I am their model. The teachers are just partners for the success I want my children to have. What I do is build in more resources for my children. School is always in session. We learn things at home. I model my expectations for education in the home environment. They see me reading so I know that they will read. They are living examples of what education means to me.

Sheila's comments illustrate her desire to find a balance between being an active contributor to her children's learning success and being overly reliant on one educational approach. Her comment about the home school being always in session doesn't impede her children's ability to learn and play. Sheila finds organic ways to incorporate learning into fun and activities which keep her children engaged and interested. She gave an example of working with her son to enhance his knowledge of applied science.

> We may use any activity to learn. Going on a bike ride. Working in a garden. In other words, I reinforce learning. I remember one day my son had to do a science experiment. What we did was work on unclogging my sink that was stopped up. We got baking soda and vinegar to unclog the sink. So basically reinforcing education, but making it make sense in real life because sometimes kids get distracted because they don't know how the information is going to help them. [Let] them understand how they can use things they learn to help at home or community environment.

Essentially, Sheila helps her children make sense of learning by being practical. She inserts abstract knowledge into a concrete activity to foster a learning environment that promotes a desire for her children to learn and takes an active role in teaching her children, facilitating learning support.

Sheila's methodology for incorporating public library resources was very telling. She had specific materials in mind that she desired to share with her children and encountered challenges in locating them. We now had a better understanding of what she wanted, how she obtained resources, and how inadequate was the supply of culturally relevant services she utilized. Therefore, Sheila was forced to find alternative ways to locate books influenced by her culture: "I get [some] books from home library ... [and I also] like to get material or books from museums like the Black Heritage Museum."

Sarah's Story: Library as Co-Teacher

Sarah and her children visit the library weekly, and it plays a large role in their lives. She began with "Mommy and Me" classes and uses the library to check out books for research papers and reports as well as for pleasure.

> There used to be a couple of homeschool programs at our main library. They offered homeschool art classes and drama classes. While my oldest was in those programs, my youngest would work on the computer using the programs they had on their system that we didn't have access to at home.

Sarah and her husband, African American college graduates in their 40s, researched homeschooling prior to becoming parents. Although Sarah acknowledges that mounting data regarding declines in Black boys' performance as early as third grade and personal observations of how Black males were treated when she served as a substitute teacher influenced their decision to homeschool, it was not until they found themselves in a community that lacked ethnic diversity that they solidified their decision. "I have homeschooled from the very beginning.... When we moved to an area that had so few Black people it was listed as 'other' in some reports, I decided it was a sign for us to homeschool our little boy."

Sarah's self-evaluation of her curricular decisions is indicative of homeschooling parents' and the self-talk that occurs, whether they are a part of a larger homeschooling network or not. "I hope their education is affected in a positive way. Some days I question if I am pushing too hard or not hard enough. If the program we chose is the right one." She takes advantage of the parent and teacher resource section of the library to find books that offer teaching tips and activities, and states that it would be difficult to fulfill her parent-teacher role without the library.

Homeschooling communities provide support that enhances parents' curriculum decisions and combat isolation and lack of socialization. Sarah appreciates the network of Black tutors and parents who pour themselves into their children's education daily to ensure their success. "We have a very strong homeschool tribe. We are a part of two communities that support our educational efforts. Watching these [parents] makes me push through when I have moments or seasons [when] I want to throw in the towel or question myself."

Homeschooling parents also struggle with homeschool tensions and boundaries. Determining the start and end times of the day, breaks, and vacations vary. "I hope homeschooling makes us closer as a family, but wearing a dual hat can be hard. Sometimes I struggle shutting it off. I have been known to bring school work on vacations. At least now I don't make them do it once we arrived at our destination."

Worth noting is how the increased incidences of racist class practices have encouraged parents to homeschool.

> The more I watch the news and see all these babies committing suicide due to bullying the stronger I feel homeschooling is our best option. Then you have the racist teachers ... you see Black kids being insulted and degraded by their teachers. Teachers making their Black students run from their white classmates in slave reenactments. Teachers calling Black students roaches and rats. I could never put my kids in that kind of environment.

Effective communication between libraries and patrons assures that stakeholders are informed of changes in programming and personnel as they impact planning and the decision-making process of homeschooling parents. Being able to utilize free programming and classes are paramount to homeschooling parents on a limited budget.

> I would love for them to bring back the homeschool classes. They already have art classes for the younger kids; why throw away the homeschool art class. My understanding is [that] the teacher who taught it left. Not sure why the person who replaced her could not offer the class for homeschoolers.

When decisions aren't communicated, parents are left to guess why changes are made and may mistakenly assume that other factors are in play. Likewise, it is important to gauge homeschool families' availability and make an effort to offer programs to meet their needs.

> They offer so many classes in the evenings, it would be great to see some of those classes offered during the day and opened up for homeschoolers. I have gone to the library and walked past computer rooms just sitting empty. Open those rooms up to homeschoolers, especially those who take online classes. Some don't have internet or a personal PCs at home, they could have homeschool co-op classes in there.

Sarah takes full advantage of the services, resources, and programming her library offers. Besides checking out books, including those on CDs, eating on site, and reserving study rooms, they use the online catalog and place holds on books. "The fact that I don't have to travel all around the city to pick up books saves me time and gas." However, the library does not allow advanced reservations of study rooms, which makes conducting a lesson nearly impossible if no room is available. The library could also extend special privileges (e.g., no due date, books due at the end of the term) to homeschool families that it offers to other patron segments, as well as reevaluate its late fee policies.

Denise's Story: Library Hopper

Denise, a married African American mother of two, decided, with encouragement from her husband, to homeschool her children when they were 6 and 11 after they attended a number of public and private schools. Due to the lack of ethnic diversity in schools among students, teachers, and administrators, and the isolation her daughter experienced in kindergarten, Denise felt that homeschooling was her only option and does not regret the decision. "When you see your kids thriving along the way, you know that you made a good decision to do what you are doing for them."

Denise realized that in order to teach her children, she had to unschool them, break habits, and understand how each of them learned best.

> And so I had to find out what [subject] areas [best] fit both of my children. I had to find out which areas [were their strengths that] would make them thrive and want to learn more and [make it] easier for me [to know what was] best for them and easier for them to learn.

Homeschooling provides her children the opportunity to decide their own interests and projects, to be a co-teacher in their learning. They are able to learn about culture within an African American inspired curriculum, and interact with other African American homeschool groups. "I am able to use their likes and strengths to catapult and organize lesson plans so that they have fun while learning." Home groups are also important in establishing connections and a sense of community.

> You have to build a village and that village needs to understand that your kids' education is important even though they are not going to a regular brick and mortar school. Everything lies on you, the books they need, science projects. Even extracurricular activities, you have to take them to those.

"We can't do homeschooling without a library." Denise uses the library not only as a resource to support her curricular planning, but also as a safe space and refuge when she needs to plan out the school year. She admits that although she could use her computer or cellphone to locate information, there is something about a physical book that sets the agenda and assists in validating information.

"The library has free resources that we can use. When my son has a paper to do, I want him to be able to find information within a book and reference books in his paper. [Kids] need to know that books are important and be able to navigate through them." The library serves other functions for Denise and her family. In addition to providing volunteer hours for her son, it serves as her teacher aide.

> We do five weeks on, one week off. During my week off I plan, and it gives the kids breaks because we don't break when everybody else breaks. I take three days of that week and I go by myself and I take all of my resources with me and I plan exactly what my children are gonna be doing the next five weeks.

The library provides free art and engineering projects. When Denise encounters a problem, librarians are quick to come to her aid. However, she patronizes several libraries, partly because some of the librarians have been reassigned. She noticed a lack of ethnic diversity in the library staff and its impact on acquisition and collections.

> There was an African American lady who worked at the library. During February she would display things about HBCUs, but they moved her and now we don't have that in the library. Even though the librarians there love my children, they don't create African American displays anymore. They may have a shelf that says African American, but they don't have anything behind it. There is no substance. It's just there because they know African Americans will be coming in there.

Not only does Denise believe there should be more African American librarians, she believes that librarians should "know more than just how to keep the library. They should educate themselves on African American history and history in general. You can't have history without African Americans." She also suggests offering additional computer classes; adding more books on African American history and art; increasing the number of programs offered for teens; advertising, utilizing, or rethinking centers if they are not being used; providing puzzles; having a designated homeschool librarian and homeschool textbooks repository; reducing annual fee to use neighboring libraries outside of home county; and providing game check outs, especially, chess. "So if the library has a spot called The Hub that's supposed to be for teenagers, but you never see any kids or anything [advertised] about it, emphasize it, make them aware. You've got to make things a little bit more interesting so that the kids will want to engage."

Recommendations

Libraries have become the go-to teaching assistance tool for African American homeschooling parents. Parents are able to think critically about the direction of their curriculum, research and write short and long terms, and design lesson plans and activities in conjunction with the library's offerings. Libraries across the nation have open robotics labs, Wi-Fi hotspot lending programs, maker spaces, creation labs, recording studios, open data, unique collections, and health care programs that lend equipment (Gascó-Hernández 2019), that can be marketed to African American homeschooling families as a way to bridge the curriculum gap that parents experience. It was clear from parents' responses that they either utilize or plan to utilize public libraries in their homeschool curriculum and personal planning. The echoing request is for libraries to frequently survey parents and provide workshops, activities, and events specifically designed for African American homeschooling families such as homeschool gatherings so that families can meet and share resources, and even a home delivery service. It would also assist African American homeschooling parents greatly if librarians hosted planning workshops to assist them in locating current research regarding effective curriculum design. Focusing on crafting an Afrocentric curriculum, as this was often cited as primary reason for homeschooling, would further the library's reach and use in African American homeschooling communities, which continue to grow.

One respondent suggested American Sign Language classes, art, and subjects that appear in traditional school settings as electives. Many libraries provide such offerings, but they may not take into consideration African American homeschooling parents who do not live in major cities. Rural African American homeschooling parents' school days may consist of a combination of online distance learning, at-home education, and part-time attendance at a brick-and-mortar school, which requires reliable transportation, and libraries to have more flexible hours. It is therefore important for libraries to gauge African American homeschooling families' availability and interests, and provide a calendar of events in advance for parents to plan their curriculum. The key goal of public libraries is to meet the needs of their patrons. Based on interviews, those living in large urban areas have more access and an easier time receiving the services they need to educate their children at home. Those in smaller, rural counties not only have to travel for similar services, but also find the lack of African American library professionals which is indicative of a larger problem, noticeably fewer collections, displays, and programming about African Americans.

WORKS CITED

Brighouse, Harry, Helen F. Ladd, Susanna Loeb, and Adam Swift. 2016. "Educational Goods and Values: A Framework for Decision Makers." *Theory & Research in Education* 14 (1): 3–25. doi:10.1177/1477878515620887.

Gascó-Hernández, Mila. 2019. "7 Unexpected Things That Libraries Offer Besides Books." *The Conversation.* April 1. https://theconversation.com/7-unexpected-things-that-libraries-offer-besides-books-111895.

Horrigan, John B. 2016. "Libraries 2016." *Pew Research Center.* September. http://www.pewinternet.org/2016/09/09/2016/Libraries-2016/.

Knott, Cheryl. 2015. *Not Free, Not for All: Public Libraries in the Age of Jim Crow.* Amherst: University of Massachusetts Press.

McQuiggan, Meghan, and Mahi Megra. 2017. "Parent and Family Involvement in Education: Results from the National Household Education Surveys Program of 2016 (NCES 2017–102)." *U.S. Department of Education. Washington, D.C.: National Center for Education Statistics.* http://nces.ed.gov/pubsearch/pubsinfo.asp?pubid=2017102.

Munzer, Tiffany G., Alison L. Miller, Heidi M. Weeks, Niko Kaciroti, and Jenny Radesky. 2019. "Differences in Parent-Toddler Interactions with Electronic Versus Print Books." *Pediatrics* 143 (4). doi:10.1542/peds.2018-2012.

Redford, Jeremy, Danielle Battle, and Stacey Bielick. 2017. "Homeschooling in the United States: 2012 (NCES 2016–096REV)." *National Center for Education Statistics, Institute of Education Sciences, U.S. Department of Education.* Washington, D.C.

Scholastic, Inc. 2019. *Kids and Family Reading Report: Finding Their Story Reading to Navigate the World.* New York: Scholastic Inc.

Specialized Services Supporting Local Homeschool Communities

CARA CHANCE *and* MEREDITH CRAWFORD

Public libraries and homeschoolers share mutual goals of learning and community building. Homeschoolers are also often ardent library supporters; home educators are available during normal work or school hours, allowing libraries provide additional programs outside of what is traditionally thought of as programming prime time. Despite this compatibility, the best way to serve this population is not necessarily apparent or fully realized. Guided by an analysis of local homeschool communities, library staff can better identify and satisfy the needs of homeschoolers. Through an evaluation of library staffing, budget, time, spaces, and current collection, libraries can offer services that effectively support the necessary components of learning and socialization within a homeschool context to better meet the needs of the community. The Lafayette Public Library (LPL) in Lafayette, Louisiana, is comprised of nine branches serving one parish of over 240,000 people, but the methodologies outlined in this essay are readily transferable to other library systems, both bigger and smaller.

Libraries provide more effective, user-centered services by assessing homeschooling needs. By doing so, library staff can:

- uncover assumptions about homeschooling
- target services and resource allotment
- conduct assessment of services
- justify services
- create a positive rapport with this patron population

A methodological and analytical approach to determining homeschool needs in a specific time and place reveals essential and delineated goals that are prioritized with input from the end user. Library services are then justified because they are meaningful to and accessed by the community for which they are co-created. Library services designed to meet these prioritized goals are effective in direction and efficient in resource allocation. The measurement of how well those accurate and specific goals are met creates assessment that further justifies services and refines services. On an intangible level, librarians broaden and deepen their knowledge and interaction with their surrounding community.

Learning About Homeschooling

The name implies that homeschooling is school done at home, usually under the guidance of an adult family member, instead of at an educational institution. In a sense this is correct, but there are varying definitions and forms of homeschooling, ranging from parents teaching their children at home to "homeschool" schools and co-ops. In addition to studies at home, homeschool students may be partially enrolled in a traditional K–12 school or college or they may only participate in extracurricular activities in a public school. Additionally, students may be enrolled in an online umbrella school that might be physically based in a different state. All such forms of nontraditional education are considered homeschooling. Noteworthy exceptions include students that are taught at home by teachers working for the public-school system. These students are considered home-bound rather than homeschooled.

At the most superficial level, information about the homeschool community is defined by state regulations delineating mandated compulsory education laws. Different states have different laws governing home education. Currently, twelve states do not require homeschool educators to report to the state. Fifteen states require the parent to notify that state that they are homeschooling. Seventeen states require that the home educator submit standardized test scores or professional evaluation, and six states require state oversight in addition to test scores (Homeschool Legal Defense Association 2018).

To further complicate the issue, each state may offer alternate options to register a homeschool. For example, LPL is in Louisiana, where home educators can either declare themselves a non-public school not seeking state approval, or they can apply for state-approved home study. Many homeschool families choose to declare themselves a non-public school not seeking state approval because they do not have to submit curricula or test scores to the State under that option. These homeschoolers often take an eclectic approach to homeschooling instead of relying heavily on textbooks. Additionally, the curriculum used for one child may not be used for another and homeschoolers may mix and match curricula within and across subjects. Many of those same homeschool families will often switch to state-approved home study when a student reaches his junior year in high school so that the student will be eligible for state-funded scholarships. The home-study option does require a curriculum outline or test score submission. These requirements change the way a family may use curricula and, as a result, the library. Libraries interested in working with homeschoolers can find information about local homeschool regulations from the Homeschool Legal Defense Association website or the Department of Education of that state.

Learning About Homeschooling Needs

Homeschooling takes many forms and is shaped by varying regulations. With such a varied approach to state registration, monitoring, and curricula use, it is apparent that library staff both identify patrons that are homeschooling and assess their needs. Methodologies that have proven effective are:

- observation and library statistics
- review of demographic information
- consultation with internal and external experts

- surveys
- interviews and focus groups

Observation and Library Statistics

Homeschoolers already come to the library. They can be recognized as families with children who often frequent the library during school hours. Observing what programs the homeschoolers attend and which collections they most consult provides preliminary information. Such information is deepened by simply asking if the family homeschools and the age and interests of the children.

Demographic Information

Sources of demographic information about homeschooling include the websites for National Center for Education Statistics (NCES), Homeschool Legal Defense Fund, and the state's Department of Education. While it may seem that reviewing demographic information is as easy as an Internet search, gathering numbers and characteristics of homeschool educators is complicated. Each state sets regulations on homeschooling and keeps different records on the number and type of homeschooling families. The states that do not require parents to report may not have an accurate count of homeschooling families in their area. Even the states that do require records on homeschool families may not make the information publicly available. As already discussed, homeschooling takes many forms, including hybrid situations where a child is enrolled part-time in an institutional setting. What counts as "homeschooling" is not hard and fast. However, when taken in context, demographic information can provide a general direction for understanding homeschooling trends and the way library services can meet the needs of home educators.

The simple count of homeschoolers, while inexact, gives indication of how prevalent the practice is locally. A large discrepancy between the number of homeschoolers in the area and the number of homeschoolers who regularly visit the library provides some insight into how many homeschoolers may be missing as patrons or hidden from library staff's view.

The geographic area that defines local homeschoolers also provides direction of/for library services. In a large city, homeschoolers may form groups in a constricted geographic area so library services can be centralized. In our area, homeschoolers tend to identify themselves as belonging to a large, multi-parish (comparable to multi-county) area known as Acadiana. They regularly travel across parish lines not only to attend homeschool functions, but also for library services, using reciprocal borrowing agreements amongst parishes.

While the cultural ties are strong within Acadiana, the draw from a large geographical area lessens the impact of regionalized socio-economic status, another important demographic marker. While home educators often live from one primary income, homeschool families are diverse in socio-economic status. In our case, the broad geographic area of Acadiana includes regions of affluence as well as economically depressed neighborhoods, whereas smaller geographic regions may have higher concentrations of a specific socio-economic environment.

A more difficult to define demographic factor that impacts library services is the reason that families chose to homeschool. The motivating factors for homeschooling are not only quite varied, but also often complex. While national studies have graphed the motivations behind the decision to homeschool, reasons often overlap, change over time, and become integrated into an overall lifestyle choice. However, how homeschoolers choose to group themselves provides insight into the importance they place on the different manifestations of homeschooling. Some homeschool groups are co-ops formed to share learning responsibilities in a school-like setting. Some groups are formed around pedagogical approaches. Others are socially based. Some are staunchly secular. Some are avowedly religious. The clustering, identity, and exclusivity of groups influence and direct library services by pedagogical representation in the library's collection as well as the structure and subject coverage of library programs. A high concentration of formalized co-ops would suggest more formalized and academic library programs whereas a large number of groups focusing on Montessori, Mason or Waldorf philosophies would suggest more open, exploratory and social library programs.

Internal and External Experts

The use of experts both internal and external to the library system is necessary to assess both the needs of the homeschool community and the services that can be provided to fulfill those needs. One example which reinforces this practice is the Institute of Museum and Library Services study "Assessment of End-User Needs in IMLS-Funded Digitization Projects" *which* found that most librarians who performed customer needs analysis for a digitization project favored consultation of internal or/and external experts (Performance Results 2003). The opinions and experience of seasoned colleagues are certainly important, but they are prey to circular reinforcement of assumptions about a specific group. External experts may expose incorrect assumptions or interpretations about homeschooling, but it is still a limited perspective. As an illustration, an LPL librarian who has ten years of homeschool experience worked with a homeschool mom with twenty years of experience and long-term active involvement in the local homeschool community to design a girls-only, hands-on program in the library makerspace for a local homeschool group. Although both the librarian and the homeschooler are intimately familiar with homeschooling, the program had to be redesigned because other members of the homeschool group balked at the exclusion of the boys. With that caveat in place, forming a relationship with an experienced and involved homeschool expert can provide general direction and background information, especially regarding state regulations. Additionally, homeschool experts are an entry point in obtaining difficult to find information, such as the number of homeschoolers in an area. They also provide access to homeschool groups and other homeschool educators, especially if they run a group.

Survey

Surveys provide a wider perspective than consulting one expert and can be easily administered online. In December of 2017, we asked three open-ended questions of two large local homeschool groups on Facebook. Based on the experience of homeschooling families that use services at the LPL, we learned that Facebook is the easiest way to access a large number of homeschool families at once. The homeschool community is very active on Facebook and there are two groups in particular which are comprised of families from many different formal homeschool groups, co-ops etc. Although Facebook is not the most reliable venue for gathering information, it is a clearing house for information and is readily accessible to many library systems. There are members that belong to both groups, with a total of 138 families in one group's Facebook page and 803 families in the second group's Facebook page. The groups have a "closed" status limiting participation to homeschool families, but it is certainly noteworthy that not all members of the group will see the Facebook post.

The questions we asked the groups were:

- What role has the Library played in your homeschooling?
- What impact has it had?
- How can libraries best serve homeschoolers?

Answers from the eleven respondents exposed the depth of the relationship between homeschool educators and the library. Homeschool educators stated that the library was an "invaluable tool," a "huge asset," and a "great go-to for our studies." One homeschooler labeled the library was a "haven," and another said it was "one of the most welcoming places in the area." Others stated that the library was "the only reason our homeschool is successful" and "LPL is the key to our successful homeschool experience." The responses also revealed that homeschoolers used the Library for collections, programs, and meeting rooms. Homeschoolers used the collections for DVDs, support for literature-based curricula, and reading for pleasure. The homeschoolers also appreciated the reciprocal borrowing system, the ability to place holds, ILL, and the new system that automatically renews material. We discovered local home educators also valued library programs for socialization and volunteer opportunities. They preferred programs scheduled before regular school was out; one of the programs, Homeschool Hangout, was mentioned by name as a program that the homeschoolers "love, love."

Notably, not all library services are tangible. Three of the respondents noted that librarian interaction was important to home education. They relied on librarians for recommendations and assistance in finding books, but they also valued the "kindness" of librarians. One said "There are always people that you can talk to who will remember you and remember your taste in reading and always have a suggestion or two for you."

Focus Groups

Focus groups deepen and broaden the discussion regarding libraries and local homeschoolers. A Google search of local homeschool groups reveals possible participants since many groups have an online presence, complete with contact information of the groups' leaders. At LPL, we invited representatives from seven local homeschool groups to discuss the Library's relationship with homeschoolers. The seven chosen groups represented a cross-section of homeschooling identities and approaches, including multiple religious, secular, and pedagogical orientations. Four people attended the discussion. We asked them:

- What is your biggest challenge in homeschooling?
- How do you use library services as a family unit?
- How do you feel the LPL meets your needs as a homeschooling family? How could we better identify your needs?
- What has been your favorite library program and why? What elements worked?
- What keeps you from accessing known resources of the LPL?
- What would you like to add to the conversation? What did we miss?

The home educators reiterated the need for librarians to proactively and positively interact with homeschool students. One educator stated the best service is "someone's thinking about me. We have this thing you might like to see." Another homeschool parent identified the "idea of the librarian who looks out for my kid" through personalized service as "one of the best things to come out of" the discussion. Other themes included the value of library collections for literature-based curricula; the desire for programs to be held before regular schools adjourn, and the need for volunteer opportunities. The home educators requested that homeschool print resources be relocated to the Children's Department on the first floor, rather than the adult non-fiction section on the third floor, since they usually have children with them and they would like to remain centralized during their visits. Homeschoolers suggested that the Library could offer resources for new homeschool families, as well as provide online resources to help homeschool families connect. They also suggested semi-annual mini expositions for families interested in learning more about local homeschool groups and exchanging educational materials. The homeschoolers stated the need for publicity of current Library services. Homeschool educators generally know where to find upcoming programs, but still feel that there are Library programs that they are missing. Notably, a home educator suggested that the Library offer a board game program. The Library had already created and advertised a board game program, which had been inspired by the interest of the homeschooler's child. The program had been discontinued due to lack of attendance. One home educator stated she uses the library all the time, but "still hasn't hit the tip of the iceberg" of library services.

Evaluation of Library Resources

The characteristics and needs of the local homeschool population provide focus, but the specific manner in which the library meets the needs of this group is determined and shaped by available resources in staffing, time, budget, space, and collections, with the biggest considerations being budget and staff.

Budget

Although the budget does not have to be large to serve homeschoolers, it determines if services can be targeted to homeschoolers as a group or whether they will be served as part of the larger civic community. The budget also determines how much outreach can be provided to homeschool communities covering large geographic area. Finally, the budget determines the number of staff who are available to serve homeschoolers.

Staffing

Staff with limited exposure to homeschooling may simply offer isolated library programs with an intended homeschool audience. However, given the gap between home education and librarianship is not huge, a single dedicated librarian could keep current with regulations impacting home education and acquaint herself with the broad scope of homeschool pedagogies. The interest of additional staff affords larger and more numerous programs as well as more integrated services in terms of reference, reader advisory, collection development and programming.

Library Collection

The size, content, and timeliness of the library's current collection shape curriculum support. Generally, a large, current, and well-maintained collection paired with the availability of InterLibrary Loan and regionalized reciprocal borrowing agreements allows home educators to explore a wide variety of topics. A collection that includes textbooks supports homeschooling in states with tighter regulations. In either case, a homeschool reference section provides support to newcomers and continued guidance to home educators, whether it covers a broad overview of pedagogical approaches or focuses on the pedagogy prevalent in the area.

Space

The physical layout of the library, as well as public meeting rooms and study rooms, affects homeschooling services. Having an informal space to gather with several tables and chairs or a seating area allows individual families and groups to meet with flexibility and accommodates informal and social experiences. Homeschool coops usually require meeting rooms on a regular schedule, which may be impacted by room availability and library policies that charge fees or limit the number of times a room can be used by a specific group or individual. Libraries with small or few rooms can support coops or family study, whereas those with numerous and large rooms additionally offer space to homeschool clubs, conventions, or science fairs.

The provision of meeting areas is an easy service to offer to a local homeschool community. Libraries with fewer staff, tiny budgets, or limited collections may still offer space to coops or homeschool clubs. Since the use of the room is self-directed, the space can serve a wide variety of homeschoolers for a range of activities, from socialization to shared academic pursuits or enrichment. While most beneficial to those of limited financial means and communities covering a wide geographic expanse, the provision of meeting areas which allow homeschoolers to meet can also be useful as a component of social learning.

How It All Comes Together at LPL

LPL serves a parish with a population slightly exceeding 240,000. The Main library is located in downtown Lafayette. Three regional branches are located in Lafayette and the nearby cities of Broussard and Carencro. There are also three small branches spread throughout the parish.

Rooms

Locally, the homeschool community uses LPL space for a variety of reasons. At least four different homeschool groups regularly meet for formal or informal shared academic pursuits. Some groups are set up as casual exchanges of academic discussions while at least three groups are formalized coops with group instruction, assignments, and presentations. One homeschool group provides hands-on science activities. Additionally, LPL offers space for groups to reserve for such activities as Homeschool 4-H, Science Club, Homeschool Chess, and Homeschool Key Club.

Collections

Lafayette Public Library provides the local community with a large collection of books, movies, video games, databases, and e-books. The Library also offers an online purchase request form, ILL, and reciprocal borrowing agreements with libraries in surrounding parishes. The homeschool community utilizes the entire collection and range of services. Additionally, the Library has garnered input from local homeschooling groups to supplement the education collection. The collection represents works from a broad range of educational theories and approaches. Books by Maria Montessori, Frank Smith, Charlotte Mason, John Holt, John Taylor Gatto, and Susan Wise cover the Montessori method, the Charlotte Mason approach, unschooling and Classical Education, while The Core Knowledge Series by E.D. Hirsh delineates grade line markers. The curriculum guide by Cathy Duffy presents an overview of homeschool approaches and curriculum. The collection accurately reflects the local homeschool community.

Programs

Many LPL homeschool patrons are regulars at library programs. However, two programs were specifically tailored for homeschoolers.

The first program, Homeschool Hangout, arose out of an observation made by the youth services supervisor at the Main Branch that there were families in the library during conventional school hours and all of the programming for five- to twelve-year-olds had been dedicated to afterschool hours. The result was the Homeschool Hangout, a monthly program that began in October 2015. It lasts 1.5 to 2 hours and has approximately 30 to 40 children and some of their accompanying adults in attendance. At first, the format was to have an introduction to the theme which included demonstrating a library resource such as TrueFlix or Tumblebooks; then introduce careers, both conventional and unconventional, for children to vote on as their favorite choice. Next, they would be separated into four groups and rotate through four stations before coming together at the end to revisit their "career choice," and to take part in the "Homeschool Hangout Symposium," when they share something about their experience from the day. Early themes such as chemistry and weather were based on trying to make stations that each involved an activity that focused on STEM, art, English language arts, and the use of authentic manipulatives and tools. Library staff then moved to integrating guest presenters to introduce a theme, like local gem and mineral society members for geology, a local musician and her children for sound and music, a high school drama instructor for a theater workshop, with activities and stations to follow. The children are encouraged to make suggestions for upcoming themes and are periodically more formally asked to contribute ideas, consequently creating programs involving puppetry, computer science, and robotics. Because of both space considerations as well as staff time involved, the program was eventually scaled down to just two or three stations and has come to involve more activities that encourage socialization and experiential learning, while bringing in the elements of STEM, art, and English language arts. Although the LPL has tried to support this program at other branches as well, it only remains consistent at the Main Library due to the availability of youth services staff. The library has tried to integrate a teen component into the program, but it was poorly attended. Teens that were attending at the time just wanted to volunteer. As our current younger homeschool patron base is aging, we have heard that there is an interest in a teen component again and are in the process of creating that opportunity.

The makerspace librarian and a homeschooler designed a series of classes for a large secular homeschool group looking for enrichment, social learning, and socialization opportunities. Classes generally lasted an hour and a half and covered the use of the laser cutter, 3D printers, microcontrollers, virtual reality, LEGO® Mindstorms robots, and problem-solving the assembly of mechanical hand. The classes took place before traditional school days ended and provided space for parents and younger siblings to congregate. Because of the inherently hands-on, enrichment-focused nature of the space, classes utilized active learning activities with minimal direct instruction or project direction from the librarian. The librarian gave a brief introduction to software and answered questions during the projects, but did not provide step-by-step directions or theoretical or academic knowledge related to the projects. Problem solving skills and software expertise came from trial and error, experience and social learning.

Home educators from an informal co-op and from a religious-bonded homeschool group also approached the librarian about classes for students. Both groups were seeking to use the specialized library resource as extracurricular enrichment. As with the previous group, the librarian clarified the student-centered nature of making pedagogy. Classes were offered during school hours and provided a place for parents to gather while the students worked.

What's Next?

Services based on the needs of homeschoolers is a circular process. Both library resources and homeschool needs change. LPL gains new information about homeschoolers, creates new services based on that information, and then evaluates and modifies the services. We return to the same starting point as libraries just beginning to explore services to home educators.

WORKS CITED

Homeschool Legal Defense Fund. 2018. "Homeschool Laws in Your State." Accessed February 17. https://hslda.org/laws.
Performance Results. 2003. *"Assessment of End- User Needs in IMLS-Funded Digitization Projects." Accessed February 17.* https://www.imls.gov/publications/assessment-end-user-needs-imls-funded-digitization-projects.

PART II

Specific Circumstances

Homeschooling, Children with Special Needs and the Library

SARAH M. SIEG

As an introduction to the topic, let's look at some definitions of what it means to be a child with special needs. A child with special needs is "working two or more years behind grade level in school subjects, has been receiving special education services, or [is] a child with any other disability that greatly impacts his/her ability to learn" (Berens et al. 2015).

The U.S. Office of Special Education Programs defines a "specific learning disability" (SLD) as a disorder

> of learning and cognition that [is] intrinsic to the individual. SLD are specific in the sense that these disorders each significantly affect a relatively narrow range of academic and performance outcomes. SLD may occur in combination with other disabling conditions, but they are not due primarily to other conditions, such as mental retardation, behavioral disturbance, lack of opportunities to learn, or primary sensory deficits [Rocco 2012].

According to a 2012 National Household Education Survey, approximately 16 percent of homeschooling parents reported "other special needs" and 15 percent reported "physical or mental health problems" as important reasons for homeschooling (Redford et al. 2017).

Reasons for homeschooling can also vary from ideological to pedagogical. An ideological decision to homeschool often stems from religious reasons, while a pedagogically motivated choice reflects a desire to provide different manners of instruction than public schools.

Some parents and families place their children with special needs into a public or private school only to withdraw them later. A motivation for withdrawal is a belief that their children's special education needs are not being met. For example, individuals with Autism Spectrum Disorder (ASD) usually are visual learners. In the public school classroom, the teaching method is more conducive to the auditory learning style.

Benefits to homeschooling children with special needs include greater parental involvement, a stronger family unit, higher self-esteem, student-paced natural learning, schedule flexibility, and increased individualization. Challenges exist as well in choosing curriculum, making connections for support either for child or parent, selecting socialization activities appropriate for the special needs of the child, and making financial decisions.

How can librarians best serve these families? In this essay we will focus on the various special curricula, special collection development, accommodations, special programming, and inclusivity for homeschooled children with ASD and Down syndrome.

Down syndrome is defined as "a chromosomal condition that is associated with intellectual disability, a characteristic facial appearance, and weak muscle tone (hypotonia) in infancy. All affected individuals experience cognitive delays, but the intellectual disability is usually mild to moderate" (U.S. Library of Medicine 2019). Every individual with Down syndrome is different and unique in their abilities.

For the purpose of this essay, individuals with ASD are assumed to fit into the following definition: "Many individuals with ASD [Autism Spectrum Disorders] experience hyper- or hypo-sensitivities to sensory stimuli and struggle with the level of stimulation … from fluorescent lights, to speakers and … to coming into physical contact with many textures and materials. Gross and fine motor skills are often poor and this can affect them negatively as well. They may experience a need to move around, and often struggle with writing, cutting, and gluing" (Hurlbutt 2012).

Remember in the midst of these definitions, library jargon, and descriptions of special accommodations, that to the family their child is not defined by ASD or Down syndrome. Their son or daughter is just like any other child: loved, wanted, and with a unique personality. Therefore, treat the child with special needs like any other child. Learn their likes and dislikes and talk to them rather than about them as if they are not there.

Several sections of this essay will address strategies and tools for working with families that care for and homeschool children with special needs. Additional resource lists, references, and website addresses are provided for each section at the end of the essay.

Special Curriculum

For the public-school teacher curriculum choices, tests, and standards are already in place. A homeschool family has the opportunity to select curriculum and research the regulations for homeschoolers in their state of residence. Depending upon the child's strengths and what areas need extra emphasis, the curriculum may be a mix of standard science, math, and language arts textbooks with additional resources. Not every family will use textbooks exclusively. The National Association for Childhood Development (NACD) program (http://www.nacd.org/) works with children and their families to create individual programs to achieve educational goals. For instance, for a family that has a child with Down syndrome, the NACD program may suggest a particular reading program, several different apps, and games to assist with math and encourage the family to teach the child life skills.

Curriculum choices will also vary depending upon the homeschool requirements in the state of residence. If the homeschooling family for a child with special needs has a curriculum in use and you are unfamiliar or being asked questions about the various curricula available, visit HSLDA (Homeschool Legal Defense Association) or Rainbow Resource's websites.

While the librarian is not teaching the curriculum, knowledge of the chosen curriculum is an asset when planning programs and developing your collection. For example, if the curriculum requires the special needs child to follow written directions, the librarian could print step-by-step instructions for the craft or activity. While this is an extra step, a simple instruction sheet can serve as a reminder that all are welcome and included.

Special Collection Development

Ellen Doman, Educational Director for NACD, requests that librarians consider "more large print books, lower shelving, more books shelved based on reading level, more aggressively interactive resource librarians because parents really underutilize this resource" (Ellen Doman, email to the author, August 27, 2018).

How can you implement these ideas in your library? If collection development and purchasing books are part of your job description, look for books that may be necessities for the homeschooling families with special needs in your community. Search your book vendor website or talk to a representative about large print or other requirements. The Amazon website is another resource to search specific print sizes or other needs.

Consider arranging your collection by reading levels, for example, into easy readers and chapter books. You can also include age ranges to offer further guidance. If your library's collection is not arranged by reading levels, visit other library systems for guidance and inspiration. As new books are added to your collection, flip through them to ascertain reading and illustration level. As you learn your collection and users with special needs, connecting them with the right book will become easier. Here are some other points to consider when purchasing or recommending titles:

- Does the library system have e-books? Research whether it is possible to enlarge fonts or change fonts on an e-reading device.
- Parents may want titles with facts to aid with reading comprehension. Does your library have an early reader nonfiction collection?
- Focus on your readers' likes rather than age or grade.
- Expect every child to learn to read.
- Offer books in audio, print, e-book, and e-audio formats.
- Share that reading a print book while listening to the audio is beneficial for developing reading skills.
- Talk to the reader, not parent or caregiver.
- Give time for the child to process information when asked a question. Wait for the count of twelve, or up to 20.
- Observe and learn from the parents, caregivers, or family as they interact with the child in the book selection process.

To be an interactive resource for your homeschooled patrons with special needs, learn your collection, get to know what your patrons need or want. Develop relationships and make it clear that you care and want to help. Be proactively available instead of sitting at the desk and waiting for patrons to ask for help. If your library has an Educator's Resource collection, add more books and subscriptions to meet the requirements of your homeschool population with special needs. Be ready with book talks and excited congratulations for your patrons' accomplishments. Create and use book lists to inform your co-workers so they are also able to answer reader's advisory questions. Include on the book lists titles featuring characters with ASD and Down Syndrome.

Accommodations

Accommodations for children with special needs will vary depending upon the child's diagnosis and abilities. Take time to plan programs considering the needs of your community's homeschool patrons with special requirements in mind. Be aware of diet restrictions, motor development, communication needs, wheelchairs and other mobility devices.

You will need to make decisions about serving food or using it for crafts during and/or after programs. Keep in mind dietary restrictions when planning food-based programs. Some families have found it beneficial for their child with ASD or Down syndrome to not eat wheat, eggs, or dairy. Food allergies and intolerances can be severe to the point that even being in the room with eggs or peanuts may lead to dangerous reactions. Take time to ask parents or caregivers about allergies and intolerances and thus prevent allergic reactions.

In terms of serving food, it is becoming more and more possible to find gluten-free and other allergy-friendly foods at big box and grocery stores. Depending on your budget and library policies, food purchasing may not be possible. For children with severe allergies, it may be simpler to allow families to bring their own snacks.

Crafts are beneficial for motor development, hand and eye coordination, following directions, allowing creativity, and life skill development. For the child with ASD or Down syndrome there may be added challenges in learning to use scissors or willingness to get messy. To ease scissor use, consider purchasing loop scissors.

Children with Down syndrome or ASD can have hearing loss, be nonverbal, or use sign language and/or PECS (Picture Exchange Communication System) to communicate. If the homeschooled children or children with special needs in your community use sign language, take the time to learn some basic signs. As you learn more sign language, incorporate signs in your programs. American Sign Language (ASL) for colors and numbers can be easily added to rhymes and felt stories when applicable. Karma Wilson's *Bear* series of picture books mold themselves easily to ASL. When Bear wants more, sign those words and encourage your program attendees to sign along. Look for other books with repetitive phrases that lend themselves easily to ASL. Practice signing and reading before presenting the program since signing while holding a book takes practice and forethought. If possible, encourage a parent or caregiver to sign the book as you read.

Other accommodations for children with ASD or Down syndrome include:

- Adjust sound levels for children who wear hearing aids.
- Look at the programming space and remove shiny bright objects that might be distracting.
- Eliminate items that can be thrown.
- If necessary, provide fidgets.
- Consider the seating. Is it possible to bring in yoga balls for chairs?
- If the library has a dedicated programming room, is it permissible for parents to use the space for quiet reading without various distractions? This is especially nice for homeschoolers so they can study away from home or meet therapists and other professionals away from home and distractions.
- Use adjustable height tables.
- What can the child with special needs handle?

- Ask parents and caregivers what they or their children need. For example, my mother did not take her four children (two of whom have Down syndrome) to storytime for the very simple reason that she had to sit on the floor and the storytime was not presented in a programming room. From a seated position on the floor she found it hard to keep three crawling children from escaping. (I was old enough to sit still.) Not all changes have to be drastic, just caring, attentive, and minimally accommodating.

Special Programming

Perhaps for the homeschooled students with special needs in your service area attending regular programming is not possible. Consider the typical storytime, a wonderful experience with shaky eggs, scarves, movement, dancing, and music. This style of presentation may not work for all children, especially children with ASD, given the sensory overload of an average storytime.

Sensory sensitive storytimes are another way to plan inclusive programs for your homeschooled patrons with special needs. When planning a sensory sensitive program or storytime, the following points should be kept in mind:

- Stick to a capella singing or simple melodies, for example, *Twinkle, Twinkle Little Star*.
- Consider making headphones available as an option to reduce noise level.
- Turn off background music.
- Have a basket of fidgets in the room.
- Be sure to communicate to parents that you do not expect children to sit still. Allow freedom of movement. The child who is running around the room is still absorbing information.
- Contain your space. If need be, use furniture to section off the program area. Bookshelves may be too visually distracting.
- Turn off fans.
- Recognize that some fluorescent lights hum and can be distracting.
- Keep supplies put away, and don't set up crafts/activities ahead of time.
- Use cushions, carpet squares, or some other objects to define seating space.
- Leave room for parents.
- Consider partnerships with local special needs support groups.
- Choose books containing repetitive text.
- Be flexible.
- Create program evaluation forms for the families, parents or caregivers to fill out. Allow them the opportunity to share what is or is not working. If your library system already has an evaluation form, review it to see if it will work for programs designed for homeschooled children with special needs. If not, create a simple form yourself. Simply ask for program date, how they heard about the program, what they liked, and if there is room for improvement.

Remember that children with special needs may have short attention span or will need advance warning in order to transition smoothly from one activity to another.

Prepare the children by having a familiar routine, a lineup of pictures showing the different activities in order of occurrence and give the children verbal clues.

The pictures used in PECS (Picture Exchange Communication System) are another resource for visual program outlines. If the homeschooled children with special needs are already familiar with these pictures, it is to your advantage to use them or create your own.

Your library system may already do special programming, such as Star Wars Reads Day, seasonal programs around various holidays or themes, and Summer Reading events. Consider hosting an additional special program and making that second program sensory sensitive. For example, a library in Georgia hosted a sensory sensitive Santa program. Families were encouraged to make 20-minute appointments with Santa in a special needs-sensitive environment.

How can you make this event happen at your library? Either start from scratch or build on an established program. When creating a new event, it is best to start planning well in advance. Buying a Santa costume and finding a library employee to portray Santa is the easiest way to go about it. Purchase a Christmas shower curtain or two, some pillows, a bench and some Christmas trees, and your picture-taking opportunity is ready.

Utilize the library calendar and a program description to clarify that this event is created for individuals with sensory sensitivities and the program is designed for homeschoolers. Either use an online registration form to gather information or follow up on the phone to determine what atmosphere is needed for each child. In this manner you can accommodate the needs of every child and provide a welcoming environment. This will also give time for advance preparation, such as dimming lights, decluttering the space, and letting Santa know what to expect and how to interact with the children.

With an already planned regular Santa event, simply schedule additional time or day when families with special sensory requirements can make appointments to see Santa. Be sure to allow transition time between Santa visits so you can arrange the room for the next attendee with unique special needs and their families.

The advantage of planning a special program for homeschoolers with special needs is their schedule. While a regular Santa event would have the best attendance during evenings or weekends, homeschoolers can come during the weekday. However, do not just assume that any weekday afternoon will work with their schedules. Like any family, homeschooling families have other commitments, and children with special needs may have regular therapy sessions or other appointments. Contact the local homeschool group or interested families and ask what day and time would work best for a sensory sensitive event and plan accordingly.

Be proactive in your program promotion. Email your contact within the homeschool special needs community and remind them about the program. If they have a Facebook page, create a template that can be updated easily, reused, and posted online. For take-home promotion of library programs, use the library calendar or create a bookmark template. Use one side of the bookmark to list books you read during a program and the other side to detail upcoming programs.

Consider hosting an Accessible Browsing time for homeschool families and their children with special needs. The Iowa City Public Library hosted this event for all ages and abilities. Recognizing that a typical library experience can be overwhelming for individuals on the ASD spectrum, the library opened an hour early on Saturday to provide a calmer, less crowded time for browsing.

How can you bring this to your library and homeschool community? As with any program, schedule a time that will work for your patrons. Prepare the library for the needs of the homeschooled individuals with special needs who will be attending.

- Think about what changes need to be made to lighting, circulation areas, the sound or volume on scanners, etc.
- Can you make the changes the night before and put the library back to normal after the event? Find a way to make the necessary changes before and after the event in a way that will flow smoothly. Allow extra time for changes in preparing for the first browsing session. If necessary, schedule extra staff or volunteers.
- Present a sensory storytime or invite a therapy animal to be in the storytime area.
- Send an email to all branch staff, not just scheduled staff, to prepare them for answering questions and for the changes directly related to the program.

Schedule either volunteers or staff members to assist with programs, not just to help the children with special needs, but also to be aware and watch exterior doors to prevent children from leaving the building without a caregiver. Additional help may be needed to post signs declaring boundaries and blocking off dangerous areas. If possible, laminate the signs for reuse. Be conscious of the wisdom of presenting programs during low traffic times when the library is not crowded and staff accordingly.

Check with your homeschool special needs community on the best day and time. If possible, find a time that will work on a monthly basis and schedule monthly programs. Take the time to think through possible issues and find solutions. For example, when scheduling the browsing hour, consider check-out length. If library items typically check out for 3 weeks but the browsing hour is a monthly program, this may lead to frustration concerning overdue books. Can your library create cards with longer check out periods?

Another challenge you may face is potential public, staff, and administrative resistance to programming designed to meet the requirements of homeschooled children with special needs. A case can be made for these programs based on need but also upon other library programs. Libraries typically host and present programs for senior citizens, anime watchers, adult book groups etc. Each of these programs is designed for specific ages and populations resulting in the exclusion of other patrons. You may find it wise to include in the program description that the program is designed for homeschooled children with special needs, but all are welcome. Libraries are there to meet the needs of their community, and programs tailored for the requirements of homeschoolers with special needs is another way to serve the community.

While there are challenges to planning and presenting programs to homeschooled patrons with special needs, the rewards are worth the effort. There is no joy like that of a mother sharing that her daughter with Down syndrome just read a 200-page graphic novel, her longest book yet! The sweet pleasure of watching a child who runs around the room during storytime choose a book and then demand to sit in your lap and read one-on-one! The successes are truly worth all the time and effort put into programming.

Resources

Curriculum

- https://specialneedshomeschooling.com/resources/ Curriculum and learning choices for homeschool students with special needs.
- https://www.rainbowresource.com/ Think of Rainbow Resource as a one-stop shop for descriptions and as a resource for parents. The list of FAQs on Rainbow Resource website includes questions about special needs curriculum choices.
- For information about homeschooling children with special needs and the requirements in your state visit https://hslda.org/content/strugglinglearner/

Collection Development

- Titles and series recommended by NACD: https://www.nacdstore.com/collections/books.
- Picture books to read with a child with special needs: https://cmle.org/2017/04/13/picture-book-suggestions-kids-disabilities/.
- A list of six titles of fiction and nonfiction featuring characters with ASD: https://cmle.org/2017/04/07/book-suggestions-autism-acceptance-month/.
- Young adult book reviews of titles featuring teens with special needs: https://hickeypicks.wordpress.com/category/teens-with-special-needs/.

Programming

- Browsing hour: https://www.libraryjournal.com/?detailStory=iowa-city-pl-institutes-autism-accessible-browsing-hour and https://www.webjunction.org/news/webjunction/autism-accessible-browsing-icpl.html.
- Sensory sensitive Santa program: https://www.albanyherald.com/news/local/sensory-friendly-santa-to-make-appearance-at-leesburg-library/article_8bd6e922-6185-5551-b472-50b0f7411600.html.
- For more information on PECS, visit: https://www.nationalautismresources.com/the-picture-exchange-communication-system-pecs/.
- St. Louis County Library's Weber Road Branch has an excellent sample of a program timeline: https://www.slcl.org/sites/default/files/social-story-wr-oct2018.pdf.
- The following web addresses offer information on supplies and presentation of a sensory storytime. https://www.alsc.ala.org/blog/2012/03/sensory-storytime-a-brief-how-to-guide/.
- The following webinar provides more in-depth information on planning a sensory storytime: https://floridalibrarywebinars.org/18413–2/.

Program Toys and Tools

- National Lekotek Center provides toys for children with special needs in order to improve their lives and facilitate playing and learning. http://www.lekotek.org/index.php.
- Retailer of products for children. Sells to schools, medical offices, private citizens and the military. https://www.sensoryedge.com/.

- AblePlay is a toy rating system designed to evaluate toys for children with special needs. http://www.minilandeducationalusa.com/able-play/.
- Egg shaped crayons for easy grip. https://www.amazon.com/Crayola-Palm-Grip-Crayons-Designed-Toddlers/dp/B0197UCD1M.
- Lakeshore offers high quality educational toys. Their special needs collection is broken down into categories based on diagnosis or developmental needs. https://www.lakeshorelearning.com/resources/special-needs.

WORKS CITED

Berens, Faith, Joyce Blankenship, Carol Brown, and Krisa Winn. 2015. *You Can Homeschool Your Struggling Learner.* Purcellville, Virginia: HSLDA.

Hurlbutt, Karen. 2012. "Special Education Teachers' Perceptions and Beliefs Regarding Homeschooling Children with Autism Spectrum Disorders." *Home School Researcher.* 27 (1): 1–9. https://eric.ed.gov/?id=ED 540710.

Redford, Jeremy, Danielle Battle, Stacey Bielick, and Sarah Grady. 2017. "Homeschooling in the United States: 2012." Last modified April 2017. https://nces.ed.gov/pubs2016/2016096rev.pdf.

Tonette S. Rocco, ed., 2012. *Challenging Ableism, Understanding Disability* San Francisco: Jossey-Bass.

U.S. Library of Medicine. 2019. "Down Syndrome." Accessed January 5, 2019. https://ghr.nlm.nih.gov/condition/down-syndrome.

Serving the Special Needs
of Gifted and Talented Children
and Their Families

Barbara J. Hampton

Sooner or later, most librarians will be inspired (and challenged) by young patrons reading far above their age peers, with surprising insights. They choose esoteric and technical books that most eschew. If you have helped these next-generation super-readers, you know the joys of serving gifted students. Six to seven percent of public school students are enrolled in gifted and talented programs, totaling over three million children (U.S. Department of Education 2016). Some parents turn to homeschooling.

Homeschoolers are avid library users for curriculum and parenting needs. Educators also need access to quality G/T resources. Gifted students, both homeschooled and traditional classroom, will benefit.

Recognizing and Supporting the Gifted

Consider resources for gifted and talented education when assisting homeschooling parents and students. Display posters describing characteristics of gifted students. If these resonate, refer your user to the associations below.

Reach out to state affiliates (NAGC "Gifted by State") for programming and contributions to your G/T collection. Your state education department or resource center may have contacts for local organizations. The Gifted Homeschool Forum "Local and Regional Support" groups are especially knowledgeable about the issues faced by homeschoolers.

Help users access these associations; besides online information, most sponsor conferences and other events for parents and students.

- American Association for Gifted Children: http://www.aagc.org/
- The Association for the Gifted: http://cectag.com/
- Council for Exceptional Children (special education resources for students with disabilities and/or giftedness): https://www.cec.sped.org/
- Davidson Institute for Talent Development: http://www.davidsongifted.org
- Gifted Child Society: http://www.gifted.org/
- Gifted Homeschoolers Forum: https://giftedhomeschoolers.org/

- Hoagies' Gifted Education Page: http://www.hoagiesgifted.org/
- Hollingworth Center for Highly Gifted Children: http://www.hollingworth.org
- National Association for Gifted Children: http://nagc.org/
- National Society for the Gifted and Talented: https://www.nsgt.org/
- Summer Institute for the Gifted: https://www.giftedstudy.org/
- World Council for Gifted and Talented Children: https://www.world-gifted.org/

For more information:

Funk, Joanne Russillo, Chandra Floyd, Cindy M. Gilson, Katherine M. Kapustka, and Feiye Yew. 2016. "Research Roundup for Parents." *Parenting for High Potential* 6, no. 1 (December): 18–19.

Haydon, Kathryn P. 2016. "The Importance of Parent Intuition & Observation in Recognizing Highly Creative Children." *Parenting for High Potential* 5, no. 3: 16–18.

Rimm, Sylvia, Del Siegle, and Gary A. Davis. 2018. *Education of the Gifted and Talented*, 7th ed. New York: Pearson.

Silverman, Linda. 2013. *Giftedness 101*. New York: Springer.

University-based G/T Identification and Assessment Centers Conduct Formal Assessments

- BESTS Above-Level Testing (Belin-Blank Center, University of Iowa) https://www2.education.uiowa.edu/belinblank/
- EPGY Talent Search (Johns Hopkins) https://cty.jhu.edu/talent/
- Duke TIP Talent Identification Program (Duke University) https://tip.duke.edu/
- Davidson Institute Young Scholars http://www.davidsongifted.org/Young-Scholars
- Western Academic Talent Search, Center for Bright Kids (Colorado, Nevada, Idaho, Montana, New Mexico, Utah, and Wyoming) https://www.centerfor brightkids.org/wats_program_overview.php
- University of Southern Mississippi, Frances A. Karnes Center for Gifted Studies https://www.usm.edu/karnes-gifted/eligibility-testing-and-psychometry-infor mation

Parent and Family Needs

When parents realize their child's G/T needs are beyond those of "just a bright kid, a good student," they seek out teaching methods and resources to keep the child excited about learning and facilitate full development.

Callard-Szulgit, Rosemary S. 2010. *Parenting and Teaching the Gifted*. 2nd ed. Lanham, MD: Rowman & Littlefield Education.

Clark, Barbara. *Growing Up Gifted: Developing the Potential of Children at Home and School*. 8th ed. Boston: Pearson/Allyn and Bacon Publishers, 2013.

Friedrichs, Terry, Noks Nauta, and Ellen Fiedler. 2016. "Recognizing and Nurturing Giftedness in Gifted Elders." *Parenting for High Potential* 5, no. 4 (Summer): 11.

Garn, Alex C., Michael S. Matthews, and Jennifer L. Jolly. 2012. "Parents' Role in the Academic Motivation of Students with Gifts and Talents." *Psychology in the Schools* 49, no. 7 (August): 656–667.

Hulbert, Ann, ed. 2018. *Off the Charts: The Hidden Lives and Lessons of America's Child Prodigies.* New York: Alfred A. Knopf.

Inman, Tracy, and Jana Kirchner. 2016. *Parenting Gifted Children 101: An Introduction to Gifted Kids and Their Needs.* Minneapolis, MN: Free Spirit.

Jolly, Jennifer L., Donald J. Treffinger, Tracy F. Inman, and Joan Franklin Smutny. 2011. *Parenting Gifted Children: The Authoritative Guide from the National Association for Gifted Children.* Waco, TX: Prufrock.

Schroth, Stephen T. and Jason A. Helfer. 2015. *Parenting Gifted Children to Support Optimal Development.* Washington, D.C.: National Association for Gifted Children.

Solomon, C.R., and Vassiliki Pilarinos. 2017. "Parenting Styles and Adjustment in Gifted Children." *Gifted Child Quarterly* 61, no. 1: 87–98.

Whitney, Carol Strip, with Gretchen Hersch. 2011. *Helping Gifted Children Soar: A Practical Guide for Parents and Teachers,* 2nd ed. Tucson, AZ: Great Potential.

Education Laws and Policies

As parents face the special needs of their G/T child, they should investigate the applicable laws and policies. The state may offer an assessment for giftedness and possibly some services (Lord and Swanson n.d.). Local support groups can supply contacts at the state and district level. Occasionally, parents seeking best options for their gifted child compare state policies and local programs across the country, then relocate.

Lord, E. Wayne, and Julie Dingle Swanson. n.d. *A Guide to State Policies in Gifted Education,* 2nd ed. Washington, D.C.: National Association for Gifted Children. [Downloadable e-book]

Roberts, Julia Link, Nielsen Pereira, and J. Dusteen Knotts. 2015. "State Law and Policy Related to Twice-Exceptional Learners." *Gifted Child Today* 38, no. 4: 215–219.

Zirkel, Perry A. 2016. "Legal Update of Gifted Education." *Journal for the Education of the Gifted* 39, no. 4: 315–337.

Homeschooling Options

Parents may prefer homeschooling, or they may opt for homeschooling because of inadequate G/T programs. Can homeschoolers meet the needs of G/T students? Kunzman (2014) documented the success of homeschooled gifted children.

Beach, Wes, and Sarah J. Wilson, ed. 2012. *Forging Paths: Beyond Traditional Schooling.* Perspectives in Gifted Homeschooling. Ashland, OR: GHF Press.

Goodowens, Samantha, and Jessica Cannaday. 2018. "Homeschooling/Unschooling in Gifted Education: A Parent's Perspective." In *Curriculum Development for Gifted Education Programs,* 172–190. Hershey, PA: IGI Global, 2018.

Goodwin, Corin Barsily, and Mika Gustavson. 2011. "Educating Outside the Box: Homeschooling Your Gifted Child." *Gifted Education Communicator* 42, no. 2 (Summer): 18–21.

Gustavson, Mika, and Corin Barsily Goodwin. 2011. *Making the Choice: When*

Typical School Doesn't Fit Your Atypical Child. Perspectives in Gifted Homeschooling. Ashland, OR: GHF Press.

Jolly, Jennifer L., and Michael S. Matthews. 2018. "The Chronicles of Homeschooling Gifted Learners." *Journal of School Choice* 12, no. 1 (January–March): 123–145.

Jolly, Jennifer L., Michael S. Matthews, and Jonathan Nester. 2013. "Homeschooling the Gifted: A Parent's Perspective." *Gifted Child Quarterly* 57, no. 2 (April): 121–134.

Kunzman, Robert. 2014. "Homeschooling Gifted Children." In *Critical Issues and Practices in Gifted Education: What the Research Says*, 2nd Ed., edited by Jonathan A. Plucker and Carolyn M. Callahan, 315–322. Waco, TX: Prufrock. Rivero, Lisa. 2014. *Creative Homeschooling: A Guide for Smart Families*, 2nd ed. [Kindle e-book]. Tucson, AZ: Great Potential.

Sargeant, Alexi. 2011. "Excerpts from the Homeschool FAQ." *Imagine* 18, no. 4 (March/April): 36–37.

Wessling, Suki. 2015. *Exploring Homeschooling for Your Gifted Learners*. Washington, D.C.: National Association for Gifted Children.

West, Cindy. 2012. *Homeschooling Gifted and Advanced Learners*. Waco, TX: Prufrock Press.

Social and Emotional Needs

G/T homeschoolers need emotional support. The growing-up years are stressful for everyone; G/T children commonly feel isolated. SENG (Supporting Emotional Needs of the Gifted) is a non-profit offering help "to guide gifted and talented individuals to reach their goals: intellectually, physically, emotionally, socially, and spiritually." Some resources (below) are written specifically for G/T children and teens.

Galbraith, Judy. 2013. *The Survival Guide for Gifted Kids for Ages 10 and Under*, 3d ed. Minneapolis: Free Spirit.

Galbraith, Judy, and James R. Delisle. 2011. *The Gifted Teen Survival Guide: Smart, Sharp, and Ready for (Almost) Anything*. 4th ed. Minneapolis: Free Spirit.

Kerr, Barbara A., and Robyn McKay. 2014. *Smart Girls: A New Psychology of Girls, Women, and Giftedness*, Rev. ed. Tucson, AZ: Great Potential.

Murphy, Joseph. 2014. "The Social and Educational Outcomes of Homeschooling." *Sociological Spectrum* 34, no. 3 (April): 244–272.

Reeves, Diana. 2014. "Teaching Your Child to Fail." *Parenting for High Potential* 4, no. 1: 14–15.

Supporting Emotional Needs of the Gifted. http://www.sengifted.org/

Whitney, Carol Strip, and Gretchen Hirsch. 2011. *Helping Gifted Children Soar*. 2d ed. Scottsdale, AZ: Great Potential Press.

Twice Exceptional and Dual Diagnosis

Parents and teachers often focus on a student's learning challenges, fearing a slide to personal and academic failure. "Twice-exceptional" students also need G/T strategies.

Barnett, Kristine. 2013. *The Spark: A Mother's Story of Nurturing Genius.* New York: Random House.

Baum, Susan, Steven Owen, and Robin Schader. 2017. *To Be Gifted and Learning Disabled: Strength-Based Strategies for Helping Twice-Exceptional Students with LD, ADHD*, 3d ed. Waco, TX: Prufrock.

Cummings. Rhoda. 2016. *The Survival Guide for Kids with LD* (*Learning Differences).* Minneapolis, MN: Free Spirit.

Franklin-Rohr, Cheryl. 2012. "Homeschooling for Twice-Exceptional Students: When Public School Doesn't Work." *Understanding Our Gifted* 24, no. 4 (Summer): 17–18.

Goodwin, Corin Barsily, and Mika Gustavson. 2011. "Homeschooling the Gifted or 2e Child." *2E: Twice-Exceptional Newsletter* 47 (July): 3–4.

Goodwin, Corin Barsily, and Mika Gustavson. 2012. "Education Outside of the Box: Homeschooling Your Gifted or Twice-Exceptional Child." *Understanding Our Gifted* 24, no. 4: (Summer) 8–11.

Kaufman, Scott Barry. 2013. *Ungifted: Intelligence Redefined.* New York: Basic Books.

Reis, Sally M., ed. 2014. *Essential Readings in Gifted Education*, vol. 7, *Twice Exceptional and Special Populations of Gifted Students,* edited by Susan Baum. Thousand Oaks, CA: Corwin.

Teaching Strategies and Curriculum

Curriculum materials developed by recognized G/T experts are available through Amazon. Some G/T research centers have associated publishing arms as well. These publishers specialize in G/T materials:

- Critical Thinking Co.: https://www.criticalthinking.com/
- Crown House Publishing (U.S.): http://www.chpus.com
- Educational Innovations, Inc.: https://www.teachersource.com/
- Eduporium: https://www.eduporium.com/
- Free Spirit Publishing: https://www.freespirit.com/
- GHF Press: https://giftedhomeschoolers.org/ghf-press/
- Great Potential Press: http://www.greatpotentialpress.com/
- Hickory Grove Press: https://www.hickorygrovepress.com/
- Kendall-Hunt K–12 (William & Mary; Mentoring Mathematical Minds): https://k12.kendallhunt.com/
- Prufrock Press (Challenging Units for Gifted Students): https://www.prufrock.com/
- Royal Fireworks Press: https://www.rfwp.com/

Gifted education is not just harder material or a faster pace but rather higher order thinking skills.

Carpenter, Dan, and Courtney Gann. 2016. "Educational Activities and the Role of the Parent in Homeschool Families with High School Students." *Educational Review* 68, no. 3 (October): 322–339.

Dixon, Felicia A., and Sidney M. Moon, eds. 2015. *The Handbook of Secondary Gifted Education,* 2d ed. Waco, TX: Prufrock.

Eckert, Rebecca D., and Jennifer H. Robins. 2016. *Designing Services and Programs for High-Ability Learners: A Guidebook for Gifted Education,* 2nd ed. Thousand Oaks, CA: Corwin.

Kaplan, Sandra, and Nancy B. Hertzog. 2016. "Pedagogy for Early Childhood Gifted Education." *Gifted Child Today* 39, no. 3 (July): 134–139.

Karnes, Frances A., and Suzanne M. Bean. 2014. *Methods and Materials for Teaching the Gifted,* 4th ed. Waco, TX: Prufrock.

Plucker, Jonathan A., and Carolyn M. Callahan, eds. 2013. *Critical Issues and Practices in Gifted Education: What the Research Says,* 2nd ed. Waco, TX: Prufrock.

Pre-K-Grade 12 Gifted Education Programming Standards. Washington, D.C.: National Association for Gifted Children. http://www.nagc.org/sites/default/files/standards/K-12%20programming%20standards.pdf.

Smutny, Joan Franklin. 2014. "Beyond School Walls: What Parents Can Do to Widen the Horizons of Their Gifted Learners." *Parenting for High Potential* 4, no. 3: 2–4.

Sparks, Sarah D. 2012. "'Hybrid' Home-Teaching Options Grow in Popularity." *Education Week* 31, no. 37 (August 8): 16.

Trefflinger, Donald J., Patricia F. Schoonover, and Edwin C. Selby. 2013. *Educating for Creativity and Innovation: A Comprehensive Guide for Research-Based Practice.* Waco, TX: Prufrock.

Wessling, Suki. 2012. "Adapting Curriculum for Gifted Learners." *Understanding Our Gifted* 24, no. 4 (Summer): 12–14.

STEM

Dailey, Debbie, and Alicia Cotabish. 2017. *Engineering Instruction for High-Ability Learners in K–8 Classrooms.* Waco, TX: Prufrock.

Donohue, Susan K., and Larry G. Richards. 2015. "FIE 2015 Special Session— Movin' Along: Investigating Motion and Mechanisms Using Engineering Design Activities." In *Frontiers in Education Conference 2015 Proceedings* 11: 22–26. El Paso, TX: IEEE.

Gann, Courtney, and Dan Carpenter. 2017. "STEM Teaching and Learning Strategies of High School Parents with Homeschool Students." *Education and Urban Society* (June). https://doi.org/10.1177/0013124517713250.

Lechner, George and Richard Kalman. (problems and strategies for Math Olympiad for Elementary and Middle Schools). Bellmore, NY: Mathematical Olympiads for Elementary and Middle Schools Inc.

MacFarlane, Bronwyn. 2015. *STEM Education for High Ability Learners.* Waco, TX: Prufrock

Merrill, Jen. 2012. "STEM?!?!." *Understanding Our Gifted* 25, no. 1 (Fall): 29–30.

Micklus, C. Samuel. (problems and strategies for Odyssey of the Mind competitions). Glassboro, NJ: Creative Competitions.

"Outstanding Science Trade Books for Students K–12: 2018." *Science & Children* 55, no. 6: 87–94. Prior years' lists are available (open-access) on the NSTA website: http://www.nsta.org/publications/#journals.

Taddei, Laura McLaughlin, and Stephanie Smith Budhai. 2017. *Nurturing Young Innovators: Cultivating Creativity in the Classroom, Home, and Community.* Portland, OR: International Society for Technology in Education.

Tassell, Janet, Margaret Maxwell, and Rebecca Stobaugh. 2013. "CReaTE Excellence: Using a Teacher Framework to Maximize STEM Learning with Your Child." *Parenting for High Potential* 3, no. 2: 10–13.

Zaccaro, Edward. (math challenge and problem-solving books). Bellevue, IA: Hickory Grove.

Moral and Spiritual Development

Bowkett, Steve, Tim Harding, Trisha Lee, and Roy Leighton. 2011. *A Moon on Water: Activities, Games, and Stories for Developing Children's Spiritual Intelligence.* Bethel, CT: Crown House.

Montgomery, Diane, and Mary Walker. 2012. "Enhancing Ethical Awareness." *Gifted Child Today* 35, no. 2 (April): 95–101.

Sisk, Dorothy A. 2016. "Spiritual Intelligence: Developing Higher Consciousness Revisited." *Gifted Education International* 32, no. 3 (September): 194–208.

Tirri, Kirsi. 2011. "Combining Excellence and Ethics: Implications for Moral Education for the Gifted." *Roeper Review* 33, no. 1: 59–64.

Distance Learning

Distance learning options are important, particularly for expertise in upper-level classes. Blair (2011) and Potts (2017) report on the experiences of homeschoolers with distance learning. Some of the G/T centers offer their own distance learning programs and may require pre-qualification; others are open to all. The library can facilitate distance learning by providing internet and computer access (video connections may require high-speed internet service), study rooms, and exam proctoring. The library and the user should warm up to online classes with some single-session events to perfect policies and operations.

- Art of Problem Solving: https://artofproblemsolving.com/
- Bird Sleuth (Cornell University Ornithology Lab): http://www.birdsleuth.org/
- Johns Hopkins University Center for Talented Youth:
  https://cty.jhu.edu/ctyonline/index.html
- Stanford Online High School (Stanford University):
  https://ohs.stanford.edu/school-where-gifted-students-thrive
- Duke Talent Identification Program eStudies (Duke University):
  https://tip.duke.edu/programs/estudies
- K–12: http://www.k12.com/
- University of Nebraska–Lincoln Independent Study High School:
  https://highschool.nebraska.edu/
- The Virtual High School: http://vhslearning.org/
- Youth Digital (online tech courses): http://www.youthdigital.com/

Academic Competitions

The thrill of competition can be a powerful inspiration for students and bring much-needed recognition to the academic achievements of the participating students. Many competitions are online. Selected programs are listed below; Karnes and Riley (2014) and Tallent-Runnels and Candler-Lotven (2008) provide more extensive lists.

- BroadcomMASTERS (Society for Science and the Public): https://student.societyforscience.org/broadcom-masters
- Intel International Science and Engineering Fair (Society for Science and the Public): https://student.societyforscience.org/intel-isef
- F.I.R.S.T.: https://www.firstinspires.org/
- International Mathematical Olympiad: https://www.imo-official.org/
- Math Olympiads for Elementary and Middle Schools: http://www.moems.org/
- Mathcounts: https://www.mathcounts.org/
- NASA Design Challenges and Competitions: https://www.nasa.gov/aero research/resources/design-competitions
- National Geographic Geography Bee: https://www.nationalgeographic.org/bee
- Odyssey of the Mind: https://www.odysseyofthemind.com/learn_more.php
- Regeneron Science Talent Search (Society for Science and the Public): https://student.societyforscience.org/regeneron-sts
- Scripps National Spelling Bee: http://spellingbee.com/
- U.S. National Chemistry Olympiad (ACS): https://www.acs.org/content/acs/en/educationstudents/highschool/olympiad.html
- U.S. Physics Team (International Physics Olympiad): https://www.aapt.org/physicsteam
- U.S.A. Computing Olympiad: http://www.usaco.org/
- International Olympics in Informatics: http://www.ioinformatics.org/index.shtml
- U.S.A. Biology Olympiad: https://www.usabo-trc.org/

Classes and Enrichment Programs

Special events, individual classes, and summer collegiate G/T programs afford another source of high-level learning. These programs are very popular and fill up early. Consistently, students identify the pleasures of meeting other students who share a common interest and ability as a particular benefit (See Berger [2016] for additional locations).

- Stanford University Summer Pre-Collegiate Institutes: https://summerinstitutes.stanford.edu/
- University of Iowa, Belin-Blank Center: http://www2.education.uiowa.edu/belin blank/students/default.aspx?o=0&s=class-&g=/
- Johns Hopkins University, Center for Talented Youth: https://cty.jhu.edu/programs/
- Duke University, Duke TIP Programs: https://tip.duke.edu/programs
- Canada/USA Mathcamp: http://www.mathcamp.org/
- Center for Bright Kids: https://www.centerforbrightkids.org/

- College of William and Mary, Center for Gifted Students: http://education.wm.edu/centers/cfge/precollegiate/index.php
- Western Kentucky University, Center for Gifted Studies: https://www.wku.edu/gifted/students/index.php
- Drury University, Center for Gifted Education: http://www.drury.edu/gifted-education
- University of Southern Mississippi, Frances A. Karnes Center for Gifted Studies: https://www.usm.edu/karnes-gifted

Acceleration and Early College

Many G/T students are academically and developmentally ready for a higher school grade or college studies well ahead of their age-peers. With a fluid and customizable curriculum this is easier for homeschoolers to accomplish. Some have expressed concerns that acceleration emotionally harms students. However, since Southern and Southern's (1991) seminal study, more than twenty-five years of studies have consistently shown that students placed with age-peers rather than academic peers also face emotional stresses. Occasionally, students enroll at local colleges several years ahead of their age-peers, with considerable public relations fanfare from the college. The important issue is matching the student to the right college, both academically and socially. G/T homeschool parents will find the resources (below) helpful in making that assessment.

Acceleration Institute: http://www.accelerationinstitute.org/

Assouline, Susan G., Nicholas Colangelo, Joyce VanTassel-Baska, and Ann Lupkowski-Shoplik, eds. 2015. *A Nation Empowered: Evidence Trumps the Excuses Holding Back America's Brightest Students, Vols. 1 and 2.* [Kindle e-book] Ames, IA: Belin-Blank.

Hertzog, Nancy B., and Rachel U. Chung. 2015. "Outcomes for Students on a Fast Track to College: Early College Entrance Programs at the University of Washington." *Roeper Review* 37, no. 1 (January): 39–49.

Howley, Aimee, Marge D. Howley, Craig B. Howley, and Tom Duncan. 2013. "Early College and Dual Enrollment Challenges: Inroads and Impediments to Access." *Journal of Advanced Academics* 24, no. 2 (May): 77–107.

McClarty, Katie Larsen. 2015. "Life in the Fast Lane: Effects of Early Grade Acceleration on High School and College Outcomes." *Gifted Child Quarterly* 59, no. 1 (January): 3–13.

Pagnani, Alexander R. 2014. *Early Entrance to College as an Option for Highly Gifted Adolescents.* Washington, D.C.: National Association for Gifted Children.

Siegle, Del, Hope E. Wilson, and Catherine A. Little. 2013. "A Sample of Gifted and Talented Educators' Attitudes about Academic Acceleration." *Journal of Advanced Academics* 24, no. 1 (February): 27–51.

College and Career Planning

Whether a G/T student enters college early or in the same age group as his or her peers, parents will want to build a file of application material, college requirements and matches, evaluations of programs and colleges, and academic records. Middle-school age students may have little interest in something that seems far off and little comfort level discussing these goals with strangers who tower over them. Homeschooled students won't have the school guidance counselor's direct contacts with the college admissions folks. Parents should review the resources below to stay ahead of the curve.

Berger, Sandra. 2014. *College Planning for Gifted Students,* 4th ed. Waco, TX: Prufrock.

Goodkin, Susan. 2012. "Ten Tips for College Planning." *Parenting for High Potential* 1, no. 6 (April): 12–15.

Imagine [magazine written for gifted students gr. 7–12]; recurring columns: "Exploring Career Options," "Planning Ahead for College," "One Step Ahead," and "Students Review a College.: Baltimore: Center for Talented Youth, Johns Hopkins University. https://cty.jhu.edu/imagine/index.html.

Wilson, Hope E., and Jill L. Adelson. 2012. "College Choices of Academically Talented Secondary Students." *Journal of Advanced Academics* 23, no. 1 (February): 32–52.

Gifted Education Collection Development

The books recommended in this essay are available through publishers and online retail booksellers. Build a collection development plan that recognizes the variety of users and materials, keeping in mind your library's existing policies. For example:

- Facilitate searches by homeschool parents, homeschool students, and professional staff with appropriate access points (e.g., catalog subject headings per LC or Sears protocols). See Library of Congress's Children and Young Adults Cataloging program for alternative entries "tailored to the needs of children and young adults": https://www.loc.gov/aba/cyac/childsubjhead.html.
- "Gifted" is the primary LOC subject term for these materials. Popular alternatives include able, bright, exceptional, high IQ, intellectually excited, high-potential, smart, genius; with curriculum described as advanced, accelerated, enriched, challenging, differentiated, above-level, creative. Incorporate your users' terms in alternative portals to your collections and services: pathfinders, Wordles™, website links, press releases, promotional materials.
- Does the catalog entry identify an intended reader by reading level: Lexile® number, Flesch-Kincaid scale, or a descriptive term? Illustrate the categories with the Lexile Map provided by MetaMetrics (2017). Explain the letter-prefix (MetaMetrics 2018) Lexile Codes used to highlight variations within a level of difficulty, particularly "AD: Adult Directed: Better when read aloud to student rather than having the student read independently"; and "NC: Non-Conforming: Good for high-ability readers who still need age-appropriate content."
- A "Parents and Teachers" shelf in children's room simplifies family library visits and allows adults to integrate children's materials in lesson plans more easily.

Research and Resource Centers

Few outside the library world know about the resources of special and academic libraries available to the general public. Extensive holdings pertaining to G/T students can often be found in specialized state education resource centers, colleges with schools of education, and G/T education centers. Some outstanding G/T centers are noted below.

- American Psychological Association, Center for Gifted Education Policy: http://www.apa.org/ed/schools/gifted/index.aspx
- Boston University, Program in Mathematics for Young Scientists: http://www.promys.org/
- College of William and Mary, Center for Gifted Education: http://education.wm.edu/centers/cfge/
- College of William and Mary, TAG Families of the Talented and Gifted: http://www.tagfam.org/
- Davidson Institute for Talent Development: http://www.davidsongifted.org
- Drury University, Center for Gifted Education: http://www.drury.edu/gifted-education
- Gifted Development Center: http://www.gifteddevelopment.com/
- The Hollingworth Center for Highly Gifted Children: http://www.hollingworth.org/
- Jack Kent Cooke Foundation: http://www.jkcf.org/news/research/ Johns Hopkins Center for Talented Youth: https://cty.jhu.edu/
- Northwestern University, Center for Talent Development: https://www.ctd.northwestern.edu/
- Purdue University, Gifted Education Resource Institute: https://www.education.purdue.edu/geri/
- Southern Methodist University, Gifted Students Institute: https://www.smu.edu/simmons/Community/GSI
- University of Connecticut, Renzulli Center for Creativity, Gifted Education, and Talent Development: https://gifted.uconn.edu/
- University of Illinois, Girls Adventures in Mathematics, Engineering, and Science: http://wie.engineering.illinois.edu/k-12-programs-resources/games wyse-camp/
- University of Iowa, College of Education, Belin-Blank Center for Gifted Education and Talent Development: https://www2.education.uiowa.edu/belin blank/
- University of Louisiana, Center for Gifted Education: https://curriculum.louisiana.edu/about-us/centers/center-gifted-education
- University of Minnesota, School of Mathematics Center for Educational Programs: http://www.mathcep.umn.edu/
- University of Southern Mississippi, Frances A. Karnes Center for Gifted Studies: https://www.usm.edu/karnes-gifted
- University of Wisconsin, Wisconsin Center for Academically Talented Youth: http://www.mathcep.umn.edu/
- Western Kentucky University, Center for Gifted Studies: https://www.wku.edu/gifted/

Miscellaneous Resources

Collecting and organizing them, curating them, and making them accessible are complex tasks that should start with a framework and include routine review and updates.

- File pamphlets and newspaper clippings, catalogues, program materials, non-profit G/T organizations, newsletters. Follow your institution's protocols in duplicating or digitizing items.
- Online resources (websites, e-journals, databases, etc.) are perfect for a library resource guide. Caution! Regular curation and updates are critical.
- Help G/T families access materials beyond your collection with pathfinders, reading lists, pamphlets, catalogs, and online resource guides. Suggested resources are included in this essay.
- Assemble information from your state and local education agencies concerning G/T students and the services provided (e.g., identification, testing, enrichment programs, specialized schools, etc.).

Connecting with the G/T Community

Point interested G/T homeschoolers to a few select social media accounts. With children involved, particularly children remaining at home, privacy issues should be paramount. Limit "follows" to well-known organizations, such as these:

- Johns Hopkins CTY: @CTYJohnsHopkins
- Kendall Hunt PreK–12: @KendallHuntK12
- Free Spirit Publishing: @FreeSpiritBooks
- WCGTC: @wcgtc
- NAGC: @ NAGCGIFTED

Language Arts

Customize! Don't categorize (not every G/T student is a computer geek). Don't restrict students' resources to standard reading levels and subjects. Get to know their interests and show them a range of related sources. Ask students to recommend books; a home-school or G/T support group may be willing to fund some new titles for the library. Well-chosen fiction offers bibliotherapy possibilities. Become familiar with the details of fiction before you recommend, as some popular titles may not be appropriate, portraying G/T children in a negative light, or including disturbing dystopian or violent themes, or mature sexual content. Halsted (2009) offers an extensive list of high quality books for gifted readers, together with insightful discussion points and suggested bibliotherapy themes and reading levels. Her 2008 article outlines important criteria in selecting books.

Great Books Foundation. Junior Great Books (K–5) and Great Books Seminar (6–12). https://www.greatbooks.org/great-books-k-12-programs/

Great Books Foundation. Great Books Now (lifelong learning). https://www.greatbooks.org/great-books-now/

Gunter, Glenda A., and Robert F. Kenny. 2012. "UB the Director: Utilizing Digital Book Trailers to Engage Gifted and Twice-Exceptional Students in Reading." *Gifted Education International* 28, no. 2: 146–160.

Isaacs, Kathleen T. 2016. *Excellent Books for Early and Eager Readers*. Chicago: ALA Editions.

Job, Jennifer, and Mary Ruth Coleman. 2016. "The Importance of Reading in Earnest." *Gifted Child Today* 39, no. 3: 154–163.

MetaMetrics, Inc. 2017. Lexile Map (8.5 × 11, with details): https://lexile.com/wp-content/uploads/2017/08/8.5x11-Lexile-Map.pdf

Saccardi, Marianne. 2011. *Books That Teach Kids to Write*. Santa Barbara, CA: Libraries Unlimited.

VanTassel-Baska, Joyce. 2017. "Curriculum Issues: The Importance of Selecting Literature for Gifted Learners." *Gifted Child Today* 40, no. 3: 183–184.

VanTassel-Baska, Joyce, Bronwyn MacFarlane, and Ariel Baska. 2017. *Second Language Learning for the Gifted: Connection and Communication for the 21st Century*. Washington, D.C.: National Association for Gifted Children.

Walsh, Rosalind, Jennifer Bowes, and Naomi Sweller. 2017. "Why Would You Say Goodnight to the Moon? Response of Young Intellectually Gifted Children to Lower and Higher Order Questions During Storybook Reading." *Journal for the Education of the Gifted* 40, no. 3: 220–246.

Student Research and Writing

Teachers and parents struggle against the "plague of plagiarism" among students, made epidemic with the ease of Google™ searching and cut-and-paste report writing. With many G/T students likely headed to college, graduate school, and research institutions, it is especially important that they master critical analysis of sources, synthesis of ideas, crediting sources, and understand the nature and seriousness of plagiarism. It's a tall order, but one that librarians are well-equipped to handle. At a minimum, good style books and online citation guides should be available to facilitate good research writing. Homeschool parents should incorporate these standards in their instruction as well. Most of the works below are written at the high school level, although some are noted as juvenile works.

Ballenger, Bruce P. 2016. *The Curious Writer, MLA Update*, 5th ed. Boston: Pearson.

_____. 2017. *The Curious Researcher: A Guide to Writing Research Papers*, 9th ed. Boston: Pearson.

Clapper, Nikki Bruno. 2016. *Learning About Plagiarism*. North Mankato, MN: Capstone. [juvenile]

Fields, Jan, and Scott Altmann III. 2013. *The Purloined Story*. Minneapolis, MN: Magic Wagon. [juvenile]

Fisher, Douglas, Nancy Frey, and Diane Lapp. 2012. *Teaching Students to Read like Detectives: Comprehending, Analyzing, and Discussing Text*. Bloomington, IN: Solution Tree.

Gauthier, Gail. 2001. *The Hero of Ticonderoga*. New York: Puffin Books. [Juvenile]

Geddes, Kimberly A. 2011. "Academic Dishonesty Among Gifted and High-Achieving Students." *Gifted Child Today* 34, no. 2 (April): 50–56.

Loewen, Nancy. 2009. *Just the Facts: Writing Your Own Research Report*. Mankato, MN: Picture Window Books.

Siegle, Del. 2017. "The Dark Side of Using Technology." *Gifted Child Today* 40, no. 4 (October): 232–235.

Turabian, Kate L.; revised by Wayne C. Booth, Gregory C. Colomb, Joseph M. Williams and the University of Chicago Press editorial staff. 2013. *A Manual for Writers and Researchers of Papers, Theses, and Dissertations: Chicago Style for Students and Researchers*. 8th ed. Chicago: University of Chicago Press.

Journals

Many important journals are included in databases to which you have access through your state or regional library consortium. A helpful table is included in Cannaday (2015). If you don't have full-text access, users can search journal archives through the publisher (e.g. Sage Journals). The Davidson Institute has an online Article Database (see below) indexing relevant articles. Subscriptions to a non-profits journal is often included in membership. Ask your users who are members to donate back issues to the library.

- *Advanced Development*
- *The Challenge: Magazine of the Center for Gifted Studies*
- *Exceptional Children*
- *Gifted Child Quarterly*
- *Gifted Child Today*
- *Gifted Children*
- *Gifted Education International*
- *Gifted and Talented International*
- *High Ability Studies*
- *Imagine*
- *Journal for the Education of the Gifted*
- *Journal of Advanced Academics*
- *Journal of Secondary Gifted Education*
- *Parenting for High Potential*
- *Roeper Review*
- *Teaching for High Potential*
- *Teaching Exceptional Children*
- *Understanding Our Gifted*
- Article Library Database, Davidson Institute for Talent Development: http://www.davidsongifted.org/Search-Database/topicType/5/entryType/1

Works Cited

Berger, Sandra. 2016. *The Best Summer Programs for Teens: America's Top Classes, Camps, and Courses for the College-Bound*. Waco, TX: Prufrock.

Blair, Randee. 2011. "Online Learning for Gifted Students from the Parents' Perspectives." *Gifted Child Today* 34, no. 3: 28–30.

Cannaday, Jessica. 2015. "A Review of Current Gifted Education Journals: Information for New Faculty."

International Journal of Education and Social Science 2, no. 11 (November): 1–8. http://www.ijessnet. com/wp-content/uploads/2015/12/1.pdf.

Halsted, Judith Wynn. 2008. Appropriate Content for Gifted Readers. Duke University Talent Identification Program. http://www.davidsongifted.org/Search-Database/entry/A10716.

_____. 2009. *Some of My Best Friends Are Books: Guiding Gifted Readers from Preschool to High School,* 3rd ed. Scottsdale, AZ: Great Potential.

Karnes, Frances A., and Tracey L. Riley. 2014. *The Best Competitions for Talented Kids: Win Scholarships, Big Prize Money, and Recognition.* Waco, TX: Prufrock.

Kunzman, Robert. 2014. "Homeschooling Gifted Children." In *Critical Issues and Practices in Gifted Education: What the Research Says,* 2nd ed., edited by Jonathan A. Plucker and Carolyn M. Callahan, 315–322. Waco, TX: Prufrock.

Lord, E. Wayne, and Julie Dingle Swanson. n.d. *A Guide to State Policies in Gifted Education,* 2nd ed. Washington, D.C.: National Association for Gifted Children. [Downloadable e-book.]

MetaMetrics, Inc. 2008. Lexile Measures at Home. https://lexile.com/wp-content/uploads/2017/08/Lexile-Measures-at-Home.pdf.

_____. 2017. Lexile Map (8.5 × 11, with details)—https://lexile.com/wp-content/uploads/2017/08/8.5x11-Lex-ile-Map.pdf.

_____. 2018. About Lexile Codes. https://lexile.com/parents-students/find-books-at-the-right-level/about-lexile-text-codes/.

Nichols, Teresa M. 1993. "A Study to Determine the Effects of the Junior Great Books Program on the Interpretive Reading Skills Development of Gifted/Able Learner Children." (Paper presented at the Annual Meeting of the Mid-South Educational Research Association, Knoxville, TN, 11–13 Nov. 1992).

Potts, Jessica Alison, and Skip Potts. 2017. "Is Your Gifted Child Ready for Online Learning?" *Gifted Child Today* 40, no. 4 (October): 226–231.

Southern, S. Thomas, Eric D. Jones, and William T. Southern. 1991. *Academic Acceleration of Gifted Children.* New York: Teachers College.

Tallent-Runnels, Mary K., and Ann C. Candler-Lotven. 2008. *Academic Competitions for Gifted Students,* 2nd ed. Thousand Oaks, CA: Corwin.

U.S. Department of Education, National Center for Educational Statistics. 2016. *Digest of Educational Statistics 2015.* https://nces.ed.gov/pubs2016/2016014.pdf.

VanTassel-Baska, Joyce. 2017. "Curriculum Issues: The Importance of Selecting Literature for Gifted Learners." *Gifted Child Today* 40, no. 3: 183–184.

Educating Homeschoolers with Learning Differences Using Design Thinking and Continuing Education Resources

Angiah Davis *and* Cordelia Riley

Homeschool groups use the public library as a place for social connectivity to other parents and students and as a resource to supplement learning. With more and more parents turning to homeschooling methods to educate their children, librarians are faced with providing information and resources to parents and students in a somewhat unfamiliar territory: educating homeschool students with learning differences. This essay explores resources available for this audience and shares continuing education opportunities for librarians. For purposes of this essay, a person with learning differences will be defined as someone who learns differently from the majority of students. Specifically, we examine students with dyslexia. The terms learning differences and learning disability may be used interchangeably.

There are different types of learners and various learning styles. Some students learn best by doing; they are kinesthetic learners. Other students may learn best by hearing; they are auditory learners. Most people who study types of learners are scientists, psychologists, teachers, instructional designers, and curriculum specialists. These are trained professionals who are familiar with this subject matter. But what if you are a librarian, information professional, educator, or parent who is responsible for teaching students with learning disabilities, or you need to find resources to assist with teaching homeschoolers with learning disabilities? Where would you begin?

Librarianship is both an art and a science. Librarians must be creative to find a resource for a library user that is not on the library shelves. Librarians must be creative when funding is unavailable for programming. Librarians also observe what their communities need and experiment daily with new and unfamiliar subject matters. However, most librarians do not learn about the science of teaching in library school. That is more of the role of an instructional designer. The instructional designer uses design thinking as a way to solve an instructional problem in a systematic way. Using ADDIE (analysis, design, development, implementation and evaluation), an instructional design model, the instructional designer would first complete an analysis, design a prototype, develop instructional strategies, implement the lesson, and finally conduct an evaluation. In the case of the homeschooled dyslexic learner, the instructional problem is how to teach this student, but more importantly, how to reach the student. With this in mind, librarians and parents can apply instructional design thinking to their homeschool lessons.

Defining Dyslexia

According to the International Dyslexia Association:

Dyslexia is a specific learning disability that is neurobiological in origin. It is characterized by difficulties with accurate and/or fluent word recognition and by poor spelling and decoding abilities. These difficulties typically result from a deficit in the phonological component of language that is often unexpected in relation to other cognitive abilities and the provision of effective classroom instruction. Secondary consequences may include problems in reading comprehension and reduced reading experience that can impede growth of vocabulary and background knowledge" [International Dyslexia Association 2019a].

Do you remember the episode of *The Cosby Show* titled "Theo's Gift" where Theo discovered that he had a learning difference? That learning difference was called dyslexia. Although Theo was much older when he learned about it, his parents embraced his learning disability by seeking help from a school counselor. For years, Theo believed that he was not that smart. As a result of his diagnosis through testing, he had to change the way he studied to improve his grades. Theo had a tutor to help him. However, with homeschoolers there is no school counselor. So, how do you know if your child has dyslexia? How would you know what steps to take to seek help for your student? In the past, dyslexia was seen in a negative light, but now there is more understanding and assistance available. More and more people are realizing the importance of dyslexia testing. Recently, the Governor of the State of Georgia signed legislation, SB 48, requiring the screening of every kindergartner for dyslexia. Additionally, students in the first through third grades showing signs of dyslexia will be referred for dyslexia screening. The SB 48 also requires the Department of Education to make a dyslexia informational handbook available to local school systems and provide professional development for teachers on the subject. This is a huge win for students, parents, and educators because studies have shown that "[w]ithout targeted interventions, children with dyslexia are unlikely to ever become proficient readers, which has significant long-term implications. The data shows that kids who can't read proficiently by the third grade are more likely to drop out of school, and chances are tripled for students who come from a low-income household. Students with dyslexia in particular are more prone to depression, anxiety, and even suicide, which can be linked to the shame and stigma of not knowing how to read" (Korbey 2019). It is also important to note that dyslexia is genetic. There is no cure for it.

So far, we introduced a good general understanding of dyslexia and the importance of having tools to assist people with this condition. But let's face it, a librarian usually does not have a training of an instructional designer. As such a librarian, what resources could you use to assist parents and yourself with learning more about dyslexia?

Dyslexia Case Example

Meet Ian. Ian is a very smart and talented child in the third grade at a public school. It was recently noted in a parent-teacher conference that Ian learns differently. He has difficulty reading. As a result, Ian has been labeled as a student with special needs. Because he is now in a known special needs class, he is bullied and develops behavior problems. Worried about his education, safety, and self-esteem, Ian's parents decide to pull him out of the public school and homeschool him. Ian's mom was told by a friend that the public library can help. Ian's mom decides to visit the public library to look for resources that can assist her and her child. They leave with a few outdated books on dyslexia, all that they could find. Now Ian's mom is wondering if homeschooling is truly the right option for her child. She feels that she has nowhere to turn. Perhaps, Ian and his mother's experience could have been better if their librarian was aware of resources to assist them.

The decision to homeschool is not a choice made lightly. Most parents who have a child with the learning difference of dyslexia often do so after seeing little to no progress in their child's education. The parents/guardians discover their children's learning differences and want to find what their children need to close the gap to be on par with their neurotypical peers or the majority. The parents/guardians quickly learn that the school may not be providing their children with free and appropriate education, because the school system may not be testing students for dyslexia, despite the information that suggests that fifteen to twenty percent of the population may have symptoms of dyslexia (International Dyslexia Association 2019b). The parents may not be immediately made aware that their children have dyslexia. They become disillusioned with the school system because of the lack of information and support.

The support schools often offer to the children with learning differences are not structured literacy methods. If the schools do not test for dyslexia, then they do not have programs to provide the needed remediation. In these instances, parents have to find what their child needs and whether or not what schools offer satisfy these needs. They often watch their child fall further behind and use the information they collect to show that the programs offered by the school system do not work for their child. As a result, the child may be pulled from the public school system; now it is parents' responsibility to address their children's learning differences and determine how and where to educate their students.

The library plays a key role in helping parents build the toolbox of resources they will need to take on the role of a homeschool educator. Dyslexia of Southside of Metro Atlanta shared some goals that can be used to assist parents who are homeschooling children with dyslexia: connect with parents; educate ourselves; educate community; provide resources to schools, community, and others (Dyslexia of Southside of Metro Atlanta 2019).

Parents need to know that they are not alone. The library can sponsor programs and invite speakers in to talk about dyslexia. The library can offer space for the groups so that parents can meet each other and learn more about their child's learning difference. Children with dyslexia may have suffered at school and had to fight the labels of being called lazy, unmotivated, and unengaged. Their parents had to fight the accusations of not being involved in their child's education; had to repeatedly take their children to the doctor to have their vision tested; thought that maybe the dyslexic child would outgrow this condition; all while trying to explain that their child with normal or above-normal intelligence had an issue with copying from the board and following oral directions. By joining the support groups at the library, the parents can shift their focus to educating their children as well as having conversations with other families who share similar goals, fears, and struggles.

Parent-led grassroots organizations such as Decoding Georgia work to support and educate the community about dyslexia. The library can participate in these efforts, for example, by providing materials that will help parents understand their child's learning difference and the issues it can cause with the self-esteem and behavior; therefore supporting their education as well as education of their children.

Design Thinking Applied

Earlier we mentioned that librarians and parents should use the design thinking approach when it comes to instruction for their homeschooled dyslexic learner. These basic design skills can be adapted to a wide variety of settings, inside as well as outside of the classroom. There are various types of instructional design models. We will discuss the ADDIE model, where ADDIE is an acronym for the five steps of this model: analysis, design, development, implementation and evaluation.

The first stage, analysis, is the foundation of ADDIE. In this phase you analyze the broad goals for the lesson or program. What is it you are going to achieve? How many modules/units do you want to design? You need to analyze learners, analyze tasks, and develop instructional goals and objectives.

For the step two, the design phase, you need to identify the learning objectives for each unit/module and the learning assessment; sequence instructional tasks; identify instructional strategies; consider text and multimedia design.

In step three, the development phase, you should develop your instructional strategies and plan the logistics. What strategies do you want your students to learn? Do you want to do online or face-to-face lessons? How do you want to group your students? What tools and materials do you want to use? Develop instructional materials, justify their use, and consider delivery methodology.

In the fourth step, the implementation phase, try out your lesson plan or unit with students. In order to do this, develop a facilitator guide, consider instructional environments, study instructional delivery and sequencing, and discuss assessment strategies.

In the final phase of the ADDIE model, develop an evaluation process and align it with instructional goals. This step is comprised of a formative and summative assessment. Formative assessment takes place in each phase of ADDIE and provides ongoing feedback from the learner to the instructor. Summative assessment evaluates learning at the end of a unit.

The ADDIE model is flexible and functions as a cycle. At any time one can revisit each step and refine it. This systematic approach to instructional design will help parents, teachers, and librarians deal with complex situations, such as, for example, a previously described situation with Ian and this mother. ADDIE helps one identify an entry point for the project and guides through the subsequent steps. Using instructional design will consistently produce efficient and effective learning as long as instructional modules are revised and refined to meet the current needs of the learner.

Continuing Education Resources

We recommend the following continuing education resources:

- Library Services to Special Population Children and Their Caregivers: A Toolkit for Librarians and Library Workers. http://www.ala.org/alsc/lsspcc-toolkit
- Decoding Dyslexia. This resource is a parent-led grassroots movement. Each state has a Facebook page dedicated to their work. This group advocates for several policy goals regarding dyslexia. http://www.decodingdyslexia.net/
- Edutopia is an online community that shares knowledge of what works in pre–K–12 education. Search topics such as dyslexia, teacher development, and technology. You can become a volunteer facilitator and write for Edutopia. https://www.edutopia.org
- International Dyslexia Association identifies resources in your area, such as conferences and free webinars, as well as articles on homeschooling students with dyslexia. You may track your state's legislation on dyslexia and follow the organization on social media. https://dyslexiaida.org
- Learning Disabilities Association links to publications and websites on learning disabilities, advocacy, disability rights, and state resources. https://ldaamerica.org
- Microsoft and Made By Dyslexia have partnered to promote the awareness of dyslexia through an online course geared towards educators and parents. Visit https://education.microsoft.com/ and search for "dyslexia awareness."
- National Center for Improving Literacy (NCIL) is a partnership among literacy experts, university researchers, and technical assistance providers, with funding from the United States Department of Education. Visit the Kid Zone which features games, books, and other resources. Learn about Bookshare, an accessible online library for people with print disabilities. https://improvingliteracy.org/
- Universal Class is an online continuing education resource. Its homeschool section contains courses that deal with learning disabilities. There are courses in behavior management, understanding learning disabilities, special needs 101, and confidence building. There are other courses for educators, librarians, parents, and homeschool students. All courses are self-paced. Keep track of your learning by signing in and earning a certificate. These courses may be free through a local library. https://www.universalclass.com/
- Understood site helps students ages 3–20 with learning disabilities. You can chat with an expert, participate in webinars, read personal stories, and learn about common challenges and assistive technology. On this site we learned about Doctor Dyslexia Dude who is an African-American superhero character with dyslexia. https://www.understood.org
- The mission of the Yale Center for Dyslexia & Creativity (YCDC) is to increase awareness of dyslexia and its true nature, specifically, to illuminate the creative and intellectual strengths of those with dyslexia. You can find research on dyslexia and use the toolkit which includes talking points about dyslexia, printable materials, and a social media awareness campaign. Through our research on the website, we found that in 2016, the YCDC piloted a program to

improve the knowledge and awareness of dyslexia among public librarians in the Atlanta area. https://dyslexia.yale.edu/
- KidsHealth website provides information on learning disabilities, specifically dyslexia, such as articles, facts sheets, and helpful tips on dealing with bullying. Do you know if your state has a homeschool group organization? These organizations can point you in the right direction for legal assistance, curriculum, and other support that you may need. www.kidshealth.org

More Ideas

Help homeschoolers with a learning disability by bringing in a therapy dog. Studies show that this educational initiative helps children improve language and literacy skills. Students may read to a dog in a fun relaxed atmosphere which helps decrease stress for reluctant readers or readers with a learning disability. Reading to a therapy dog can raise self-esteem, motivate speech, and build confidence. If you are interested in having a therapy dog come to your library, contact Therapy Dogs International: https://www.tdi-dog.org/default.aspx.

Promote services such as Overdrive and BrainFuse as well as the databases that offer narration to parents who wish to educate their dyslexic child at home. There are other things the library can offer to help enrich children's worlds with a love for the written word. The library can provide a maker station that parents can use for multisensory teaching. It can also offer access to learning materials such as The Barton System (https://bartonreading.com/) or Toe by Toe (https://toe-by-toe.co.uk/) which were developed for parents wishing to teach their dyslexic children.

Just as children of various ethnicities and backgrounds need to see themselves in the reading material, so do children with learning differences. Books written by individuals such as Henry Winkler, who is dyslexic and uses a dyslexic font in his books, is a great way to have kids see themselves in the books. This will help counter the negative images and allow children to become more tolerant of others.

Below is a selected list of additional titles for students, parents, librarians, and educators:

Berninger, Virginia Wise, and Beverly J. Wolf. 2009. *Teaching Students with Dyslexia and Dysgraphia: Lessons from Teaching and Science*. Baltimore: Paul H. Brookes Publishing Co. Learn about the different types of dyslexia and how to match teaching methods to fit a child's specific type of dyslexia.

Braun, Hannah. 2018. *Learn to Read: For Kids with Dyslexia: 101 Games and Activities to Teach Your Child to Read*. Emeryville, California : Zephyros Press. This book makes reading engaging for the dyslexic learner. It is recommended for ages 7–12.

Foss, Ben. 2016. *The Dyslexia Empowerment Plan: A Blueprint for Renewing Your Child's Confidence and Love of Learning*. New York: Ballantine Books. This book is a must for a parent whose child's self-esteem may have suffered at school where this child has been labeled as unmotivated, lazy, or non-engaged.

Henry, Marcia Kierland. 2010. *Unlocking Literacy: Effective Decoding & Spelling Instruction*. Baltimore: Paul H. Brookes. Parents will study terminology, such as morphology, etymology, and orthography. They will understand why their children need to learn in an explicated fashion in order to spell and decode words.

Hunt, Lynda Mullaly. 2015. *Fish in a Tree*. New York: Puffin Books. A story about a girl with dyslexia who overcomes her learning disability with the help of her teacher. A good read for tweens.

Kilpatrick, David A. 2015. *Essentials of Assessing, Preventing, and Overcoming Reading Difficulties*. Hoboken, New Jersey: Wiley. Teachers will learn how to choose the correct evaluation tools so that children can make adequate progress and be successful in school.

Moraine, Paula. 2012. *Helping Students Take Control of Everyday Executive Functions*. London: Jessica Kingsley Publishers. All children have to learn how to plan and organize their work. This book can help all children, including the ones with dyslexia, learn planning and organization.

Oelschlager, Vanita, and Joe Rossi. 2012. *Knees: The Mixed-Up World of a Boy with Dyslexia*. Akron, Ohio: VanitaBooks. A fourth-grader, Louis the Third, teaches us about dyslexia in a fun way.

Pagliano, Paul J. 2012. *The Multisensory Handbook: A Guide for Children and Adults with Sensory Learning Disabilities*. Abingdon, Oxon: Routledge. The author explains that learning requires the use of multiple senses and provides multisensory stimulation ideas.

Shaywitz, Sally E. 2012. *Overcoming Dyslexia: A New and Complete Science-Based Program for Reading Problems at Any Level*. New York: A.A. Knopf. Dr. Shaywitz, is a co-founder and co-director of the Yale Center for Dyslexia & Creativity. Her work explains how the brain learns to read and describes the differences in the brain of people with and without dyslexia.

Thus far, we have discussed the definition of dyslexia, the importance of using design thinking when preparing instruction for the dyslexic homeschooler, and shared books, and online resources for continuing education for librarians and homeschool educators. All of this information sounds great in theory. However, we know studying this information can be time-consuming. So we want to leave you with practical, simple, and low-cost best practices that you can implement today.

Start small. Create a display with some books from the library that may be checked out by library users and include free information material about dyslexia during National Dyslexia Month in October. Library users like to take things home. If you do not have books, or your books are outdated, create a display of famous people with dyslexia. You can print out photos or use their biography books to display.

Consider starting a support group for homeschoolers with learning differences. Many parents who come to the library for a specific program often network with each other to learn about resources that can help their child improve both educationally and socially. Start a group at your library and invite speakers to discuss learning differences. In the age of social media, you can connect to online groups to learn more information and stay abreast of current trends in homeschool education for learners with disabilities.

Educate yourself about learning differences. Search for books and research articles on dyslexia, multisensory learning, and learning disabilities.

Provide the environment that allows parents/guardians to network so the parents can create a space to educate their children with support from the community. Having community and creating an atmosphere for support is a recipe for success. Librarians are here to help connect parents with resources to help people with dyslexia succeed.

WORKS CITED

Dyslexia of Southside of Metro Atlanta. (2019). Accessed May 3. https://ga.dyslexiaida.org/support-groups/.

International Dyslexia Association. 2012. "Why Homeschool a Student with Dyslexia." Accessed May 3. https://app.box.com/s/rkd9hm3egekiay2floohqj8iv2xsew1c.

_____. 2019a. "Definition of Dyslexia." Accessed May 3. https://dyslexiaida.org/definition-of-dyslexia/.

_____. 2019b. "Dyslexia Basics." Accessed May 3. https://dyslexiaida.org/dyslexia-basics/.

Korbey, Holly. 2019. "Unraveling the Myths Around Reading and Dyslexia." George Lucas Education Foundation. Accessed May 29. https://www.edutopia.org/article/unraveling-myths-around-reading-and-dyslexia.

Wiley, John. Georgia General Assembly. (2019). "Senate Bill 48." Accessed May 29. http://www.legis.ga.gov/legislation/en-US/Display/20192020/SB/48.

PART III

Programs and Case Studies

Learning in the Library

SARAH POLACE, AMY DREGER
and MEGHAN VILLHAUER

With the number of homeschoolers on the rise, the library offers the perfect location to present programming that meets the needs of these children. Homeschooled families are typically frequent library users who enjoy attending library programs and using library services. Creating programming just for them can help homeschooled children develop a deeper connection to their library and feel welcome.

Deciding What Programs to Offer

Talking with parents is the best way to determine what kinds of homeschool programs to offer at your library. See what might be lacking in their curriculum. Find out what parents do not have the time or resources to cover or in which subjects they would like to dig a little deeper. Many families will pay expensive fees for their children to attend classes at museums and other organizations. Library programs are free and can be very enticing for families on a budget.

Presenting homeschool programming also allows children's librarians the chance to present school-age programming during the morning or early afternoon, when traditional students are in school. This helps prevent non-homeschool families from signing up for programs reserved for homeschoolers.

Keep in mind that homeschooling families typically like for their children to learn together if possible. Offering a program that encompasses a wide range of ages can be very attractive to families. Some programs are better equipped to handle this challenge than others. Use your judgment and make adjustments if necessary.

Building Your Base

Once you have decided to present a homeschool program in your library, the next step is finding your audience. Begin conversations with families that you know homeschool their children. Let them know about your program. In most cities, homeschoolers are a relatively tight-knit community. Families join co-ops and frequently meet with other homeschool families. Ask them to spread the word. Seek out homeschool groups on social media or online listservs and ask the moderators if they can mention your program. Utilize in-library marketing to advertise the event. Once you lead a successful program, word will spread, and families will fill up your attendance and wait lists. Most homeschool families are willing to travel to attend quality programming.

Cuyahoga County Public Library in greater Cleveland, Ohio, offers a variety of homeschool programs at several branches. Here are some examples.

Home School Geography Classes

Background

Students meet once a month at the Orange Branch of Cuyahoga County Public Library during the school year. About 20 children attend each month; they are between the ages of six and fourteen. This program lasts an hour and a half and offers students an immersive learning environment where they explore history and customs from countries around the world.

At the end of each school year, students select the countries that will be covered in classes the following school year. Students are encouraged to select countries from each of the continents.

Sample Geography Class for the Country of Morocco

At the start of the class discussion, students sit on the floor facing the projector screen. Students and librarian review the countries they previously studied during the school year and find them on the class map. Each country they have "visited" is labeled with a colorful dot sticker.

The librarian asks the students if they have anything they would like to share about the country. Whether it is an object they own from the country, a visit, a local experience involving the country, or any facts they may already know.

The class discussion utilizes a PowerPoint presentation with the following subjects included on the slides (subjects do tend to vary slightly with each country, but this is a standard format that can be followed with additional tweaks made by each librarian doing the program). Librarians can ask questions during the presentation to allow students to join in on the discussion or do the presentation as more of a lecture with questions and comments at the end. This would depend on each librarian's teaching style. Plan for about a 30-minute discussion.

1. Opening slide shows the country's flag and the words "Welcome to Morocco."
2. Embedded in the slide show is a YouTube video where several common words and phrases in Arabic are taught to the students.
3. Also included in the slide show is a short travel video about the country. These videos can be found on YouTube, but be sure to preview each one.
4. A world map highlighting the location of Morocco on the Earth.
5. A close-up map of Morocco showing the different regions, the capitol, and some major cities.

    6. A map showing the size comparison between Morocco and the United States.

    7. A few slides highlighting images or information that discusses briefly the history of the country.

    8. The current leader of the country.

    9. A slide showing the country seal and symbols. National bird, flower, tree, animal, etc. Some countries do not have a national symbol for each of these groups.

    10. A slide showing a one-dollar bill along with the exchange rate between the country and the United States. In the case of Morocco, the slide would show a $1 US bill along with nine and a half Moroccan Dirham coins as the current exchange rate is $1 USD = 9.41 Moroccan Dirhams.

    11. Show images from several cities and natural landmarks. Some examples for Morocco would include:

- The capital city Rabat
- The largest city Casablanca
- Marrakech—another important city in Morocco
- The Sahara Desert along with a map showing the expanse of the desert across Northern Africa.
- The Atlas Mountains
- Ouzouad Falls—Second highest waterfall in Africa.
- Chefchaouen—a smaller mountainside city where all the buildings are painted blue.
- Any other places the librarian wishes to include in the presentation.

    12. Islamic Calendar—describe the differences between the Gregorian calendar used by many countries including the US and the Islamic calendar.

    13. Discussion of the holiday Ramadan.

    14. A YouTube video of a traditional dance. This is a great way to see traditional clothing worn by people for special occasions, hear samples of music, and often hear their language used in song form. Again, be sure to preview any YouTube videos prior to sharing with the class.

    15. Animals native to Morocco.

    16. Inventions or discoveries from Morocco—for instance, the first university (the University of Al Quaraouiyine) is in Fez, Morocco and was founded by a woman named Fatima al-Fihri in the year 859.

    17. Extra slides to consider including at the end may show samples of art work from the country at your local art museum and any photos needed to help illustrate the crafts or activities.

Once the presentation is over, allow time for students to make any additional comments or ask questions. Tell them about the various activities available at stations around the room. While students are engaged in activities, play quiet background music from the country.

Offer a variety of learning experiences to meet the needs of different learning styles. Have tables set up around the perimeter of the room. Students can move freely between tables exploring the activities. Here are some sample stations:

Art Activities

Study traditional Moroccan geometric patterns. Look at some examples of Moroccan patterns found on tiles, carpets, clothing and ceramics. Provide coloring sheets for students to color printed patterns or scraps of paper, scissors, and glue to create their own designs.

A fun activity can be making a lantern for Ramadan. Students can glue pieces of colorful tissue paper to the outside of glass jars. Put a small LED light inside the lantern to see the beautiful, colorful glow.

Computer Activities

Find a child-friendly game either on a computer or iPad for children to play. Or, in the case of Morocco, use a website, like Google Translate, to translate the child's name into Arabic.

Building Activities

Use LEGO® blocks to build something representing the country you are learning about. For Morocco, the children could build a desert scene, the Atlas Mountain range, a Mosque, or a building with the traditional arched doorways found throughout Morocco.

Local Games

Look for popular indoor games from the country.

Green Screen

Students take turns standing in front of the green screen to have their photo taken in the country they learned about. Look for green screen apps in the app store for either iPad or Android devices. Photos can be emailed home to the parents directly from the tablet. Suggest to families to print these photos and use in a project at home. For instance, a journal page, a pretend scrapbook page detailing their "visit" to the country, or pamphlet-type guide to the country.

Stamp Passport

At the end of the class give each student a passport stamp. Use round label stickers to make passport-style stamps using clip art.

Incorporating the Library Class with Learning Done at Home

Since a majority of the learning for homeschool families is led by the parents, consider offering families handouts to take home which might assist them in making lesson plans based on the library class. Handouts for a geography program might include:

- Country facts at a glance sheet. Some suggestions for the facts: continent country is located on; capital city; population size; national animal, bird, flower, and

country seal; samples of currency; some common words and phrases in their language with translation; popular names; national anthem in original language and translation, etc.
- Worksheets for students to complete at home, for example, an outline map for students to label and color in the country they learned about or a flag coloring page which includes basic country facts
- Internet links for families to find out more information about the country; also include online resources offered by library (such as Living Language and/or Culture Grams)
- Book list with fiction, non-fiction, movies, and music titles related to the country
- A list of upcoming library programs that might pertain to the country
- Suggestions for cultural events in the area
- Passport with fields to fill out country name, capitol, language(s) spoken, continent, space to draw the flag, spot to stick on passport stamp
- Display books about Morocco for families to check out after the program.

Homeschool Science Classes

Background

The Orange Branch of Cuyahoga County Public Library offered science classes for a few years before switching to geography. The science program was structured similar to the geography class described above. The group met once a month for an hour and a half and discussed either a scientist or inventor. Sometimes the class focused on a scientific concept and discussed the history of how that concept transformed through the years.

Sample Science Class

Begin the program with a PowerPoint discussion about the topic the class is learning about. Include notable people and inventors associated with each topic. Discuss the history and take a look at what might be coming in the future. Include photos and videos to help illustrate your talking points. Topics might include:

- History of movie making
- How flight works
- Hot air balloon science
- Electricity
- History of automobiles
- Evolution of computers
- Photography
- The science of microscopes and what you can see with them
- History of telecommunications

Arrange tables around the room with a variety of activities relating to your topic. Similar to the geography portion mentioned above, try to include activities that appeal to different learning styles. Some examples:

- If the topic is automobiles—set up a LEGO® assembly line where students each choose a part of a LEGO® car to assemble. The first student creates a base (using either a single flat piece or building from small bricks), the next student adds wheels to the body, then the third adds LEGO® bricks around the edge to make the sides of the car, etc.
- For photography, try using sun print paper. Students take the paper outside and place objects on it. After a few minutes the sun bleaches the paper. Quickly submerge the paper in water and the image will set. This is a great way to illustrate how printing photos in dark rooms works.
- For hot air balloon science, look online for free computer games that mimic the skills needed to fly a hot air balloon. Also try using a hair dryer to fill a small garbage bag with hot air. Once the bag is full, turn off the hair dryer, release the bag, and watch it float upwards.
- For a movie-themed class have children make a flip book so they can see object permanence in action.

Homeschool Art Explorers

Background

Once a month during the school year, approximately 30 homeschool children between the ages of six and sixteen gather at the Beachwood Branch of Cuyahoga County Public Library for the Homeschool Art Explorers program. Each month, they learn about the life and art of famous and sometimes not-so-famous artists.

The program began during a conversation with a homeschooling mother. Children's Librarian Amy Dreger wanted to reach out to the homeschool community and had considered the idea of offering an art class once a month. She mentioned the idea to the mother who thought it would be a great fit for homeschooling families, especially since they often don't have time to fit art into their curriculum. The mother offered to help Amy advertise the program through her co-op and gave her suggestions for other online places to promote the program.

The first session of Homeschool Art Explorers, which featured Andy Warhol, was filled to capacity. The need to heavily advertise dropped considerably as most families signed up for an entire year's worth of the programs. Because some families have stuck with the program for the four years that it has been offered, the challenge is to keep it fresh and come up with different artists each month.

Along with accomplished fine artists, Homeschool Art Explorers has also showcased illustrators and lesser-known artists. Care is taken to include racially diverse artists and both men and women. Featured artists have included:

- Andy Warhol
- Georgia O'Keefe
- Grandma Moses
- Mary Blair
- Dr. Seuss
- Jean-Michel Basquiat
- Faith Ringold

- Salvador Dali
- Romare Bearden
- Frida Kahlo
- Eric Carle
- Paul Gaugin
- Mary Cassatt
- John James Audubon
- Horace Pippin
- Norman Rockwell
- Pablo Picasso
- Jerry Pinkney
- Sandro Botticelli
- Paul Klee

Program Format

Students gather on the floor facing a projection screen. Offer a slide presentation that focuses on the artist's life, art training, challenges and major works. This presentation should be more of a conversation with the students, rather than a lecture. Ask lots of questions and allow them to express their opinions about the art. If applicable, read a picture book about the artist or show a brief video of them at work. Show the children the art project they will be working on, in the style of the artist that was just discussed. You can find project ideas online or come up with your own designs inspired by the artist's work. Send the children to the tables where art supplies have already been laid out. Let them create their artwork. Circle around the room offering praise and answering questions. Provide a display of books related to the artist, the art form that they represent or the time period in which the artist is from.

Allow two hours for this program. The presentation portion lasts approximately 30 minutes, with the remainder of the time earmarked for art creation. Many students will not need that much time to make their art, but others who enjoy the process, will take the full amount of time.

Supplies

The Homeschool Art Explorers program requires the purchase of art supplies beyond the usual construction paper, crayons, markers, scissors and glue sticks. Once items are purchased, they can generally be used many times before having to replenish. A well-stocked art cupboard should include the following:

- watercolors
- tempera paints
- paintbrushes
- oil pastels
- chalk pastels
- fine-line black markers
- paint trays
- colored pencils
- white mixed-media paper

- bowls for rinsing brushes
- newspapers for covering tables

Plan on one item per two students. If you are expecting 30 students, have 15 trays of watercolors, 15 packs of oil pastels, 15 paint trays, etc. Note that specific art projects might require additional items.

Homeschool Art Show

If you notice that you have the same families attending your program each month, you might want to consider hosting a Homeschool Art Show. Let families know in September that you are planning the event for late spring. Ask them to hold on to their pieces and bring their two favorites to one of the last sessions of the school year. Be sure that students' names are printed on the back of the painting along with the names of the artists whose work inspired the pieces. Mount the artwork on black construction paper, make labels with the child's first name and the artist's name, and hang them in a prominent place in the library, such as a meeting room. Offer a reception for families on the opening night of the art show.

Homeschool Book Discussion

Background

Book discussions allow homeschool participants the opportunity for social interaction with their peers. In addition, they are exposed to new books that may not be part of the homeschool curriculum. A quarterly homeschool book discussion was presented for several years at the former Parma-South Branch of Cuyahoga County Public Library. The program was part of a monthly homeschool series that also included art, science and music programming.

The most difficult part of planning a homeschool book discussion is selecting a book for the group to discuss. Because homeschool programs are offered for a wider age range, it is important to select a book that will be appropriate for all ages. The older readers will read the book on their own while younger participants may have the book read to them. This program began as a discussion for grades K–5; a middle school group (grades 5–8) was added when some of the participants began to age out of the younger discussion level. This age division lines up well with the natural division between middle-grade literature and teen books in the library.

Here are a few things to take into consideration when selecting a title. Select titles that are available in multiple formats. Many families prefer to listen to the book on audio as a family. Be sure to select titles that have numerous copies available so that each child or family can check out a copy of the book.

Families homeschool for various reasons and some families choose this option because of religious or conservative values. Classic titles often meet their needs better than contemporary ones. Some of the classic titles used for discussion included:

- *Mr. Popper's Penguins* by Richard and Florence Atwater
- *A Mouse Called Wolf* by Dick King-Smith

- *Sarah Plain and Tall* by Patricia McLachlan
- *The Mouse and the Motorcycle* by Beverly Cleary
- *Flat Stanley* by Jeff Brown
- *Stuart Little* by E.B. White
- *The Cricket in Time Square* by George Selden
- *The BFG* by Roald Dahl

Among more contemporary titles there were:

- *Because of Winn-Dixie* by Kate DiCamillo
- *The Talented Clementine* by Sara Pennypacker
- *Frindle* by Andrew Clements
- *Dinosaurs Before Dark* by Mary Pope Osborne

Preparation

1. Read the book. This may seem obvious but it is important to re-read the book even if it is a title you have read before so that it is fresh in your head.

2. Write or find discussion questions about the book. For many popular titles, discussion guides are available on publisher websites.

3. Look for related materials such as videos that can be shown to expand on the book.

Program Format

The program begins with a discussion of the book. Setting up chairs in a circle or semi-circle works well for the discussion portion of the program. Begin with a question that each person will answer such as "what was your favorite part of the book?" to ease them into the discussion and make sure everyone has an opportunity to participate. From there you can move to the prepared discussion questions. The discussion portion of the program can last anywhere from ten to thirty minutes depending on how talkative the group is and how much there is to discuss.

The extension activities will vary depending on the book but could include watching a related video or clip of the author or listening to a sound clip from the audio book. If the book has been turned into a movie, a selection from the movie could be shown for a comparison discussion. A movie license with public performance rights is needed to show the movie in the library. Trivia is another fun way to extend the discussion of the book.

Find a related craft or activity that accompanies the book. For example, a talent show was held after reading *The Talented Clementine*. For *Flat Stanley*, use rolls of kraft paper to trace flat versions of the participants that they can color and decorate. Provide a display of other books and audio books by the same author or books about topics discussed in the story. Pass out the books for the next discussion.

Sample Program Outline for *Beezus and Ramona* by Beverly Cleary

Supplies

- crayons
- safety scissors

- pencils
- handouts
- nametags

Program

Book Discussion—30 minutes. You can discuss the book, show the movie trailer or a clip from the movie, and compare the book to the movie/trailer.

Extension Activity—10 minutes. Complete the "Are you a Beezus or Ramona?" quiz. It might be necessary to read the questions/choices out loud for the younger kids who do not know how to read yet.

Craft Activity—20 minutes. You can offer "Ramona's Fortune Teller" or "Do Not Disturb Door Hanger" crafts. Both of these, as well as the quiz above, are available in the Ramona activity booklet on Beverly Cleary's website (The World of Beverly Cleary, 2010). If there is time at the end of the program, roll out a large piece of white kraft paper and have the kids work on a mural like Ramona did with her dad in the movie.

Home School Technology Programs

Technology programs are a nice complement to traditional homeschool curriculum because they offer the opportunity to use technology that families may not be able to purchase on their own. Here are some examples of technology programs that would be effective for a homeschool audience.

- Robotics—LEGO® Mindstorms NXT/EV3 and LEGO® WeDo offer educator curriculum that can be adapted for library learning.
- Makey Makey®—Learn about circuits and make anything conductive into a keyboard or game controller.
- Coding—The ability to code is an important part of digital literacy in today's world. The website Code.org® offers a variety of Hour of Code programs that introduce students to basic coding. The website Scratch™ and the app Scratch Jr.™ offer options for learning visual coding and basic block coding for children and teens.
- Stop motion animation—Use tablets with a stop motion app to create digital "flip books." This can be incorporated with green screen technology to add various backgrounds.
- 3D design—Learn the basics of 3D design in Tinkercad™ and create a 3D design to be printed on the library's 3D printer.

Offering homeschool programs at the library is an approachable way to expand your program offerings to a new audience. These attendees may already be library regulars or new customers. In addition, the programs allow attendees the opportunity to interact with their peers while expanding on homeschool curriculum.

WORKS CITED

"The World of Beverly Cleary." 2010. Accessed February 15, 2018. http://www.beverlycleary.com/.

Topic-Based Programming for Homeschoolers

Leah Flippin

Prior to my career in librarianship, I spent 16 years homeschooling my own children. Closely understanding this audience, I continuously take steps in my current position to facilitate their learning and meet their other important needs. I created a webpage for our library emphasizing low-cost and free resources for homeschoolers along with links to the basic information and local co-ops. During the last two years, I have developed programming for area homeschoolers based on topics of interest. In this essay, I am recommending programs that are of general interest to homeschoolers and can be adjusted, as needed, for your library's resources.

Getting Started

Examine the following points when considering a program:

- Do you have the staff, materials, budget, and space to handle the desired program?
- Is it appropriate for the library just to offer a room and for homeschoolers to provide speakers, materials, and equipment?
- Should you provide an outside speaker or presenter instead of a staff member to facilitate a program?
- Should you limit the subject programs to 4–6 annual programs or offer weekly or monthly ones?
- Should you incorporate hands-on family-based programs that appeal to a general audience as well as homeschoolers?

Researching Materials

There are many ways to find materials for homeschool-friendly programming. Try Pinterest and include the keyword "homeschool" along with the topic. You can also browse homeschool sites like 123Homeschool4Me (https://www.123homeschool4me.

com/), A2Z Home's Cool (https://a2zhomeschooling.com/), and Freely Homeschool (https://freelyhomeschool.com/) for ideas. You will have many resources available in your library's collection, but as you make your choices, examine potentially controversial topics and consider potential differences in your attendees' family values.

Marketing Strategies

Create a branding and a logo and publicize on social media sites. Reach out and network by posting online directly to co-op Facebook pages, contacting by phone or e-mail, and setting up listservs. The Facebook posts have an option to check the number of potential attendees to give an idea of how many to expect. If the library user checks "interested," a reminder will be sent nearer to the date. Some libraries prefer a more accurate record of expected attendees for planning purposes by establishing a registration process.

Encourage co-workers to offer informational handouts whenever a library user mentions homeschooling. We have a Homeschool Resources Guide that provides general homeschooling information like local co-ops, teaching tips, and collection resources. At our library website (http://weatherfordtx.gov/Library), we have a webpage dedicated to homeschool resources (www.weatherfordtx.gov/WPLhomeschoolresources). I post local resources as well as free and low-cost website links as an additional service to area homeschoolers.

Program Formats with Examples

Decide if you want programs with the same general topic that can be periodically repeated or series of programs that deal with different topics based on seasons, homeschool basics, or local interests. Gather information on best days, times, and topic interests for programs. The following are examples of programs, classes, series, and standalones that will benefit your homeschoolers as well as other audiences.

Backyard School Series

This series is a good example of a topic-based outdoors programming that changes with the seasons. It allows including projects and ideas from multiple subjects, not just science and nature studies. Be creative and find ways to incorporate hands-on activities that emphasize math, reading, spelling, writing, and art. These can be simplified to fit the younger crowd, or made more elaborate for additional age groups. I promote these programs as family-based so everyone can attend, and usually give out an information resource or materials for the parents to continue working with the topic at home as a supplement to curriculum. The program is loosely based on seasonal subjects, ideas, and alternatives:

1. Leaves (Fall)

or:

- Apples

- Geology
- Harvest
- Nuts
- Pumpkins
- Trees

2. Ice and Snow (Winter)

or:

- Birdfeeders and bird boxes
- Nature collage or center
- Winter gardening

3. Flowers (Spring)

or:

- Birds
- Bugs
- Gardening
- Herbs and seeds
- Kites
- Nature journaling
- Pond life
- Rain and rainbows

4. Water Fun (Summer)

or:

- Astronomy
- Camping
- Forest
- Fourth of July
- Ocean
- Outdoor treats
- Shells and fossils

You can conduct a presentation with demonstrations or make the program participatory with a class format. Under the presentation model, I display and explain slides as an information session, answer questions, and provide demonstrations, a display, or examples. This type of program is geared more towards the teaching parent. Often, I offer handouts for duplicating the process at home along with some related ideas and explanations for curriculum support. I prefer to choose selections for several different subject areas. Feel free to limit yours to one subject, like science, to make it more manageable for your situation. Using the class model, you supply the materials, demonstrate the project, and then explain "why" or provide additional related information.

Another option is a family-based program (or group program) which encourages participants to work as a group (or family) to complete a project; it may be a solution for homeschoolers looking for activities that include a wide range of ages. Additional forms of group programming could include speech/debate teams, homeschool choirs, competitions (spelling bee), contests (art, writing), show and tell, and other activities that require group participation. These could be combined with topics as well. For example:

- The debate team topic for this month: "Is technology changing people for the better or the worse?"
- The homeschool choir will be practicing selections of operas from the Romantic era this semester.
- This month's homeschool spelling bee will focus on words you should know for the SAT.
- Art contest requirements for this semester: landscape paintings using impressionism techniques.

Sample Walk-Through

I began by creating a graphic for marketing purposes that could be repeated for the general topic (Backyard School), with a subheading of the specified topic (Water fun). Then I researched a variety of hands-on activities that could be recreated at home. I used Pinterest and *Maker Lab Outdoors: 25 Super Cool Projects* by Jack Challoner to get some ideas.

I utilized a presentation model that included the following demonstrations:

- Water squirter math game (https://www.kitchencounterchronicle.com/water-squirter-math-game/)
- Make your own microscope (https://childhood101.com/science-for-kids-how-to-make-a-microscope/)
- Exploding baggies (https://buggyandbuddy.com/baking-soda-vinegar-science-experiment-exploding-baggies/)
- Melting candy magic (https://www.funwithmama.com/easy-skittles-rainbow-kids-candy-science-experiment/)
- Floating ink designs (https://www.craftymorning.com/floating-stick-man-trick/)
- Leak-proof bag experiment (https://funlearningforkids.com/leak-proof-bag-science-experiment-kids/)
- Bubble foam (https://busytoddler.com/2015/11/bubble-foam/)
- "Rainy" day impressionism art (https://www.123homeschool4me.com/impressionism-art-project-for-kids/)

First, I walked through the activities and requested help, as necessary, from audience members. Afterwards, I explained the material, discussed the demonstration, and asked and answered questions. The remaining time was reserved for the presentation slides. These included activities that covered various age levels and subject areas and allowed parents to ask any questions or offer ideas to each other. I provided paper copies of the slides for parents to take home for their family and placed the remaining copies in our homeschool area display (Dewey Decimal Classification 370s) for those who missed the event. Another option would be to arrange the slides into a booklet format and offer to parents to take home as a curriculum resource. In your handouts, include any citation information on the source of the projects for future reference and to give credit to the original creator.

Homeschool Basics (Individual Program Ideas)

Below are examples of basic topics of interest to homeschoolers that can be repeated as needed, either as stand-alone programs or series.

Homeschool 101

Programs related to the basics of homeschooling are usually well attended. I cover state laws, teaching methods, popular curricula, local co-ops, and library resources in this presentation. I offer this program in late July either annually or every other year if it conflicts with summer reading schedules. Some libraries may decide to present this program more than once a year as some parents may start considering homeschooling mid-way through the regular academic year.

College and Career Prep

This program can be offered any time, but earlier dates in the school year offer additional planning time for parents. Covering options after high school, you will walk parents through the college admission process and give insight into how homeschoolers can transition more easily into that environment. Also include information on careers, trade schools, entrepreneurship, freelance work and other unconventional paths like a gap year.

Curriculum Swap

Offer a time and place for homeschoolers to exchange materials. I provide a handout of literature and curriculum suggestions from the library as a supplement.

Lapbooking

Lapbooking, and its companion method, notebooking, are terms that are almost exclusively used by homeschoolers. It is an original and creative format of research reporting by the student. The Homeschool Share website offers free templates for this style at https://www.homeschoolshare.com/. A lapbook or notebook can be made of any material, but its most unique characteristic are foldables, like mini-booklets, flaps, and wheels. The child cuts, decorates, fills out, and arranges these foldables, scrapbook-style, with information. The result is a beautiful keepsake that also functions as a record of the student's work. The notebook version for the older child simplifies the work into 3 ring binders with decorated sheets that focus more on writing skills. A series by Carson-Dellosa (2016) has a subject-based workbook series called *Interactive Notebooks* that simulate lapbooks. For programming purposes, this works best as an interactive class. I include samples of various styles to create the background of a lapbook. Then I provide a collection of the different foldables for participants to paste to the background. They cut, color, and decorate according to the theme and take it home to complete the research and information.

Nature Journaling

Observation of nature as part of science study is a great way to provide hands-on learning. Parents interested in a Classical or Charlotte Mason teaching approach are especially fond of this record-keeping option. A nature journal can include samples of flowers, leaf rubbings, drawings, poems, and descriptions. It gives students time to reflect and observe the natural order of science all around them and raise questions for further research. The journal also encourages writing skills and creativity while creating a record of schoolwork. Nature guides, sketching art books, and science encyclopedias will be of extra help; a fun title to use for the younger child (age 4–8) is *Backpack Explorer: On the Nature Trail* by Oana Befort (2018). I do a presentation demonstrating to parents the best ways to help a child create a journal, what to include, and how to observe. I offer ideas on creative ways to express information and encourage exploration and research, including suggestions for library collection items. I display some of these items at the presentation so library users can check them out immediately following the program.

Special Needs Homeschooling

The challenge of teaching children with learning disabilities or special needs is a concern for many parents. They obtain help from therapists and treatment centers, but these do not usually focus on academic skills. When my autistic child was receiving treatment, our family learned the basics of Applied Behavior Analysis (ABA) therapy, and the treatment center assigned an education specialist to help develop an academic program for us to implement. It might be helpful for the library to bring in an ABA therapist to explain the basics of this method, or help parents find local resources for their child's specific needs. I realize that most libraries won't have a staff member who has experience in this area, so it may be best to bring in a guest speaker. If I were doing a presentation, I would emphasize the need for parents to allow the children to move at their own pace and use activities that support their learning style. For the more severely disabled children, I would focus on academic skills that are more aligned with life skills: sight words, reading, basic math, counting money, and telling time. Prepare activities related to "work tasks" for the day, using a visual schedule or list to follow. There are many book titles that explain ABA therapy and its implementation, but it is best understood by observation. Other options for special needs programming could include a special needs story time or a hands-on workshop. I would also encourage parents to bring samples of projects they do with their children. It would benefit the special needs child to explore the samples, giving other parents an idea of what type of activities peak their own child's interest. It will be helpful to offer materials recommending help with different education issues of special needs children, for example, remedial reading for dyslexia or teaching social skills for people with autism. Some libraries provide story times for mentally disabled individuals using PECS (Picture Exchange Communication Symbols).

Picture Study

A picture study is an art appreciation activity. It is usually offered in a class format, where students observe the displayed work of art and learn about the artist. This type of program can be followed by "homework" where students and parents can continue working on various aspects of the subject after the library program is over. Encourage students to become familiar with the person behind the work, recommending biographies or biographical DVDs from your library's collection. Then discuss the art piece, ask students to describe it (on paper or verbally), and replicate. Allow the students to form their own opinions on the style and beauty of the piece and consider various forms of narration for expressing their personal taste and observation. For example, younger children could be prompted with questions that they answer verbally. Those students who are comfortable writing can narrate what they observe on paper or create a story for the work of art. History buffs may enjoy doing research on the author with provided resources. Older students with an interest in art skills may prefer an attempt at imitating the work or art techniques of the piece.

Organizing the Homeschool Home

The inside of a homeschool home often differs from a typical home. Depending on the parental teaching approach, it could resemble a simulated classroom or be blended into daily family life. A program where participants share ideas and swap organization tips would be beneficial. Librarians can be especially helpful with creative suggestions for organizing materials. I would offer this program as a presentation and include photographic samples and basic tips on organization like color coding, thematic boxes, work tubs, alphabetical or numerical solutions, and appropriate containers or furniture options. Allow those who have a problem to share their challenges and then ask for audience input. Look for materials in the collection that deal with organizing the home as well as solutions specific to homeschooling online.

Homeschool Fair

This event at our library is one of the best attended for the entire year. The optimal times to schedule this program are in June, July, or early August. We contact local businesses, co-ops, therapy centers, entertainment venues, and others who have options or discounts for homeschoolers. The focus is more on businesses and organizations that can provide extra-curricular and social supplements rather than academics, although some participants will be local co-ops and private schools that can offer classes for homeschoolers. Each participating business and organization receives an event table where they can display and distribute materials. They are not allowed to collect any membership dues or sign someone up on site, but they can create a contact list of interested attendees.

Typical Programs Modified

Enhance or duplicate typical programs that the library already provides and modify them for topic-based programming that might be of interest to homeschoolers to motivate participation. For classes or programs that take place during the school day, consider these options.

Book Groups

Form a book group for students to participate. Select titles from library staff's ideas or vote on a list of suggestions by the group members. Organize a "book review" presentation where students recommend the book to others in the group. To make it more educational, allow students to present the review in a format of their choice: PowerPoint slides, video-sharing, podcasting, public speaking, writing, art, etc.

Animals

Bring in a guest speaker with some animals and you will always have an enthusiastic group of kids show up. Some homeschool families may also have experience with and knowledge about certain animals and their care, and might want to share this with the group. Select a scientific class (e.g., reptiles) or a specific animal (e.g., pygmy goat) to use as a theme for a program. If appropriate and possible, consider having the program outdoors.

Arts and Crafts

Present an art or a craft program based on specific art movements or styles for the older students; or consider creating a comic book. The younger students would enjoy themes like "Sensory Art" or "Paper Crafts." The messier the better!

Community Garden or Nature Center

For some outdoor learning, create a space on your library campus for a community garden. Homeschool students and other patrons can volunteer to care for the garden. Organize a nature center with items to examine indoors or consider a nature experience outside for hands-on exploration. Build bird feeders and houses, plant a butterfly garden, and have nature play activities.

Computer Classes

Numerous topics can be considered for these classes, such as programming, graphic design, website design, networking, social media safety, research skills, etc. Stay updated on the current and most popular tech developments. Try to find a staff member, a parent from the homeschool community, or a community partner who is enthusiastic and skilled enough to offer some program options.

Cooking

Cooking is a popular activity, and can be tied to a theme related, for example, to geography or culture studies. Keep in mind allergies and food restriction policies of your library. If you cannot cook or distribute food at your library, you can still provide handouts and materials with information.

Cultural Studies

Select a country or state and research information to present to students. Developing activities from all subject areas (geography, math, science, history) would be welcome to homeschoolers, as many enjoy the unity study approach. You can do this with any topic, but cultural studies are particularly popular with homeschoolers. Include recipes, clothing, and other hands-on experiences when possible. Encourage everyone to bring something of interest to share.

Drama Club

Thespians anyone? An introduction to theatre and an informal performance is just the thing to really understand the art of acting. Consider a simple musical to liven things up, and base it on a theme each year. Hold auditions to give students more performing experience. Keep the number of rehearsals around 8–10; this should be adequate for most simple productions. Set a date for a dress rehearsal and performance. Invite the public to attend.

Games and Gaming

For those who would like a break from studies, gaming provides a way to relax and meet with others. Escape rooms are increasingly popular and would be a great addition for puzzle solving and logic skills. You can find helpful resources for these activities online or try *Escape Rooms and Other Immersive Experiences in the Library* by Ellyssa Kroski (2018).

LEGO Club

Using LEGO blocks, children can work together or individually to create projects or answer a challenge. This takes thinking skills like planning and teamwork, and the setting can also be a great non-threatening exercise for social skills development. Each meeting could be based on a theme and expanded to many academic subjects.

Music Programs

Music and movement classes for the younger students are always popular and are easy to tie into themes based on seasonal topics or children's books. For the older students, consider someone to lead a choir, ensemble, or string quartet. Develop these meetings into topic-based programming by specifying a genre for the semester or year. Selections from musicals, chansons, or folk songs are a few examples of topics to cover in choral music.

Public Speaking

Explore and choose themes in advance to allow students time to prepare. Add a discussion option to presentations. Employ the traditional forms of speech preparation as well as digital options. Provide ice breakers that help students work on communication skills. Consider creating debate teams and provide prompts to get debates started; be sensitive to differing family values. Encourage the students to research and work together for a lively debate. Bring in the students' families and the public at large for the final debate.

STEM/STEAM

There are many ways to incorporate STEAM learning across all ages. Demonstrations and participation are key elements of these subjects. You can set up stations for individual projects, organize team activities, or conduct a class. Themes for STEAM programs and stations can include LEGO design, Scratch, Robotics, weather, construction, chemistry, Minecraft, etc.

Show and Tell

Show and tell is a great option for homeschool families. The age of the student is not as important, so this would work for a family-based program. You can specify a theme or topic to cover for each meeting to narrow down the choices. This type of program offers an opportunity for homeschool students to express themselves in a social setting while also honing important public speaking skills. You provide the location and keep the flow going. There may be something you can "show and tell" that would be very interesting to kick off each meeting. It is often difficult for homeschoolers to create this type of an experience at home, so it's a simple way that libraries can contribute to the homeschool community.

Writing Lab, Workshop, Contest or Club

Encourage children to express themselves on paper. Some of these programs can be based on a theme for those eager wordsmiths who enjoy a challenge. The theme could have specific parameters. For example, create a dialogue using characters in a book and see if the other participants can guess who "wrote" it. Share a writing prompt, photo, or painting and have everyone give a response. Have a system in place for critiquing each other's work to provide the best positive experience for feedback.

Additional Topics for Older Students

In addition to topics mentioned above, older students may find the following subjects and angles helpful for general skill-building, college preparation, or workforce:

- Car purchase and maintenance
- Carpentry
- Electronics
- Engine Repair
- Entrepreneurship
- Fashion design
- Jewelry design
- Needlework
- Photography
- Videography

- Survival skills
- Woodworking

With topic-based programming, you can focus on local homeschoolers' needs in your community and offer educational experiences they may not be able to find elsewhere. This strengthens the image of the library as a place where lifelong learning takes place, and where you can assist parents with academic resources that support a child's success.

WORKS CITED

Befort, Oana. 2018. *Backpack Explorer: On the Nature Trail: What Will You Find?* North Adams, MA: Storey Publishing.
Carson-Dellosa. 2016. *Interactive Notebooks.* Greensboro, NC: Carson Dellosa Publishing Company.
Challoner, Jack. 2018. *Maker Lab Outdoors: Super Cool Projects.* New York: DK Publishing.
Kroski, Ellyssa. 2018. *Escape Rooms and Other Immersive Experiences in the Library.* Chicago: American Library Association Editions.

Providing Vibrant Social Opportunities for Homeschooling Families

HOLLY S. HEBERT

Introduction

While there is a common misconception that homeschooled children lack social interaction, additional opportunities provided by the library are often valued and welcome. According to homeschool researcher Richard Medlin, homeschoolers want their children "to learn to respect and get along with people of all ages and backgrounds. They use a wide variety of resources outside the family to give their children the opportunity to interact with others" (Medlin 2013, 287). Seventy percent of homeschoolers use the library as a resource in their educational process. Libraries can be a dynamic community hub for homeschooling families fostering social interaction for children and parents. Tom Bruno, a librarian, highlights this in his article "Homeschool Resources That Extend the Curriculum and Build Community." He states, "not only can library programming supplement the homeschooling curriculum but it can also provide invaluable opportunities for socialization as well" (Bruno 2017). This essay will highlight some specific ways that libraries cultivate opportunities for social interaction.

Libraries as a Community Space

Libraries evolved long ago from book repositories into community spaces where many different types of social activities happen on a daily basis. Libraries today offer activities and programs for all ages, as well as meeting spaces, collaborative spaces, and now makerspaces. On any given day, a scan of the local library shows people browsing for materials, doing homework, going to a business or club meeting, using the computers, doing yoga, participating in programs for all ages, being tutored, or attending a class about genealogy or computers. Truly, everyone uses the library. It's a great place to see a cross-section of society.

Libraries in our society today often serve as a "third space." First coined by Ray Oldenburg, this term "refers to places where people spend time between home ('first' place) and work ('second' place). They are locations where we exchange ideas, have a good time, and build relationships" (Butler and Diaz 2016). In a more recent Brookings Institute article titled "How Public Libraries Help Build Healthy Communities," the authors argue that public libraries fit firmly into this third space. "A reason public libraries are seen as such important third-place institutions is that they and their librarians have gradually taken on other functions well beyond lending out books" (Cabello and Butler 2017). Librarian Tom Bruno concurs and states "The public library is often a nexus for the community, a safe space for people of all ages to come and learn and experience new things. As such it is a perfect supportive environment for homeschoolers" (Bruno 2017).

So it comes naturally that homeschooling families would find libraries a great place not only for educational resources but also as a place to gather formally and informally and take part in the many programs and services that the library has to offer. Librarians wishing to see how libraries are serving homeschooling families can find examples from all over the country in the professional literature, on library websites, and by networking with other librarians. The following examples are just a sampling of how librarians are working with homeschooling families all over the country.

Providing Excellent Customer Service to Homeschooling Families

Before going further, it's important to do a self-check in regard to customer service. A library that delivers poor customer service will not have vibrant programs, attract users, and, therefore, will not have a thriving social environment. If changes need to be made, consider making them before trying to reach your homeschooling customer base.

When preparing to offer any kind of activity or event, it's important to consider the user experience from a patron's point of view. Customer service is important in every aspect of library service and is essential in welcoming and keeping homeschooling families. No different from any other patron group, homeschooling families want to feel welcome and respected. In 2016, trainer Laurie Brown presented a workshop called, "How to Deliver Great Library Customer Service" which included her Top 10 Service Guide. Librarians serving homeschooling families will benefit from following these tips.

1. Have trust: assume people are telling the truth.
2. Say "yes,": make their day, find a way to say "yes" if at all possible.
3. Give alternatives: if it's not possible to say "yes," explore other options.
4. Be approachable: look up, smile, make eye contact and acknowledge.
5. Be respectful and kind: they'll remember how you made them feel far longer than what you told them.
6. Be flexible: don't get hung up on the rules.
7. Be patient: don't get frustrated with challenging customers and don't be afraid to ask a co-worker for assistance.
8. Keep it simple: do what you can to make it easy for the customer.
9. Be positive: your mood is contagious, spread some happiness.
10. Do the right thing: when in doubt, trust your gut [Brown, 2016].

Timing of Activities

A survey of library websites shows that most programs and activities for home-schooling families are planned between 10 a.m. and 2 p.m., with the majority being held between 1 p.m. and 2 p.m. which seems to be the sweet spot for homeschoolers. This timing is also good for libraries because it is often a less busy time and librarians can focus on the attending homeschooling group. Homeschoolers also attend programs that aren't specifically designed for them, but most activities marketed to homeschoolers will be held on weekdays before public and private schools get out for the day.

Managing Multi-Age Activities

While librarians are used to creating programs for specific age levels, creating multi-age programs for homeschooling families can be more challenging as they may have children in several different age ranges. Adrienne Furness, in her webinar "Helping Home-schoolers in the Library," mentions that successful programs for homeschoolers often "have the widest age range and programs geared towards the whole family. If you have five kids at home and two kids can attend a program at your library and the other three can't that is probably going to be something that is going to dissuade you from going to the program." Multi-age programs are natural for homeschooling families. Librarians can play to this strength by having older children help younger children (which they are already accustomed to doing at home) and utilizing parent volunteers. Other strategies for multi-age activities include team teaching with another librarian and creating stations around the room for different age groups (Furness 2012).

Integrating Homeschoolers, Public Schoolers and Private Schoolers

Who should be included? Some programs will be geared towards homeschoolers just by the nature of the program or because it is offered during brick-and-mortar school hours. Other programs will attract mostly public or privately schooled students. Every library population is different and it might take some trial and error to find the right balance. At times, homeschooling families might ask for separate programs, and libraries will have to decide if they can accommodate that. Summer reading programs are a good example. Most likely, it's just not feasible or desirable to run two separate summer reading programs. In order to keep everyone happy, reading challenges should be broad enough to include all interests.

Children's story times organically attract homeschooling families and non-homeschooling families alike. Story times often include a craft, signing, or some other activity related to the story and are geared towards younger children.

The Spring Hill Public Library in Tennessee hosts a monthly Saturday chess club for school aged children. There are also chess competitions hosted at the library, and although the teams are sometimes divided into school teams and homeschool teams, still, everyone is there playing. The library also has a monthly Saturday Pokémon Club for school aged children (Spring Hill Public Library 2019).

Shawna Sprague, librarian at the Evans Public Library in Illinois, hosts Fantastic Fridays club which includes a craft and storytelling time and is open to children up to age 10. The club is held every month in the afternoon, with a different theme chosen for each gathering (Shawna Sprague, personal communication, March 28, 2019).

Tapping into the escape game craze, during school breaks, the Omaha Public Library has hosted escape game rooms with teams signing up according to grade level. It also hosts Nerf war lock-ins and uses the whole building as the playing field. These events attract homeschoolers as well as public and private schoolers and are a great success (Melanie Webb, phone interview, March 29, 2019).

Meet and Greet/Open House

One of the first activities libraries should offer to their homeschooling communities is some sort of meet-and-greet event, where homeschooling families can come to the library, learn about library and homeschooling resources, and have time to meet other families. This can be a formal or informal affair. Some libraries time these to coincide with the start of the school year. Even though there is no formal start of the school year that is common for all homeschooling families in an area, there is a general starting time, especially for co-ops and tutorials. A meet-and-greet event can be offered every year if the homeschool community has a frequent turnover of residents, for example, when the library is located near a military base or a university campus. If that is not the case, such an event can be offered once every few years.

In 2017, the Omaha Public Library hosted a successful Back to School Ice Cream Social for homeschoolers which was advertised on their website and was attended by about 50 people. Youth Services Librarian, Melanie Webb, reported that they plan on offering it again soon. She paid particular attention to her patrons' needs; for example, she was extremely conscious about food allergies and dietary concerns as she found that many of her homeschooling families deal with these issues (Melanie Webb, personal communication, March 29, 2019). Indeed, many homeschooling families have children with food allergies, and that may be one of the reasons why they homeschool. According to a study at the University of Maryland, ten percent of families who have children with food allergies choose to homeschool to keep them safe. Librarians should be aware of food and also sensory issues when planning events and programs (Bollinger et al. 2006, 418).

Meet-and-greet activities provide opportunities for families to network with each other, which is especially important for those families who are just beginning the journey of homeschooling.

Information Fairs, Panels and Workshops

Homeschooling parents are often looking for more information to help them as they educate their children. Whether it is a parent who is just curious about homeschooling, or someone starting their first year as a home educator, or a homeschooling veteran, having specific events geared towards educating parents is a great way to attract and keep homeschooling families. Information fairs can include library resources, vendors, curriculum, etc. Libraries can host panels comprised of homeschooling parents, students, librarians, community members, and co-op leaders. The Home School Legal Defense Association (HSLDA) conducts workshops, as well as regional, state, and local homeschooling organizations. These types of events can be held in the evening or on weekends when more parents are available. With homeschooling families, often one parent will attend while the other stays home with the children. While informative, these events also provide opportunities for parents to network, share strategies, and socialize with other homeschooling parents.

Speaking in Front of a Crowd

One experience that homeschooled students might miss, unless their parents are purposeful in arranging it, is an opportunity for public speaking. In public schools, most students are required to take a communication class where they have to speak in front of an audience; one of the earliest examples is show-and-tell in kindergarten. Libraries have found several ways to provide homeschoolers with these types of opportunities.

The Arlington Heights Memorial Library in Illinois hosts a Lunch Bunch for homeschoolers. According to librarian Christina Giovannelli-Caputo, the children bring their lunch, and there is a show-and-tell time which gives them an opportunity to share in front of others (Giovannelli-Caputo, phone interview, March 29, 2019).

Brenda Mills, branch librarian at the Scotland Neck Memorial Library in North Carolina, believes in encouraging others in the community to engage in homeschooling activities. The library hosts an Art Show for homeschoolers, and the local arts council is invited to be involved. Students display their art around the library and talk about their work. The library also hosts a science fair where community leaders and professionals knowledgeable in those areas act as judges and students are given the opportunity to explain and showcase their projects (Brenda Mills, personal communication, March 27, 2019).

The Omaha public library hosts a yearly spelling bee which is registered with the Scripps National Spelling Bee just for homeschoolers. According to librarian Melanie Webb, official Scripps National Spelling Bee word lists are given out ahead of time and medals are awarded by the homeschool association. Winners are eligible to advance in the contest (Melanie Webb, phone interview, March 29, 2019). A Google search showed that participating in the Scripps National Spelling Bee is popular all over the country. Events have been held at the Bethlehem Public Library in New Hampshire, the Chapel Hill Public Library in North Carolina, and the Ilsley Public Library in Vermont, among others.

Involving the Community

Local communities are full of professionals who can be utilized. Jackie Hicapie, Youth Services Librarian at the Union County Public Library in New Jersey, recommends inviting speakers from the community to present specific topics. Ask local business owners to share how they run their businesses. Skilled workers are often of special interest. Bring in employees from the local hardware store to provide hands-on activities in addition to a short lecture. The police and fire departments are also often willing to share what they do in the community to keep everyone safe (Jackie Hincapie, phone interview, March 27, 2019).

Makerspaces

Makerspaces are all the rage at libraries across the United States. Utilizing 3D printers, laser cutters, media studios, woodworking, electronics stations, letterpress printing, and needle crafts, makerspaces are great for STEM and STEAM projects, as well as for building community. According to Kristin Fontichiaro, "Makerspaces are not just stuff or places. In thriving makerspaces, there is a culture as well, one that prioritizes community, mutual support, and a noncompetitive atmosphere" (Fontichiaro 2018, 222). In other words, makerspaces are made for human interaction and community building among participants. The possibilities for programs are limited only to the imagination of the librarians, space and staff limitations, and, perhaps local fire codes. For example, when the library at Abilene Christian University opened their makerspace in 2015, they had no idea that it would be so popular with the homeschooling community. Created as an academic makerspace, it is open to students, faculty, and to the public. As a result, the Maker Academy was born, where homeschoolers, as well as kids who attend public and private schools, are invited to participate in summer day camps offered to elementary and middle school ages (Baker 2018).

Digital Media Studios

Many libraries now have a digital media studio that is located either in their makerspace, or separately. Both Arlington Heights Public Library in Illinois and Nashville Public Library in Tennessee have professional grade recording studios.

Studio NPL at Nashville Public Library often has homeschoolers using their equipment and space for a variety of programs and activities. According to Niq Tognoni, Studio Coordinator, "one homeschool group uses Studio NPL as the 'venue' for their final semester performances and projects. We provided them with a microphone, theatre seating, and spotlights for their dances, songs, poems, and short stories that were written as part of their semester finals." Another group used their studio to record a self-produced album (Niq Tognoni, personal communication, April 16, 2019). The digital media studio at Arlington Heights Public Library was funded by the Friends of the Library and is open to all users from the community, according to librarian Christina Giovannelli-Caputo. They also have had students record songs and community members record commercials. They have staff who assist with the studio and show people how to use it. She emphasizes that libraries can often utilize the talents that their staff already have to help run the studio. Library staff often have talents separate from their library duties that can be discovered when projects like a digital media studio are implemented (Christina Giovannelli-Caputo, personal communication, March 29, 2019).

Homeschool Band and Instrument Tryout

Ask anyone who has ever played an instrument in a band or orchestra, and they will tell you that it requires not only mastery of the instrument, but also following the conductor and learning to blend in with fellow musicians. It's a team effort.

Although not all libraries will have the space or soundproof area to accommodate a band, hosting a community band performance is a great outreach to the community. In the western suburbs of Chicago, West Suburban Home School Band (WSHSB) is a concert and marching band with upwards of 200 members (West Suburban Home School Band 2019). Several libraries in the area have been able to partner with WSHSB and invite them in for a concert and an instrument tryout. According to their website, the Woodbridge Public Library hosted WSHSB for the Homeschool Instrument Tryout Program in 2018. Homeschoolers were invited to try out marching band instruments (Woodridge Public Library 2018). WSHSB has also come to the Glen Ellyn and Carol Stream libraries. According to Kate Easley at Glen Ellyn, "At my library, almost the whole band came and played a concert which was really fun (and very loud!) After that they did an instrument tryout. They did the same instrument tryout at Carol Stream. It was very successful here. The band is the West Suburban Homeschool Band so they like having an opportunity to recruit new members, and the kids loved getting a chance to try out the instruments" (Kate Easley, personal communication, April 10, 2019).

Just Hanging Out

Of course, there can be time set aside for informal gatherings as well. Hangouts are popular times when homeschoolers can socialize, play games, have snacks, watch movies, etc. Christina Giovanelli-Caputo at Arlington Heights Memorial Library offers a homeschool hangout and says, "Homeschool Hangout is a laid-back program where youth socialize and parents have a chance to chat and collaborate" (Giovanelli-Caputo 2018, 45). Building in some non-structured time can give everyone a chance to socialize without an agenda. Many libraries host monthly hangouts with set times, but, of course, sometimes hangouts just organically happen.

Homeschooling Families in Advisory Groups

Libraries often have advisory groups that meet and discuss a variety of issues that are relevant to their interests. The Teen Advisory Board (TAB) is a good example. TABs usually meet once a month to discuss wanted and needed materials, services, and programs, and often join in planning events. If the homeschool community at a library is large enough, a homeschool parent advisory group might be formed as well. They can discuss and suggest materials, help manage a homeschool collection, plan events and activities, and be a sounding board for librarians. Christina Giovanelli-Caputo at Arlington Height Memorial Library recommends forming a Homeschool Advisory Team "where parents and youth can advise the library of their needs and identify the way the library can serve them" (Giovanelli-Caputo 2019, 29). As with any group, members will arrive and depart, and dynamics will change from year to year. It is up to the librarian to facilitate and moderate the group and ensure that it runs smoothly. For teens especially, this might be their first opportunity to interact in this kind of advisory group and can become a meaningful experience.

Book Clubs and Book Award Programs

Book clubs are a mainstay at libraries and can take on many forms. There can be book clubs for homeschool parents who want to read a specific book geared towards their interests. Book clubs can be for certain ages, and also multi-age, for homeschoolers, as well as for all other students. Book discussions are a great opportunity to learn how to share in a group and form relationships.

One especially empowering opportunity exists in Nebraska, where the state book award is called the Golden Sower Award. According to librarian Melanie Webb, traditionally students in public and private schools were the ones who were able to vote on three grade levels of books to win the Golden Sower Award. Now, however, homeschool students can also vote for books at their public library and have a say in which books win the Golden Sower Award each year (Melanie Webb, phone interview, March 29, 2019).

Volunteering

Libraries also provide a unique opportunity for volunteering. Both adults and homeschooled students can volunteer. From shelving materials to clerical work, tutoring, helping with programs, assisting users on computers, and even teaching classes, there can be a job for everyone. While most libraries have age limits for volunteers, they generally allow starting as early as during teen years. Brenda Mills at Scotland Neck Memorial Library has had former homeschoolers who first came to her programs as students, then became volunteers, and at least one became an employee (Brenda Mills, personal communication March 27, 2019). What a great way to recruit future librarians.

Not Just for Humans

Who says socializing is just for humans? Libraries also offer chances to socialize with a variety of animals. PAWS to Read is a popular nationwide program that brings in specially trained dogs and cats to libraries and other organizations so that children can read to them. In addition to improving reading skills, reading to these furry animals can "foster positive social interactions [because animals] provide a safe, non-judgmental presence for struggling readers" (PAWS to Read 2016).

Besides dogs and cats, libraries often host other creatures. A recent Google search found that The Rochester Hills Public Library in Michigan offers a large fish tank in the children's area. The youth services area in The Forest Park Public Library in Illinois houses a pet turtle named "Shelly." In Arkansas, the Craighead County Jonesboro Public Library has had a menagerie of creatures over the years, with a hedgehog and fish being the current residents. The Homewood Public Library in Alabama hosts a raptor day where the Alabama Wildlife Center brings several feathered friends to visit and the New Castle Public Library has a resident cat named Stacks who has his own Instagram account at https://www.instagram.com/stacksthelibrarycat/.

There are many benefits of having animals in the library. Some families can't have pets for different reasons, and the library offers a safe and controlled environment for engaging with them. Again, allergies should be a consideration, and each library has to determine what is best at their organization.

Partnering with Seniors

What if libraries brought together two groups of users who are often at the library at the same time, homeschoolers and senior citizens? There are several ways that libraries can create opportunities for these two groups to interact and learn from one another. The timing would work for both groups since homeschoolers like to come during school hours and seniors don't have work time constraints and often visit the library during the daytime. Bringing these groups together might foster intergenerational relationships that they might not have otherwise. Homeschooling families might live far from their extended families and so might the seniors. Libraries could host a board game time which could also include puzzles, and card games. One perfect combination might be genealogy and local history research. Other opportunities might include sewing, needlework, woodworking, and cooking. Many libraries have started seed libraries. What better way to utilize a collection than to do some gardening together? Perhaps include Master Gardener Association in the area and/or the local 4H club which often have a homeschooling group.

Conclusion

While this essay lists many ways that homeschooling families can and do socialize at the library, it is impossible to describe everything that exists in different parts of our country in different types of libraries. This essay only scratches the surface of the variety of opportunities out there. The options really are limited only by the imagination of librarians and maybe a few practical concerns. The author is hopeful that she achieved her goal of presenting a selection of activities to spark an interest and give a starting point and a few ideas to professionals and administrators.

Works Cited

Baker, Laura. December 12, 2018. "Extending Our Reach: Using Day Camps at Academic Library Makerspaces to Include Homeschoolers" April 4, 2019. http://www.inthelibrarywiththeleadpipe.org/2018/day-camps-makerspaces-homeschoolers/.

Bollinger, M.E., L.M. Dahlquist, K. Mudd, C. Sonntag, L. Dillinger, K. McKenna. 2006. "The Impact of Food Allergy on the Daily Activities of Children and Their Families." *Annals of Allergy, Asthma and Immunology* 96 no. 3: 415–421.

Brown, Laurie. October 13, 2016. "How to Deliver Great Library Customer Service." (ALA Ecourse). Accessed April 4, 2019. https://www.slideshare.net/ALATechSource/how-to-deliver-great-library-customer-service.

Bruno, Tom. December 11, 2017. "Homeschool Resources That Extend the Curriculum and Build Community" Accessed April 4, 2019. https://medium.com/everylibrary/homeschool-resources-that-extend-the-curriculum-and-build-community-1dba830c799b.

Butler, Stuart M., and Carmen Diaz. September 14, 2016. "'Third Spaces' as Community Builders" *The Brookings*, Accessed April 4, 2019. https://www.brookings.edu/blog/up-front/2016/09/14/third-places-as-community-builders/.

Cabello, Marcella, and Stuart M. Butler. March 30, 2017. "How Libraries Help Build Healthy Communities." *The Brookings*. April 4, 2019. https://www.brookings.edu/blog/up-front/2017/03/30/how-public-libraries-help-build-healthy-communities/.

Fontichiaro, Kristen, ed. 2018. "Creation Culture and Makerspaces." *Information Services Today: An Introduction*, edited by Sandra Hirsh. 220–228. Lanham, MD: Rowman & Littlefield Publishers.

Furness, Adrienne. April 18, 2012. "Helping Homeschoolers in the Library." (Webinar). April 5, 2019. http://librarylinknj.org/content/helping-homeschoolers-library.

Giovanelli-Caputo, Christina. 2018. "Hanging with My Homies: Engaging Homeschoolers in Library Services" *Voice of Youth Advocates* 41, no. 5: 45.

_____. 2019. "Hanging with My Homies: The Homeschool Revolution" *Voice of Youth Advocates* 41, no. 6: 29.

Medlin, Richard G. 2013. "Homeschooling and the Question of Socialization Revisited." *Peabody Journal of Education*, 88, no. 3: 284–297.

Paws to Read. 2016. "About." Accessed April 23, 2019. https://www.pawstoread.com/about.html.

Spring Hill Public library. 2019. "Calendar of Events." Accessed April 12, 2019. https://springhilltn.libcal.com/.

West Suburban Home School Band. 2019. Accessed April 12, 2019. http://www.wshsb.org/index.htm.

Woodridge Public Library. 2018. "Homeschool Instrument Tryout Program." Accessed April 23, 2019. https://www.woodridgelibrary.org/homeschool-instrument-tryout-program.

Public Libraries Serving as Homeschool Hubs

LESLIE PAULOVICH

This essay is intended to be a guide for turning your library into a homeschool hub. Topics include outreach, evaluating library resources, specific program ideas, and collaborating with other libraries. The essay follows a case study on the Robinson Township Library, a public library in the suburbs of Pittsburgh, Pennsylvania, serving 22,000 residents (U.S. Census Bureau 2016). To increase library usage among homeschooling families the library took steps to develop a strategic plan. The process included questionnaires to better understand the needs of homeschooling families and to determine how the library could fulfill those needs. The library then used those results to design and provide suitable services. The library also collaborated with regional partners to expand services and develop best practices.

Outreach

Do you have a homeschooling demographic? Depending on your state's laws and regulations, you may be able to find out how many homeschooled children are living in your demographic area by visiting your state's education website. Most states require homeschooling families to report their education status to education officials. Other reputable resources for obtaining homeschooling statistics is the National Home Education Research Institute and the National Center for Education Statistics. Using the 2016–2017 statistics reported from the Pennsylvania Education Department, the Robinson Township Library was able to determine that there are 170 homeschool students living within a six-mile radius of the library. This information confirmed that there is a need for homeschool services.

The first step to serving homeschooling families is to locate the families living in your library's demographic area and make initial contact. Chances are that homeschooling families are already visiting your library. Pay close attention to the families that visit the library during regular school hours. Even if you only have one homeschooling family visiting your library, you have a gateway to many other homeschooling families as well. Homeschooling families rely on each other for support and tend to collaborate often. If you currently do not have homeschooling families attending your library, you will have

106

to find other ways to make initial contact. Online searching and social media can be a great start. Many homeschool groups use social media, for example, Facebook, and have a dedicated social media page to share events and other resources. Families are often members of a homeschool co-op which can be found through a quick internet search.

Once you have identified at least one homeschooling family, make contact, introduce yourself, and state your intentions. Parents will be more likely to open up to you and trust you if they know your intentions are to help and serve their family. Unfortunately, some homeschooling families have a mistrust of institutions due to how their family may have been treated in the past. Get to know the parents and children in order to build a trusting relationship. Start to uncover the needs of homeschooling families through conversation. Listen to parents when they express their needs. Parents may not be aware of what resources or programs you can offer, so often you will need to interpret conversation and be creative to provide services. Parents will not say, "We need social activities or makerspaces" instead parents will say, "I wish my son/daughter could meet other kids his/her age" or "It would be nice if I had the space to do science experiments at home."

Collect Information

Another way to get to know your homeschooling families is through surveys and questionnaires. Questionnaires and surveys are a great way to obtain information and collect feedback. Designing an effective questionnaire can be tedious, but luckily, in a public library setting, you don't have to be too formal. Your patrons probably wouldn't mind answering multiple surveys if you didn't get the information you needed the first time around. While each library may be seeking different information, there are two questions you should always include on your questionnaire: "What are your children's ages?" and "What is your availability (days and times)?" Many homeschooling families prefer daytime programs rather than evening programs, so if you are only offering programs for school-age children in the evening, you may be missing out on program attendance.

To get as many respondents as possible, be sure to offer your questionnaire in many different formats including an online version. Some parents may have time to fill out the questionnaire while visiting the library. Others may want to take the questionnaire home to fill out later. In the latter case, be sure to include a secure location for the patron to drop off the questionnaire. Always make the privacy of your patrons a top priority. In some cases, your patron may not want to fill out a questionnaire at all. To get around this incorporate your most important questions into conversation while collecting verbal answers. Also, always give an online option for convenience. There are a lot of free online survey builders available such as Survey Gizmo, Survey Monkey, Survey Planet, Google Forms, and Typeform. Once you have developed your questionnaire, ask your homeschooling families to share it with other homeschooling families on their social media pages.

The Robinson Township Library designed two different questionnaires. The first questionnaire sought to discover the families' reasons for homeschooling, which resources homeschooling families use, and which resources they are lacking. The second questionnaire focused on library use among homeschooling families. The library specifically wanted to know if homeschooling families were using the library, if they were aware of the resources available at the library, and which resources they were using. The questionnaire responses were evaluated and used to develop and implement library services tailored to homeschooling families.

Below is a small sample of the questionnaire results in which thirty-three separate families responded.

1. What factors influenced your decision to homeschool?

- 30 percent Child with autism
- 20 percent Mistrust of school systems
- 20 percent Flexibility
- 10 percent Child with special needs other than autism
- 10 percent Child with special talents

2. When choosing to homeschool, what support and resources did you find readily available?

- 24 percent Facebook social group
- 20 percent Online support
- 20 percent Other homeschool families

3. Describe any disadvantages you face while homeschooling.

- 20 percent Lack of social interaction/feel isolated
- 15 percent Curriculum expenses

4. Describe how the public library is currently supporting your homeschooling needs?

- 36 percent Books
- 33 percent Library programs
- 6 percent Computers/internet access

5. Describe solutions/suggestions for the public library to better serve homeschooling families.

- 40 percent Host more frequent programs for homeschooling families
- 15 percent Host more programs for teens during school hours
- 10 percent Provide curriculum-based materials that can be borrowed from the library such as textbooks and microscopes
- 7 percent Host multi-age programs

6. Describe what types of programs you would like to see at the library.

- 88 percent Curriculum-based programs in subjects such as science, history, geography, foreign language, computers, literature, and writing
- 18 percent Hobby-based programs such as knitting, sewing, music lessons, and fandom
- 15 percent Life skills programs such as fire safety, cooking, credit cards, and checking accounts
- 6 percent Fitness-based programs

The results indicated that homeschooling families are using the library, but desire more from the library, specifically more programming and curriculum-based materials. It was also revealed that homeschooling families desire social support as well as a safe place for their children to learn and interact with other children. It had also been discovered that differentiated instruction, inclusion, and sensory-friendly environments are important due to the number of children with exceptional learning needs.

Evaluate Library Resources

Take inventory and evaluate your library's resources. To effectively serve home-schooling families, you must know what your library can offer. Besides the obvious, libraries have many resources that are appealing to homeschooling families. Your job is to identify those resources and then find a way to deliver them to your intended audience. For example, does your library offer online databases? Databases are a great tool for teens writing research papers. Does your library have a meeting space? Homeschooling families need a space outside of the home to work on school projects, enjoy social time, and collaborate with other families. Does your library offer any unique collections such as microscopes or STEM kits? Homeschooling families like to enrich their curriculum, but often find that resources can be expensive and not worth the investment for short-term use.

The Robinson Township Library has a small physical library space of 3,000 square feet and a collection of 25,000 physical items. With limited space and collection being a barrier, other resources had to be considered. The library focused on four major resources:

1. Interlibrary Loan. The library relies on interlibrary loan for day-to-day operations, but interlibrary loan also gave a unique opportunity to borrow special educational kits from other libraries including microscopes.

2. Programming Space. The library has access to a separate programming space not within the library with optional seating and tables. This space can be used to host multiple programs simultaneously while accommodating different age groups and different interests. In addition to programming, the space can be used to homeschool families to collaborate and meet with other families.

3. Human Resources. Many librarians have additional skills or hobbies that can be incorporated into programming, such as knitting, sewing, and photography. This minimizes having to find and pay an outside entity to provide such services for programs. Another librarian has an education background which is helpful for writing and evaluating learning goals.

4. Databases. Many families were not aware of the databases available through the library. The library used this as an opportunity to boost usage by incorporating databases into programming.

Library Programs for Homeschooling Families

When planning homeschool programs, keep your audience in mind. Homeschooling families are often seeking educational programs to supplement their child's learning needs outside of the home. When designing homeschool programs, outline specific learning goals and how the program achieves them rather than just planning an activity. Even when you are planning social activities, establishing learning goals is important. Your learning goal should reflect the type of social interaction you are hoping to see as an outcome of the activity such as teamwork, verbal communication, or non-verbal communication.

Book Clubs

Facilitating book clubs is not a new or original idea, but they are often overlooked when developing library programming for children. Librarians have put such a tremendous focus on STEM programs that traditional library programs seem to have been forgotten. In addition to the traditional value of book clubs, homeschool children also benefit from having an instructor outside of the home, peer support, and peer collaboration. This is especially important for those homeschool students who may lack peer interaction at home. Book clubs are also an opportunity to introduce storyboards and writing prompts.

Curriculum-Based Programs

It is important to incorporate educational programs that meet specific and predetermined learning goals for homeschooling families. Learning goals can include subject learning such as math, reading, and science; or developmental enrichment such as constructing, organizing, and applying knowledge. Through conversation and questionnaires, you will be able to uncover what key learning areas your homeschooling families are seeking.

At the Robinson Township Library there was a strong interest in curriculum-based programs in subjects such as history, geography, and science. In addition, many parents expressed the desire for their children to experience a classroom setting with an instructor outside of the home with peer-to-peer interaction. To fulfill those needs, three unique library programs were designed specifically for homeschool students, Passport Pals, Zoo Keepers, and Travel USA. All the programs were designed for elementary-aged children but could be easily adapted for other ages.

Passport Pals

Passport Pals received the 2017 Best Practices Award for exceptional service to school-aged children, their families, and caregivers from the Pennsylvania Library Association. The focus and goal of the program is to give children an opportunity to explore other countries and cultures by promoting a sense of inclusion and respect for others. At each one-hour session, children get to "travel" to another country and explore. Children receive their own play passport, world map, country fact sheet, recommended book list, country-themed bookmark, and get to enjoy crafts, games, and snacks from other countries and cultures.

The program can apply many different learning goals. It enriches children by providing resources to expand language learning, foreign or domestic, strengthen reading skills through recommended books lists, learn basic geography, and use creative thinking and expression in cultural arts and history. The program has also found ways to incorporate STEM through crafts and activities. For example, one activity provides the children with recycled materials and they must try to build the Eiffel Tower out of the given supplies.

Zoo Keepers

Zoo Keepers is a winner of the 2018 Best Practices Award for exceptional service to school-aged children, their families, and caregivers from the Pennsylvania Library Association. The focus and goal of the program is to give children an opportunity to explore wild animals that live at the zoo, their natural habitats, and what it takes to be a zoo keeper. Each one-hour program focuses on a different animal at the zoo. Children receive their own Zoo Keeper folder, Zoo Keeper checklist, zoo sticker map, animal fact sheet, animal trading card, recommended book list, and get to enjoy crafts, games, and STEM activities. Children also get to view a live web cam of the animal from a zoo or conservation site.

Zoo Keepers is a fun learning opportunity that can apply to many different learning goals including social responsibility. The program also focuses on animal and environmental conservation, which helps kids make smart decisions about recycling and other issues. In addition, Zoo Keepers enriches children by providing resources to expand learning in the following areas: strengthen reading skills through the recommended books lists; increase knowledge of biological science, environment, and ecology; learn basic geography and physical characteristics of places and regions; and develop decision-making skills and responsible behavior.

Travel USA

The focus and goal of the program is to give children an opportunity to explore the United States, state-by-state. During each one-hour program session, children get to take a "road trip" to a different state and learn about the culture, geography, food, language, landmarks, and more. Children receive a map of the United States, a state flag sticker book, a state information sheet, a recommended reading list, a state-themed bookmark, and a key chain to collect souvenir license plates from each state visited. Children also get to enjoy crafts, games, and STEM activities.

Travel USA touches upon multiple learning goals such as geography, history, reading informational text, science, and art. Sample activities include building a suspension bridge to represent the Golden Gate Bridge, exploring and creating Andy Warhol's pop art, and constructing igloos.

Passport Pals, Zoo Keepers, and Travel USA can be easily implemented in any library setting. Learning materials for each program are available online. There is no cost or fee to download the materials. Crafts and activities can be performed with basic craft supplies such as scissors, glue, construction paper, etc. If you have an extremely low budget or limited supplies, homeschooling families may be willing to bring their own supplies or make small donations to the library. For more information and material downloads, visit LibrarianGoals.com.

Enrichment Programs and Special Visitors

Introduce local community leaders to your homeschooling families. Reach out to the police department, fire department, and local government. They can provide enrichment in fire safety, self-defense, and civic topics such as voting. If your police department does not have a K–9 unit, try reaching out to another police department or a countywide K–9 program. Visits from the K–9 unit are very exciting as well as educational.

Bring nature indoors. Reach out to local farmers or county parks to bring nature to the library. Chick hatching is a very popular event that takes place each spring. Many local farmers are willing to host a demonstration to educate students. Many county and state parks offer free educational programs to schools and libraries such as information sessions on birds, insects, animal tracks, and foliage. Try reaching out to animal shelters who often host animal educational programs. In addition, many private animal enthusiasts are available to host live animal shows at your library for a small fee.

Provide opportunities for students to experience culture. Many museums, art galleries, and theatres have outreach/traveling programs. Try to pick a program that accommodates various ages, or one that works in stations. These programs tend to have a higher price tag, so you will want an activity that can benefit the most number of children. If you do not have the budget, try reaching out to a local theatre/dance studio. Usually the instructor is willing to do a free workshop or show in exchange for the free publicity and marketing.

Multiple Age Programs

Many homeschool families reported that age restrictions on library programs were burdensome due to age differences between siblings. Designing a quality program to accommodate all ages can be extremely difficult. It is challenging to find an activity that is developmentally appropriate for various ages and yet is appealing to all ages. Hobbies tend to fill this gap in programming quite well. Activities such as knitting, sewing, painting, pottery, photography, and screen-printing have worked well at my library. Group projects are also helpful, such as using Cardboard Creator® where kids get to build their own creations using cardboard and basic tools. It is helpful to have teens assisting young children. Another solution is to offer an additional space for siblings during an age specific program. For example, offer a play space for younger siblings or a lounge space for older siblings to hang out. Social events such as parties, games nights, and movies, can also be very beneficial for children of all ages.

STEM Programs

It is essential for all children to have access to STEM programs and makerspaces. It is especially important for libraries to offer such resources to homeschooling families since many families may not have the space or resources to do so at home. STEM opportunities offered to homeschooling families at the Robinson Township Library include Cardboard Creator®, LEGO® clubs, Makey Makey®, forensic science activities, health career exploration, science experiments, cooking and science, coding, and green screen technology.

Collaborating with Other Libraries

By collaborating with other library professionals, you will get an amazing amount of feedback and new ideas. You may discover that other libraries have been hosting homeschool programs all along and you can learn a thing or two. Maybe other libraries are not serving homeschool families and you can teach them a thing or two. Either way, it is an invaluable opportunity to brainstorm with peers.

Develop Best Practices

Work with your peers to develop best practices for serving homeschool families. These practices will help you maintain the quality of your programs and work as a guide for self-assessment. Below is a list of best practices developed at the Robinson Township Library.

1. Plan events with specific learning goals. Homeschooling families are looking to enrich their children's education with unique experiences. Providing specific learning goals will attract homeschool families.

2. Provide opportunities for social interaction. Homeschooling families want their children to have frequent social experiences outside of the home. Be sure that your programs include activities that promote social interaction such as group work, games, discussions, and playtime.

3. Schedule around your patrons. At the Robinson Township Library, it was found that homeschool families were more likely to visit the library during the day, but you should always discuss scheduling with your patrons to see what days and times work best for their schedule.

4. Ask for feedback often. Keep up the conversations and surveys even after you have established program attendance. Patron needs can change frequently and it is important to keep up with those trends.

5. Reach out to other libraries. Seek professional advice from other library professionals. This may also open up the opportunity for additional supplies or resources that you did not have access to before. Schedule around one another for maximum attendance. If your neighboring library were to host a homeschool book club on Tuesday mornings, you certainly would not want to host a homeschool book club on Tuesday mornings. Instead, offer a science program on Wednesday mornings.

6. Be sensitive to children with special needs or talents. Provide sensory-friendly options and host programs that can easily be adapted for students of all abilities. Allow parents and caregivers to participate during programs to ensure the most comfortable experience.

Additional Resources

By reaching out and making relationships with other libraries, you may be opening the door to an array of new resources beyond interlibrary loan such as programming kits, robotics equipment, microscopes, science kits, tablets, and curriculum materials. The Robinson Township Library staff members gained access to educational materials that were previously only available to another library's staff. Having access to the new materials helped enrich programming while saving money in the programming budget.

Expand Services to Homeschool Community

Homeschooling families often must travel to find resources and enrichment programs. Not all the families you serve will live in your community. By working with neighboring libraries, you will be able to expand services to homeschooling families in your area. Expanding services also helps take some of the pressure off of your library. It would be unrealistic, and extremely time consuming, to prepare all of the enrichment services that homeschool families are seeking. Working with a network of libraries provides adequate support for individual libraries and thorough services for homeschooling families.

Becoming a homeschool hub is a process that takes time, creativity, and ongoing assessment. The Robinson Township Library has been providing services to homeschooling families for about 18 months. In the beginning, the library only offered one homeschool program per month. Now, the library offers seven different homeschool programs per month. Scheduling has proven to be challenging, but assessing the schedule every four months has minimized scheduling conflicts. It is important to keep up with the needs of homeschooling families by continuously having conversations with parents and children, have a suggestion box on hand at all times, and send out at least three questionnaires/surveys per year for evaluation and continued strategic planning.

WORKS CITED

Paulovich, Leslie. 2018. "Librarian Goals with Leslie (blog)." https://www.librariangoals.com/.

U.S. Census Bureau. 2016. *American Community Survey 5-Year Estimates Kennedy Township.* http://census reporter.org/profiles/06000US4200339312-kennedy-township-allegheny-county.pa/.

U.S. Census Bureau. 2016. *American Community Survey 5-Year Estimates Robinson Township.* https://census reporter.org/profiles/06000US4200365352-robinson-township-allegheny-county-pa/.

Washington, Monica. 2017. *Home Education Synthesis Report 2016–2017.* Harrisburg: Pennsylvania Department of Education.

Revitalizing Homeschool Programming for Public Libraries

A Case Study

CASEY O'LEARY *and* RUTH SZPUNAR

In the fall of 2015, Mooresville Public Library focused their homeschool programing efforts into a STEAM-based program and a book club. In this essay we will discuss how these changes were implemented and how they revitalized Mooresville Public Library's homeschool community.

Getting Started

Mooresville Public Library first began hosting a homeschool program in September 2006, titled Homeschool Hour, which was held for one hour, twice a month, during the traditional school year (September-May), for students between the ages of six and twelve.

The program covered a variety of topics, such as American pioneers, kite building, musical instruments, and reader's theater. On average, 28 children and their parents participated in each session in the first year, reaching a peak average of 31 participants per session in 2012. The program's name had also changed to Homeschool Group @ the Library.

While the bimonthly sessions remained consistent, additional programming was added in subsequent years with varying success. In 2008, Mooresville Public Library held a Homeschool Spelling Bee, with the winner participating in a regional spelling bee as part of the Scripps National Spelling Bee program. The spelling bee continued for two additional years, but was cancelled due to declining participation. In 2011, homeschooled students were offered the opportunity to participate in a theater production, written and directed by the Youth Services Librarian; the program was again offered in 2012. Both productions, "Sleeping Beauty" and "The Wizard of Oz," saw attendance of over 100 patrons and allowed students to learn about the dramatic arts through literary connections.

Before 2013, homeschool programming was facilitated by the head of the children's department. Beginning in the fall of 2013, homeschool programming was assigned to the school-age programmer, since the students were primarily school age. The program focused on topics that would encourage circulation of the juvenile non-fiction collection, and the program was renamed Homeschool Library Explorers to reflect the "exploration" of the library's juvenile collection. Topic selection was at the discretion of the facilitator, and teaching style varied with each facilitator. Attendance began to decline with turnover in the position of school-age programmer. The library struggled to find someone who could meet the wide range of abilities and interests among homeschool programming students. The position was part-time, so those seeking full-time employment would only remain in the position for a matter of months.

When full-time early literacy librarian Jess Frederick took over facilitation of Homeschool Library Explorers in the fall of 2015, she decided on a STEAM-based focus for the sessions. STEAM, or Science, Technology, Engineering, Art, and Math, "has been kind of a buzzword" in libraries, according to Frederick. "We were talking about STEAM and how important it was, and I thought, 'this really isn't my wheelhouse, but I want to do it. I want to try.'"

Initial Planning

Programming was broken down into two components: Homeschool Library Explorers with a STEAM focus, and Homeschool Book Club. Homeschool Library Explorers was scheduled bimonthly, with topics selected by Frederick; the book club was held once a month. Parents dropped off their children and then remained in the library during the sessions.

Homeschool Library Explorers sessions, for children ages six to twelve, were focused on topics successfully used by other librarians, located via blog posts and other online sources. Programming ideas are shared freely among public librarians, and programming that had been successfully facilitated at another library meant greater success for Frederick. Topic selection was also influenced by the juvenile non-fiction collection and the availability of library materials on that topic. Sessions that incorporated projects with inexpensive, easily accessible materials for a large group were often chosen, such as bridge design with mini-marshmallows and toothpicks.

Homeschool Book Club was tailored for students in grades 3–5, encompassing the ages of the majority of regular homeschool programming attendees who were capable of reading independently. The Indiana State Library circulates book club kits for children, and that became the go-to resource for selecting titles for book club gatherings. Book club kits were delivered via interlibrary loan, and students signed out a copy and returned it after the book club meeting. Occasionally, the library purchased multiple paperback copies of titles from Amazon or discount bookstores, and created book club kits to be stored at the library. These kits have also been used to facilitate outreach book clubs in local schools, resulting in increased circulation of materials and opportunities to partner with other organizations.

Program Goals

The primary goal of homeschool programming was creating additional educational opportunities for area homeschool students at the library. Mooresville Public Library's own mission statement reads, "The library is committed to supporting lifelong learning by serving as a center for self-education," and that educational focus extends to students' future endeavors. Frederick shared, "Especially for future jobs, I think it's really important, because a lot of the STEAM fields are the ones where you can actually get a job right now … if you go to college you can actually maybe get a job out of college…. I was kind of passionate about helping them prepare for later in life."

The library also saw the programs as an opportunity for homeschool students and their caregivers to socialize with peers. Students had the opportunity to develop friendships before, during, and after sessions. While children learned collaboratively in the program, caregivers could talk to other homeschooling parents and share ideas and information. Alternatively, parents could find a quiet place in the library to work or enjoy some time away from their children.

Lastly, the library sought to improve programming and increase circulation of its juvenile materials. Homeschool parents had expressed appreciation for science and art programming because both areas can be challenging for homeschooling in terms of knowledge and resources. STEAM-based programming would incorporate age-appropriate topics and concepts, presenting them in fun and interesting ways. Attendance would be a clear indicator of the success or failure of the program, as would the circulation of juvenile nonfiction materials related to program topics.

Budget

Homeschool programming was considered part of the annual programming budget, rather than given a standalone budget. Mooresville Public Library receives children's programming funds from an endowment, and part of those funds paid for homeschool programs.

The sessions often used items already owned by the library; for example, a session about bridge architecture might include an activity building with Legos from the children's area. Many activities required minimal supplies that could be purchased locally. More expensive supplies were usually ordered online and could be used more than once, such as child-sized plastic magnifying glasses.

Programming costs also included occasional visits from artists and science and technology experts. Local teaching artists were booked through a program called Arts for Learning, with the cost of hosting an artist averaging $85. Occasionally, a friend or family member pitched in too: Frederick's husband, a computer scientist, facilitated several computer programs about coding at no cost to the library.

Homeschool Library Explorers

Frederick usually began the planning process at least three weeks in advance of the session date. She chose an experiment, craft, or experience that sounded engaging to her, and completed the activity herself to ensure she could achieve the desired outcome. Next, she defined an objective for the session: what did she want the students to understand when they left the session?

Frederick would then research the topic online to find out what other children's librarians had done in terms of programming, and adapt successful session ideas to her particular group of students. After outlining the basic session plan based on the objective, Frederick would pull relevant library materials for a display. Online videos or photos were often used; one session about caves incorporated an online tour of a famous cave in Europe. Occasionally, PowerPoint was used to share multiple images or videos with the students.

Prior to each session, Frederick made sure to write out each step of the session in detail, adding lecture notes so she felt more prepared for class day.

Homeschool Book Club

The title for each month's book club was provided one month prior to each book club session. Frederick would read each book, then research activities and crafts that went with the story. A favorite regular activity, "Vote with Your Feet," offered students the opportunity to express their opinions about a book by standing close to or away from a paper on the floor, containing a written statement about the book. For example, after reading *From the Mixed-Up Files of Mrs. Basil E. Frankweiler* by E.L. Konigsburg, Frederick placed a piece of paper on the floor that read, "Claudia and Jamie made a good decision when they ran away from home." Participants could move away from the paper if they disagreed, but place their feet near or even on the paper to show agreement. Their responses helped lead the book discussion.

Book club gave homeschool students the chance to read books from a variety of authors and genres that they may never have discovered on their own. It also gave them a chance to discuss books with their peers and engage in deep thinking about each title.

Community Connections

Guest speakers, teachers, and performers were an invaluable tool in developing strong homeschool STEAM programming at the library. Their specialized knowledge of particular subjects meant that the students could go more in-depth with the topic from a reliable source.

Guests also took the pressure off Frederick, giving her time to work with individual students during guest visits, as well as avoiding the expectation that she would have to "know everything" about STEAM.

Mooresville Public Library's most popular homeschool session was led by the local Soil & Water Conservation District, who parked a mobile garden in the library parking lot and presented gardening basics to the students. Land-grant universities, like Purdue University, have similar programs through the Cooperative Extension System and often work with schools and libraries to offer programming. Local Master Gardeners groups or the Department of Natural Resources are also good resources for guest presenters.

Another guest who received positive feedback from students and parents was Japanese calligrapher Garret Uyeno. He is a teaching artist through Arts for Learning, an organization that facilitates arts programming at schools and libraries by connecting teaching artists to venues. Uyeno offered a Japanese calligraphy workshop for homeschool students. He provided supplies and facilitated the class. The cost to the library was less than $100, and provided a unique experience for the students.

Occasionally, as mentioned earlier, a friend or family member can help out at no cost to the library. A library patron who trains service dogs gave a presentation to the students and brought along a furry friend. A local retired teacher presented a class about Indiana history to students. When the library partnered with a local elementary school to host children's author Tom Watson, homeschool students were encouraged to read his books, then invited out to lunch in between school presentations to spend time with the author.

Future plans for guest visits include partnering with a local college observatory to discuss astronomy; inviting scientists to come in and talk about research; creating opportunities for students to learn about the financial planning required to start a business from local small business owners; and asking local police officers to present information about police dog training.

Marketing

Marketing at Mooresville Public Library is the responsibility of the programming staff. Frederick often did her own marketing or used other children's department marketing resources. Each program was listed on the library's online calendar, accessible through the library website. Programs were also listed on paper fliers containing library programming for children. Homeschool programs were promoted on the library's social media accounts: Facebook, Twitter, and Instagram.

Often, participants found out about the library's programming through word-of-mouth. Homeschooling parents would invite other families to join them for Homeschool Library Explorers, and the guests would become regular attendees. Word-of-mouth was invaluable when Frederick took over homeschool programming, since marketing resources were limited and she was a stranger to most of the parents and children.

Evaluation and Impact

The primary evaluation tools for the success of homeschool programming were attendance and caregiver feedback. Attendance is tracked by session each month by the program facilitator, then included in annual library statistics reports to the Board of Trustees.

In terms of attendance, "Homeschool Library Explorers" has been a huge success. In two years, there were 33 sessions with over 500 total students. "Homeschool Book Club" has discussed 20 titles, with 228 total students. In comparison, Mooresville Public Library programming for the same age group, but not specific to homeschool students, showed fewer than five students per session during the school year. Homeschool programming students participated consistently and in larger numbers than those of the same age who participated in other library programs.

Additional feedback on the programming was received through a survey written by Ruth Szpunar. The surveys were given to both caregivers and students at the beginning of a recent session in paper format, with an online version available. Participants were told that library staff would not look at their responses, and were encouraged to share their feelings openly and honestly. Each completed survey was sealed in an envelope and given to Szpunar to compile.

Nine homeschool caregivers completed the survey. Sixty seven percent of those surveyed rated the programming at the top of the rating scale provided, and said that they bring their children to 75–100 percent of homeschool programming.

Seventeen homeschool students completed the survey. When asked about their favorite part of "Homeschool Library Explorers," 53 percent said their favorite part was the activity offered in each session. They were also asked how they felt about the program, and every child selected a positive response, saying they liked or loved the programming.

The STEAM focus has been a huge success. When students and parents were asked what topics they'd like to see in the future, all but one topic (history) was STEAM-based. Parents were enthusiastic about the homeschool programs, as was evident from the following quotes from their responses:

- "It has been amazing! It opens up their learning and gives them time to learn alongside other kids."
- "They love that they get to do a variety of hands-on projects."
- "Many times they are learning about things I wouldn't have ever thought to introduce them to."

Lessons Learned

When asked what tips she would give to other librarians implementing homeschooling programming, Frederick had a few thoughts.

First, she encouraged librarians to set a very intentional classroom atmosphere. Most homeschool students are not used to raising their hands before they speak. She consistently encouraged them to do so, and built a culture where this became the norm. She shared that after months of work in this area, regular attendees helped remind new attendees to raise their hands before speaking. She also had the following advice for handling students who want to interrupt to share everything they've learned on a topic with you. She uses the phrase: "Let me go through my notes, and if I forget something, then you can share it at the end!"

She also said that sometimes the programming was difficult for younger students who needed one-on-one help for some activities. She especially enjoyed days when guest speakers were present because it allowed her to spend more time working with students rather than presenting. She also suggested limiting written activities, or offering an alternative (such as drawing, retelling, or building).

Future Plans

Frederick recently vacated her position as homeschool programmer. A newly hired Children's Librarian has taken on responsibility for Homeschool Library Explorers and Homeschool Book Club, and plans to continue offering similar programming options for the next four months, and then evaluating the success of the programs. This librarian applied for the position with previous experience in homeschool programming at another local public library; those skills will come in handy to facilitate similar programming at Mooresville Public Library.

A recent addition of a part-time Teen Librarian to Mooresville Public Library means there is potential for adding homeschool programming for teens. Caregivers have expressed interest in such programs, but further evaluation of the needs of this particular age group, as well as their availability, is required before moving forward. Fall 2018 would be an ideal time to consider implementing homeschool programming for teens.

Conclusion

Homeschool programming in public libraries meets the needs of both homeschool families and libraries by providing educational programming and community building using library resources. Mooresville Public Library's decision to offer STEAM-based programming to homeschoolers has resulted in consistent program attendance, high programming statistics, and positive caregiver feedback and program support. No special training is required to facilitate homeschool STEAM programming, just the willingness to thoughtfully research topics that offer educational opportunities for students. Homeschool STEAM programs can be facilitated with a minimal budget, and can provide a wealth of opportunities to partner with community members and organizations. Homeschool programming fulfills the library's mission to "support lifelong learning" by offering programs and resources for educating members of the homeschool community.

Appendices

I. Topic Ideas

Food Science	Bridges	Beginning Coding
Volcanoes	Friction	Bubbles
Meteorites	Pi Day	Plants
Flight	Finances	Slime
Candy Sushi	Service Dogs	Balloons
Gingerbread Houses	Mummies	Titanic
Art & Recycling	Earthquakes	Magnetism
Tools and the Brain	Owl Pellets	Watershed
Robots	Japanese Calligraphy	

II. Suggested Resources

ONLINE

Association for Library Service to Children (ALSC) Blog (http://www.alsc.ala.org/blog/category/programming-ideas)

Science-Technology Activities & Resources for Libraries (STAR net)—STEM Activity Clearinghouse (http://clearinghouse.starnetlibraries.org)

Show Me Librarian Blog (https://showmelibrarian.blogspot.com)

TeachEngineering STEM curriculum for K–12 (https://www.teachengineering.org)

BOOKS

Ardley, Neil. 2014. *101 Great Science Experiments*. New York: Dorling Kindersley Limited, Inc.

Churchill, E. Richard, Louis V. Loeschnig, Muriel Mandell, and Frances W. Zweifel. 2014. *365 More Simple Science Experiments with Everyday Materials*. New York: Black Dog & Leventhal Publishers.

Cook, Trevor. 2011. *Awesome Experiments for Curious Kids*. London: Arcturus.

Doudna, Kelly. 2016. *The Kids' Book of Simple Everyday Science*. Minneapolis, MN: Scarletta Kids. (Doudna has also written an entire series called Super Simple Science for ABDO Publishing Company.)

Margles, Samantha. 2013. *Star Wars: Science Fair Book*. New York: Scholastic Inc.

Maynard, Christopher, Christopher Maynard, and Christopher Maynard. 2006. *Science Fun at Home*. New York: DK Publishing.

Spangler, Steve. 2012. *Naked Eggs and Flying Potatoes: Unforgettable Experiments that Make Science Fun*. Englewood, CO: Steve Spangler Science.

VanCleave, Janice Pratt. 2007. *Great Science Project Ideas from Real Kids*. San Francisco, CA: Jossey-Bass. (VanCleave is a popular standard for science projects and has published many books on the subject.)

III. Survey Forms

HOMESCHOOLING AND LIBRARIES SURVEY—FOR PARENTS

1. How long have your children been coming to homeschool programming at the Mooresville Public Library? (Choose one answer.)

- Less than 1 year
- 1–2 years
- 2+ years

2. What percentage of homeschool programs do your children attend? (Choose one answer.)

- 75–100%
- 50–75%
- 25–50%
- 0–25%

3. Why do you bring your children to homeschool programming? (Check all that apply.)

- Socialization
- Hands-on projects
- Exposure to books
- Learning opportunities
- Curriculum support
- Other:

4. Please rate the homeschooling programming offered on a scale of 1–10

- Worst 1 2 3 4 5 6 7 8 9 10 Best

5. How do you feel about guest presenters? (Choose one answer.)

- They're fantastic!
- They're ok
- They're terrible!

6. Are there specific guest presenters you'd like to comment on?

7. Are there organizations or people you would like to see as guest presenters?

8. What topics would you like to see more programs about?

9. What impact has the homeschooling program made on your homeschool?

10. Anything else you'd like to share on this topic?

HOMESCHOOLING AND LIBRARIES SURVEY—FOR CHILDREN

1. What is your favorite part of homeschool library explorers?

2. How do you feel about homeschool library explorers? (Choose one answer.)

- I love it!
- I like it
- My mom or dad makes me go
- I only come because my friends are there
- Other:

3. How do you feel about guest presenters other than Miss Jess? (Choose one answer.)

- They're great!
- They're ok
- They're terrible!
- Other:

4. Are there specific guest presenters you'd like to comment on?

5. What topics would you like to see more programs about?

PART IV

Beyond the Public Library

Parents' Night Out

Heidi S. Busch

Paul Meek Library on the campus of the University of Tennessee at Martin has hosted several Parents of Homeschool Students Information evenings. These themed evenings are meant to educate parents of the resources available to them as members of the learning community. The library staff has worked with a wide variety of organizations both on and off campus to ensure that the parents not only understand what the library can provide, but also how it can serve as a portal to other materials and services. This essay will elaborate on the various evenings held and resources shared during those evenings and provide the reader with additional ways academic libraries may serve all parents in their communities.

Introduction

The University of Tennessee at Martin's Paul Meek Library has hosted Parents' Night Out events for our local homeschoolers. These events take place usually in the early fall as a way for parents to learn about the resources and the people that are available to them as part of the learning community.

In the fall of 2013, a local alumni member mentioned to members of her homeschool organization that she uses the Paul Meek Library for resources to create and expand learning opportunities for her children. The members of the group thought this was an excellent opportunity and wanted to know if they could also use the library and its resources. The alumni member then approached the staff of the library and asked if the members of her group could come to the library as well. We are a state institution, so community members are welcome to come in and use our resources.

Faculty and staff of the library met together and determined that yes, as community members the group participants could use our resources, but we wanted to help them understand that we have much more than just the books on the shelves that they can see. We decided to create a program specifically for parents of homeschool students and invite them to hold one of their organization's meetings at our library.

Year 1—2013

For this first event, on September 24, 2013, we involved several members of our faculty and staff in preparation for the meeting. We called it Orientation Night for Homeschool

Parents. We emphasized that parents should treat this as an evening out and no children were to attend. Members of the faculty and staff of the library introduced the parents to the Juvenile Literature Collection, the Tennessee Textbook Collection, TEL (Tennessee Electronic Library), Government Documents, and our Learning Resource Center. After we presented a brief slide show covering these areas, attendees were divided into smaller groups and taken on tours of the building. These tours covered the Media Center, Juvenile Collection, Tennessee Textbook Collection, and Government Documents. We also explained that while they were able to use our resources in the library, they would need to obtain a guest borrower card to check materials out of the library.

Homeschool parents are treated as local educators. That means that they have the same borrowing privileges as other local teachers and are welcomed into the library to gain assistance with our resources. The parents filled out guest borrower forms and then were given information on how many resources they could check out at a time.

We also provided parents with other resources in a "goody bag" in the form of a two-pocket folder. This file folder included a library pen, information on library hours, a guest borrower form (in case they didn't have time that night to fill it out), and an evaluation form. We included the evaluation form to help us determine if the information we were presenting was useful to the parents.

From this evaluation we determined that the parents saw enough benefit from having an orientation night and would appreciate having at least one night like this per year. We also learned that we should include a map of the library in the folder of information. The parents' evaluations of the evening were full of positive remarks on how they had not realized that all these resources were available to them.

The faculty and staff later met and determined that we would hold a homeschool event for the parents at least one night per year. We also realized that there were additional resources that we might want to include and some that we might leave out the next time we presented the information.

Year 2—2014

Based on our experiences from the year before we were anxious to start planning for this year's event. We decided to call it Homeschool Brainstorm Night. In our early planning meetings, we kept in mind the positive evaluations and the comments that we had heard from the parents who had attended. Because we were working from experience this time, we had several additions to the program that we wanted to include. We also wanted to expand our "goody-bag" folders to reflect some of the things parents had told us would be helpful. We also decided to involve more people from the library who had not had the opportunity to participate the first year. The library had undergone some personnel changes and we wanted to make sure the homeschool parents met our new staff members. We also wanted to highlight some other materials and areas of the library that we thought would be beneficial for the parents and their children.

We created our "goody-bag" folders again. Each contained a map of the schedule for the evening, a map of the library, the evaluation form, and printed copies of the PowerPoint presentation. This allowed the parents to have links to the electronic resources that were available. We also included resources for children from the local Public Television Station—WLJT—located on the University of Tennessee at Martin campus.

We held Homeschool Brainstorm Night on November 6, 2014. We began in the Media Center with a brief introduction by our Library Director and an overview of the resources available in the library. Then we separated the attendees into three groups of about 7 people in each group. These groups then spent the next hour and a half rotating through three different activities. Each group spent about half an hour doing one activity and then rotated to another area of the library.

During the first activity parents learned about Electronic Resources. One librarian explained "The Best Apps for Teaching and Learning" from the American Association of School Librarians and how several of these apps could be used by homeschool parents. As was explained to the parents, they could only access these databases in the library because of the licensing agreements that are attached to the use of these resources. Another librarian then covered resources that the parents could access at the library. These resources included the Children's Literature Comprehensive Database, and Education in Video. Both librarians shared with the parents some of the resources that were available to them as residents of the state of Tennessee. These covered R.E.A.D.S. (Regional eBook and Audiobook Download System), TEL (Tennessee Electronic Library)—including the *World Book Encyclopedia* and World Book Early World of Learning, and ALA Great Websites for Kids. The librarians had highlighted the links to all online resources covered on a PowerPoint presentation which was included in a CD in the "goody-bag" folder.

The second activity involved exploring the Steven E. Rogers Media Center. The Media Center manager concentrated on the upcoming Thanksgiving and Veterans Day holidays to show one way of focusing attention in this broad collection of materials. She demonstrated how to use the Ellison Die Cutters. She also explained what educational resources were available, such as music on CD, Thanksgiving– and Native American–themed DVDs, and instructional aids, including our large art poster collection. Parents were encouraged to brainstorm what other activities or themes they might want to add to the curriculum that they were teaching. In the "goody-bag" folder the parents were given a handout covering the resources for Thanksgiving and Veterans Day as well as Ellison Die shapes of the *Mayflower*, pilgrims, and other colonial-themed objects.

Parents toured three different areas of first floor of the library as a part of the last activity. First, they were encouraged to explore the Juvenile Literature collection. Then they were given a brief tour and explanation of the Tennessee Textbook Collection. Finally, they were shown the Alliene and Jimmie S. Corbitt Special Collections area which includes the J. Houston Gordon Museum and the West Tennessee Heritage Study Center. The Museum has special exhibits and also includes replica offices of Tennessee Governor Ned R. McWherter and Congressman Ed Jones. Included in the "goody-bag" folder for this session was the handout further explaining the Tennessee Textbook Adoption Cycle and a complete list of Juvenile Award Winning titles (Caldecott, Newbery, Coretta Scott King, Batchelder, Michael L. Printz, Pura Belpre, Robert F. Sibert Informational, and Theodor Seuss Geisel) from 2000 to 2014. These titles can be found in our library's Juvenile Collection.

At the end of the evening the library staff held a closing activity where we encouraged parents to ask questions. We also invited them to enjoy refreshments and chat with others. Parents filled out the evaluation forms and offered verbal feedback to faculty and staff. We also asked those parents who had not gotten an Area Educator Borrowers card to go up to the circulation desk and get one.

The day after the Homeschool Night, the members of the team got together to review the evaluations and debrief. Overall the comments were positive. A few people mentioned that the pace of the activities was a bit too quick and perhaps we should try to do a Saturday workshop. Several also suggested providing childcare for parents during the time of the activities.

Year 3—2015

For this year, we decided that our theme would be "A Night at the Library," following the idea of the movie *A Night at the Museum*. We hoped to increase the number of parents attending this year by offering childcare as was suggested. Since we are a public institution, this meant that we needed to make sure that our student employees and adult staff were trained in the Minors on Campus policy and had background checks completed prior to the event. We also wanted to increase the homeschool community awareness of other activities beyond our library. We invited the local Public Television station WLJT to come and present. We also asked a representative from Discovery Park of America, a local history museum, to talk about programs they might have available for homeschooling families.

"A Night at the Library—Watch Everything Come to Life" was held on September 22, 2015. There were 13 parents in attendance with childcare provided for 10 children. The children participated in nature-themed activities while parents were at the evening event.

In an effort to streamline the event, we decided not to split the parents into groups this year and keep everyone in the same room. We took to heart the comments made about the pacing of the activities and tried to keep things a bit less frenetic. A brief introduction was made by our Interim Library Director, followed by a presentation by the Assistant Education Director of Discovery Park. He talked about the homeschool programs that were specifically planned for students and parents at the Park and provided other information about park activities. Next, the Manager of Education and Community Engagement from WLJT gave a presentation on designing lesson plans based on PBS Learning Media. She specifically talked about insects and ways to design lessons that would fit a variety of ages and grade levels. After that, the Electronic Resources Librarian demonstrated the Best Apps and Websites for 2015. To close the presentation portion of the evening, we conducted a brief tour of the library. We also organized a scavenger hunt of the library designed to let people explore the library at their own pace. The scavenger hunt also provided parents with an activity for their children when they returned to the library at a later date.

We closed the evening with refreshments and a time for parents to interact and reunite with their children. The children were very excited about the activities they had done. We also had books, reading posters, and other items to give away as prizes for completing the scavenger hunt. Each parent had a folder with materials from different presenters as well as from the library.

At the end of the evening we had a time of debriefing as a team. As we reviewed the evening's activities, we realized that we had not given the outside presenters a time limit which caused each of them to go over the time we had anticipated they would use. The Media Center staff and students were able to provide childcare, but learned that they would need to be prepared for a much wider range of ages and abilities. Overall, the evening was deemed a success, and we looked forward to doing the program in the next year. Some ideas that we had were increasing the number of outside presenters, thus working with our campus goals to promote university outreach. We also discussed hosting these events later in the year.

Year 4—2016

The team started planning the annual event in late August. This year we decided to host the homeschool evening, but changed the name to Local Educators Night. We did this as we had several new teachers in the area who were interested in what we were offering to our homeschool parents. Other teachers learned about the program through the public library and wanted to participate as well.

During the planning process we talked about things that had worked and not worked in the past three years. We also discussed the previous years' evaluations. People had really seemed to enjoy seeing what other activities were available in our area, and we wanted to make sure we provided information about some of these activities in our events. Suggestions for outside participants included Readers Theater, local authors, and camps offered on campus.

We decided to have a pirate theme and chose the title "Discover the Treasures." This evening was hosted on October 25, 2016, from 6:30 p.m. to 9:00 p.m. Instead of having the educators travel through the library, we kept all evening activities in the Media Center. This allowed the program to be contained and also decreased disruption throughout the library, since UTM students were studying for midterms.

Our participants were welcomed by our interim library director. We divided the rest of the evening into 15-minute time slots and made sure that presenters observed their time limits. First, the campus educational outreach office presented information on Kid College, an annual program for children, kindergarten through fifth grade, which is held on campus in the early summer. After that, local authors of children's books discussed how they do research for their writing and how educators could apply the same research methods when teaching children about local history and science. A representative from Discovery Park described programs and activities that were available to educators. The public library sent a representative to tell about teen programming and specifically discussed the creation of their new teen space. Finally, two campus professors explained how Readers Theater could be used with teaching and also included activities for singing and dancing.

When the presentations had concluded, we sent the educators out on an Informational Treasure Hunt in the Media Center. This gave them a chance to see our 3-D printer and also spend a bit more time with educational resources that they may not have seen before.

To close the evening, we held a door prize drawing where everyone was invited to choose something from the Treasure Chest. The door prize was a reading kit with books and teacher resources. The prizes in the treasure chest were a mixture of books, bookmarks, and other reading-related items. Educators were encouraged to fill out the evaluation forms and share goodies that we had brought in.

In our team meeting after the event, we shared disappointment in the low turnout.

Most of the attendees were people who were presenting that evening. We had a total of 16 people in attendance and at least 11 of them were involved in the presentations or organization of the event. Reasons for the low attendance by other teachers and home-school parents varied. A major reason was that the event coincided with other parent and child activities on campus. We did not provide childcare this time and that may have deterred some families from attending. We also wondered if we might have exhausted the community we were trying to reach and they thought they had seen all we had to offer.

Conclusion—Lessons Learned

A night out for homeschool parents can be a successful experience. We enjoyed four years of sharing resources with parents. As educators in our community, we worked together to provide opportunities for their children to have options for learning. Along the way we also learned some valuable lessons.

One of the first lessons was that we need to pick a good night. In reviewing the evaluation forms, it was often noted that having an evening event in the early fall would be a good way for parents to get ready for their school year. Another option that was suggested would be to have a workshop day or afternoon on a Saturday in late summer or early fall in order to prepare for the year ahead.

We also recognized that we need to advertise better. We need to make sure that we follow campus procedures and go through our university relations office for approval of flyers. We also should share the event with the local media. The public television station was wonderful at sharing the information, but we also should use the student-run radio station. We also could have advertised more widely by using our community message boards at the public library, the electronic message boards throughout campus, as well as a local television station's public service board.

Another concern with our advertising was that we were relying on the flyers we had created and also relying too heavily on e-mail communication. We realized that this event often is best shared by personal invitation. We needed to reach out in person and invite people through community group meetings or as individuals. The team also recognized that our flyers were not sharing the information that parking was free for that event. We learned that people did not want to come to campus, because we have issues with finding parking in the library parking lot and parking on campus can often result in off-campus people getting ticketed.

We also affirmed that we should provide childcare. That was something that was mentioned in many of the evaluations. We understood that we needed to provide training for our staff as per campus policy. Another issue that we needed to be better prepared for was making sure we had activities for a wide range of ages and abilities when providing this service. A suggestion was made on one of the evaluations that it would be good to have children and parents be involved in at least one activity together. They could then take that activity to expand upon in their teaching and learning time at a later date.

Finally, we acknowledged that although it was beneficial to plan a good mix of activities, we should not offer too many of them. We all wanted to share what was available, and many parents found that overwhelming. Parents mentioned that they enjoyed having time to speak with other homeschool parents and discuss experiences. When we began inviting other organizations to join us the third year, we limited it to two organizations and that seemed to work well. One suggestion received from an evaluation form was to have a keynote speaker and then set up different areas that parents could go to, at their own pace, to work with specific presenters or work on special projects.

We have decided to take a year off, regroup, and see if we should bring Homeschool Parents' Night Out back to life in a different format. We hope that our local homeschooling community understands that we are here to serve them and that we can provide excellent resources and activities throughout the library and can connect them to resources beyond our four walls.

Virtual Homeschooling

Aviva Ebner

Some families who opt for an alternative to traditional brick-and-mortar schools prefer a more structured curriculum than the myriad of choices typically available for homeschooling. As a result, a quickly growing population of students not attending traditional schools is now attending virtual schools. "Over the last decade, parents and students seeking a more flexible and individualized educational experience have increasingly turned to virtual public charter schools, the newest trend in an age-old U.S. debate about school choice…" (Bausell 2016). Though some brick-and-mortar settings may offer hybrid options (part of the school day or specific days on site, with the rest online), 100 percent virtual public online charter schools provide curricula, teaching, learning, and family communication through online platforms. It is important to note that there are also private school online options. However, many homeschooling families take advantage of the tuition-free opportunities made available by online public charter schools. Online charter schools are growing faster than many traditional charter schools because they do not have the same "physical constrictions and boundaries" of brick-and-mortar schools (Taylor and McNair 2018).

For the purposes of discussing the challenges and proposed solutions to serving virtually homeschooled students, a working definition of a virtual school is needed. A virtual school is one where all (or most) of the learning occurs online. As a result, traditional schools are now often referred to as brick-and-mortar schools. In online schools, learning takes place in a virtual space rather than in a physical classroom (Taylor and McNair 2018).

Why Virtual Schools?

Many online schools have some distinct advantages for families. They can offer a large variety of courses, many of which can be approved by the National Collegiate Athletic Association (NCAA) and pre-approved by universities (i.e., University of California A–G approved). As opposed to parents having to teach their children in subject areas that may not be their forte, fully credentialed teachers are available both synchronously and asynchronously to provide direct instruction and small group/one-on-one tutoring to students (depending on the structure of the online school). Teachers, students, and families can meet via video chat, virtual classrooms with special whiteboard tools, and other video platforms (i.e., Skype, Google Hangouts, Facetime, etc.). Additionally, there is an online asynchronous classroom to which most students are given access 24/7. This allows students to work at hours typically not available during a regular brick-and-mortar school day.

Challenges and Solutions to "Packaged" Online Curricula

Online schools may create their own curricula, but often use premade courses aligned to state standards, purchased from educational vendors. These "canned" courses are typically well-developed, including text, video, and drag-n'-drop activities. There are usually assignments, quizzes, and unit assessments, as well as a final exam. Unfortunately, a one-size-fits-all approach is rarely what homeschoolers are seeking, and there are always diverse learners. In fact, studies support that students value the efforts of teachers to "design and organize engaging learning activities, and provide personalized instruction" (Borup and Stevens 2017). Therefore, online educators and parents must find ways to personalize and supplement these pre-packaged courses. This is often a challenge because it is not the norm to find a librarian at an online K–12 school; the work, then falls to the teacher, the parent, and, often times, the local public library's librarian.

Curating Resources for Virtual Schools

One of the issues that often plagues such online programs is the lack of a physical library to support student research, as well as a professional development library with resources for staff. Some online schools use cumbersome methods, such as shared folders and files in Google Drive. Though these tools are highly useful and are vital for collaboration in the online environment, they are not necessarily the most efficient solution. A better solution is to create a schoolwide digital library and, clearly, to keep such a site updated by a trained and licensed librarian.

Most online schools, though, mistakenly think that a librarian is not a crucial position, since the students and teachers have access to the World Wide Web. Additionally, a single combined database would be time consuming and overwhelming for one person to create. Thus, it is best for online educators to focus on curating databases and useful resources directly pertinent to the program and curriculum. A school with limited resources can easily build out such a library using free website building platforms, such as Google Sites, Blogger, Weebly, and Wix, to name a few.

For example, A3 Education (a3education.org), a non-profit charter school district and educational consulting firm, developed a password-protected teacher resource website, under the direction of an administrator who was also fully credentialed as a teacher librarian. The website consists of multiple pages, each clearly named. The directory of pages is on the home page. Staff can click on the page list and jump directly to the topic in question. Teachers may need resources for instructing students on academic honesty, avoiding plagiarism, and media literacy, to reduce the chances of students submitting cut-and-pasted work for assignments. The site hosts a page that is filled with links to existing resources for teachers, lessons, and videos to share with students as tutorials on these topics. For instance, teachers may be faced with children who have experienced trauma. One page contains a directory of resources for supporting students who have been exposed to trauma, as well as on-demand professional development webinar recordings on the topic. Other topics covered include lessons and resources for national heritage months, new teacher resources, recommended technology tools and applications, support for annual or monthly activities (i.e., Annual Hour of Code where every staff member and student learns how to code, celebrated during National Computer Science Week), and Banned Books Week, to name a few. There are also video tutorials on how to use the various online platforms through which the online curricula are accessed.

Teachers love resources, and free resources are even more appreciated. A3 Schools further developed their professional library to include pages for each content area. Links to videos, lessons, interactive websites, and useful applications for subject-specific content are also housed on the website. As their schools expand, so do contributions to the website, so their future plans include having links for various subject areas, which would redirect their users to sites fully fleshed out with a myriad of resources specific to the subject area. Ideally, though, a school virtual reference librarian, at the very least, would be helpful for students conducting research for assignments in their online courses.

Whether a part of an online school district, such as A3 Education, or at any virtual school/homeschool, each teacher can also create his/her own webpage with links to resources specific to the courses taught by that teacher. This should be a collaborative effort on the part of staff. The benefits are worthwhile, and students can also contribute. A teacher-made website can integrate data, photographs, infographics, text, videos, and student-curated resources (Trimble 2017). Studies support that "online resources provide more joy and entertainment in the class and have a wider range of variety, including culturally oriented activities" (Khoshhal 2016). Teachers also trust other teachers, more than outside experts, for standards-aligned resources (Caniglia and Meadows, 2018). This supports the push for teachers to curate meaningful online resources and share them with other staff. In order for these resources to be well-vetted, some direction from a librarian would be recommended. Teachers have likely not been trained in the same manner as librarians in terms of identifying the most reliable, non-biased sources; there is no reference course required in most teaching credential programs.

Professional Learning Communities

Such online collaboration among colleagues has further spurred the virtual homeschooling world to allow teachers to better serve students by participating in online Professional Learning Communities (PLCs). EdWeb.net hosts such PLCs on many pertinent topics, ranging from serving English learners to integrating technology to social-emotional learning. EdWeb.net also hosts free webinars and continuing education certificates. Some schools also use their own methods of encouraging grass roots PLCs that grow organically from the needs of the students. For example, Uplift California North Charter, Uplift California South Charter, Uplift California Santa Barbara, and Uplift California Monterey all participate in online PLCs held via Google Meets and Zoom video. Staff follow a research-based model, outlined for them in prior professional development, and share materials via Google Drive. These PLCs also support the respective School

Improvement Plans (SIPs), which focus on increasing student achievement across subgroups, while supporting community engagement.

Role of the Library

Although parents can feel secure knowing that highly qualified teachers are overseeing implementation of the virtual homeschool curricula, there is still the need for students and families to have access to appropriate materials, typically found at a school or local library. Families that live within a reasonable distance of a public library are fortunate. Many online teachers will create a page with links to the local public libraries' websites, or send out emails to parents early in the year with this information. Using Google Maps, a teacher could even provide a map to families of the bus route, drive, or walking route to the nearest library, or students could be tasked with researching this information themselves. Some homeschooling families are already aware of the value of their local libraries, while others discover it for the first time when recommended by a school staff member. Some students actually prefer working on their courses at the local library, since they have access to the resources and a librarian to field reference questions. However, there are many students who are participating in virtual homeschooling due to living in isolated rural areas, suffering from severe medical conditions, and experiencing other situations that make visiting a library prohibitive. In such cases, there are several options. One option is to locate the closest public library online via Google Maps and reserve books online, then request that they be mailed to the student, who is responsible for mailing them back in a timely manner (please note that not all public libraries offer this service). Another option is to provide to families a school-created digital library page with access to free e-texts that do not infringe on copyright. Some educational vendors used by online schools have included in their fees (paid by the school) the access to such e-books.

The California State Library has offered to all California public schools, including online public charter schools, access for families to Britannica Online and Britannica Escolar, free of charge. Links to these encyclopedia databases can then be emailed to homeschooled families, or added to an existing school digital library site. This offer also includes access to Proquest, allowing students to use scholarly, peer-reviewed articles for their research projects. In California, up until this school year, access to these databases required an annual subscription fee and, with students spread across wide regions and not attending a local school site, tracking usage and administering these programs was labor intensive and cost prohibitive for independent charter schools.

Virtual Field Trips and Guest Speakers

One might assume that virtual homeschoolers are missing out on what is often a student's favorite part of school: field trips. Not so anymore. With the advent of virtual field trips, students can experience a wide range of "visits" to places a typical in-person field trip would go, as well as to destinations that would be inaccessible to students/teachers at most brick-and-mortar schools. An Internet search of "virtual field trips" results in many ready-to-go virtual visits. Additionally, online educators can piece together their own visits, or rely on Google Earth, to create virtual trips. For instance, many zoos in major cities have "animal cams" where students can log in and observe the animals and their behaviors in real time. Overall, virtual field trips are less expensive than in-person trips and usually do not have a maximum participant number set, as an in-person field trip might (Stainfield, Fisher, Ford, and Solem 2000). Participants and hosts are only limited by bandwidth. Furthermore, virtual field trips are "a flexible teaching tool, allowing inclusive learning across abilities and a range of taught subjects" (Norris, Shelton, Dunsmuir, Duke-Williams, and Stamatakis 2015).

In addition to "field trips," live events can often be attended online in real time, such as some offerings from the Smithsonian. One example is the Smithsonian's Ask a Scientist series where scientists speak in real time to students and even answer questions posed through the chat function. For virtual homeschoolers who are not being provided such experiences, digital library access or in-person access to local libraries can yield a plethora of ideas for planning an actual trip. Since virtual homeschooling involves logging into courses online, families are no longer tied down to traditional school year calendars for travel. As long as the student has access to the Internet and brings along a laptop or tablet, schoolwork can be completed at almost any time of day without resulting in a gap in the student's education, before or after a family outing at a new destination. Other recommendations that can be made to students include both virtual reality and augmented reality apps. There are many free or low-cost apps that can be downloaded to a smartphone on both the iOS and Android platforms. The student can then be immersed in experiences to which he/she would otherwise not have access.

Virtual homeschooling lends itself quite well to hosting guest speakers. Guest speakers can be invited from all over the world to interact with students in real time via video platforms. Students can meet authors, athletes, career professionals, and many other types of speakers. They can ask questions using their computer microphones or using the chat function of the platform. Vanguard Leadership Academy is one online school with a civics-minded approach to schooling that frequently utilizes online platforms for live interactions with guest speakers. Military officers, medal recipients, government officials, and service-minded organization representatives are often invited to participate in the school's weekly leadership webinars. During these meetings, there is typically a focus on a character trait necessary for leadership and for citizenship. A teacher hosts the session, posing questions to the guest speaker, and then facilitating questions from the students. Students, family members, and staff have found these personalized online interactions to be valuable and inspirational.

Virtual STEAM Makerspaces

Still, some may argue that virtual homeschools are at a disadvantage in this day and age of libraries also serving as makerspaces. However, as innovative online schools continue to evolve, they also find solutions to such issues. Cal STEAM San Bernardino is a large online public charter school serving virtually homeschooled youth in grades K–12, that has found a way to address makerspaces in a virtual environment. The concept first started with a science night for families of the online elementary students. However, this soon expanded once the staff had access to multiple webinars on makerspaces in general, as well as online resources about makerspaces. A small group of staff members, including elementary, middle and high school teachers, as well as one administrator who was a former science teacher and another administrator who was formerly a librarian, quickly turned these family nights into virtual STEAM makerspaces. The teachers could then host the makerspace live online via Google Hangouts, Google Meet, Zoom, or another video platform. The teachers prepared a list of materials that the students should have on hand during the makerspace meeting time. These materials could be found at local stores or ordered online. Sufficient lead time was given to obtain these materials; the link for the meeting, as well as the list of materials, was emailed to students several weeks in advance. Students, siblings, parents, and friends then logged in at the designated time. The teacher proposed a design challenge with a problem to solve. Students helped each other via video and chat functions, while also working in person with family or local friends. There are many grants available from a variety of sources to fund makerspaces. Educators can apply for these grants and then ship materials to their students. This can allow for more complex design challenges with materials that might not be readily available locally.

Virtual makerspaces can serve students well beyond the STEAM learning ramifications. Since online learning lends itself to individualized connections between teacher and student, schools should be taking advantage of how connected students may feel from collaborating in the virtual makerspace environment. Students may feel comfortable opening up to discuss difficult topics, such as coping with grief, in a makerspace environment, where they are busy creating (Seymour 2016). Therefore, the virtual makerspace promotes a sense of community that can double as a supportive environment, addressing the social-emotional needs of the students. "The goal of fostering a community that includes a range of students with diverse racial, ethnic, religious, political, gender, and socioeconomic backgrounds" helps create a welcoming, safe space for all students (Welch 2018).

Conclusion

All of these advances for allowing virtual homeschoolers and their teachers access to resources are wonderful, but there are some potential barriers to overcome. One hurdle is that most teachers, whether they teach at a virtual school or a traditional brick-and-mortar school, have not been trained as librarians and do not possess the knowledge base or experience to teach media literacy and digital citizenship on an ongoing basis to all students. Staff without such training may also not know how to properly vet sources for inclusion in a digital library for their students. Professional development can be provided to train teachers to work with students on evaluating online resources using the CRAAP test (Currency, Relevance, Authority, Accuracy, Purpose of the source), but the process is quite time consuming for teachers who already have other assigned duties (Duby 2018). Some online school leaders may not be aware of the value of a trained librarian, mistakenly thinking that students who have access to a laptop and the Internet have unlimited access to every needed resource. There are more potential challenges, but no matter what those are, one thing is certain: the world of virtual homeschooling has made great strides over a short period of time and will no doubt continue to adapt to the needs of homeschooled students and their families. Virtual homeschooling is not a fad; it is a quickly growing viable option for many families (Bausell 2016).

WORKS CITED

Bausell, S.B. 2016. "From the Editorial Board: Virtual Charter Schools: Where Did All the Children Go?" *The High School Journal, 99*(2), 109–112. Retrieved from https://search-proquest-com.contentproxy.phoenix.edu/docview/1760242651?accountid=134061.

Borup, Jered, and Mark Stevens. 2017. "Using Student Voice to Examine Teacher Practices at a Cyber Charter High School." *British Journal of Educational Technology*, 18(5), 1119–1130.

Caniglia, Joanne and Michelle Meadows. 2018. "Pre-Service Mathematics Teachers' Use of Web Resources." *The International Journal for Technology in Mathematics Education* 25 (3): 17–34. doi:http://dx.doi.org.contentproxy.phoenix.edu/10.1564/tme_v25.3.02. https://search-proquest-com.contentproxy.phoenix.edu/docview/2131581135?accountid=134061.

Duby, H.R. 2018. "What a Load of CRAAP: Evaluating Information in an Era of "Fake News." *Tennessee Libraries*, 68(4) Retrieved from https://search-proquest-com.contentproxy.phoenix.edu/docview/2161373282?accountid=134061.

Khoshhal, Yasin. 2016. "Busy Teachers: A Case of Comparing Online Teacher-Created Activities with the Ready-made Activity Resource Books." *International Journal of Pedagogies & Learning* 11 (3): 283–300. doi:http://dx.doi.org.contentproxy.phoenix.edu/10.1080/22040552.2016.1272535. https://search-proquest-com.contentproxy.phoenix.edu/docview/1869846079?accountid=134061.

Norris, E., N. Shelton, S. Dunsmuir, O. Duke-Williams, and E. Stamatakis. 2015. "Teacher and Pupil Perspectives on the Use of Virtual Field Trips as Physically Active Lessons." *BMC Research Notes* 8, https://search-proquest-com.contentproxy.phoenix.edu/docview/1779669628?accountid=134061, accessed January 13, 2019.

Seymour, Gina. 2016. "The Compassionate Makerspace: Grief and Healing in a High School Library Makerspace." *Teacher Librarian*, 43(5), 28–31. https://search-ebscohost-com.contentproxy.phoenix.edu/login.aspx?direct=true&db=a9h&AN=116364069&site=ehost-live&scope=site.

Stainfield, John, Peter Fisher, Bob Ford, and Michael Solem. 2000. "International Virtual Field Trips: A New Direction?" *Journal of Geography in Higher Education*24 (2) (07): 255–262, https://search-proquest-com.contentproxy.phoenix.edu/docview/214734885?accountid=134061, accessed January 13, 2019.

Taylor, Brett Ushal, and Delores E. McNair. 2018. "Virtual School Startups: Founder Processes in American K–12 Public Virtual Schools." *International Review of Research in Open and Distance Learning* 19 (1). https://search-proquest-com.contentproxy.phoenix.edu/docview/2047921736?accountid=134061.

Trimble, Leslie. 2017. "Creating Science Websites." *The Science Teacher* 84 (9) (12): 25–30, https://search-proquest-com.contentproxy.phoenix.edu/docview/1968399989?accountid=134061, accessed January 13, 2019.

Welch, Amber. 2018. "Beyond Metrics: Connecting Academy Library Makerspace Assessment Practices with Organizational Values." *Library Hi Tech* (36)2, 306–318. https://doi-org.contentproxy.phoenix.edu/10.1108/LHT-08-2017-0181.

Expanding Access

Homeschooling in the Academic Library

MARGARET DAWSON, DIANNE MUELLER
and BRIDGIT MCCAFFERTY

At the Texas A&M University–Central Texas University Library one of our primary goals is to act as a resource for the communities in our region, including the homeschooling community. The university is located in the Killeen–Temple–Fort Hood Metropolitan Area, where there is a pronounced need for homeschooling support due to our large military-affiliated population. Military families choose homeschooling at rates that are approximately double those of the U.S. population at large (Prothero 2016). This need is more pronounced because, although we have an outsize homeschool population, we have far fewer cultural institutions than other communities of a similar size. For instance, the population in our metropolitan region is approximately 40 percent larger than the nearby McLennan County, home to Waco, but unlike McLennan, we have no zoo and only few museums.

In this context, the academic library at A&M–Central Texas views itself as an important informal educational resource within our community. Though academic libraries are not traditionally viewed as a community resource, we believe that offering educational services for community groups is a natural fit for many academic libraries, because we have unique informational and educational collections. By making these already existing resources accessible to community groups and offering curricula and other support services that ensure that they are used effectively, we can easily create a new set of services that are perfectly tailored to the homeschool community.

A&M–Central Texas has developed these services with our existing educational collections, programming, and infrastructure. Notably, the purchase of these resources did not originate in service of the homeschool community. Many items were acquired to support our education students, or were bought for programming funded by the U.S. Institute of Museum and Library Services through a grant to the Texas State Library and Archives Commission. The development of specific PreK–12 educational services followed from community interest in our existing resources. This nurtured a strong commitment to impact our community with the personnel and collections we had on hand. This is the crux of our strategy—finding new ways of using personnel and resources that we already have available.

141

We are committed to this strategy because we recognize that informal educational experiences at academic libraries allow students to learn how to use libraries and interact in the higher education environment before they ever pursue a degree. By engaging children at academic libraries, we can prepare them for formal higher education later in life. We also offer resources that might not otherwise be available outside of a school, and therefore enrich the opportunities for homeschool students.

Informal Education

According to Sarah Mills and Peter Kraftl, in *Informal Education, Childhood, and Youth*, informal education is "learning that occur[s] in and through everyday life," which "can conceivably happen in an infinite array of situations, geographical and historical contexts." Mills and Kraftl argue that informal education has to meet three key requirements. First, students choose to participate and guide what will be addressed. Second, informal education involves a dialogue, and a building of trust. Third, informal education fills a gap that is identified in other, more formal kinds of learning. Academic libraries can fulfill each of these requirements in the context of serving the homeschool community by providing opportunities for youth-directed educational experiences built on a relationship of trust, and in service of providing more opportunities for homeschool kids to learn (Mills & Kraftl 2014). Furthermore, the academic library provides safe spaces for this informal learning to take place for individual families and also allows them to meet with other homeschoolers, thus creating "mini-communities" (Edwards, Unger & Robinson 2013).

Academic Libraries

Despite the importance of informal educational experiences, and the way they can prepare children for further study later in life, few homeschool parents have the funds to acquire books and other resources to the extent available in a school library. To this end, academic libraries can be a rich source of support for homeschool families, supplementing what is available at local public libraries and ensuring that homeschool students have access to the many collections they need to be successful.

We recognize that there are many excellent public libraries that can fill this need on their own, especially in major metropolitan areas, but working in our region, we find that some rural public libraries, as well as those in communities that are struggling financially, do not have all of the resources that could prove useful for homeschool students. Moreover, some of the public libraries in our region have missions that privilege collection use over long term collection building for research purposes, which leads to aggressively weeded nonfiction collections. These limitations can be problematic for homeschool families, who often want a wide variety of resources to ensure that their children receive the best education possible.

Academic libraries tend to have broad, research-oriented collections, with less focus on high use items. These libraries also often have collections of resources to support teachers-in-training and access to faculty expertise in developing programming for groups of community members. These resources ensure that academic libraries have opportunities that some public libraries might not in service of this community. Further, academic libraries are often located in, and serve, rural communities or regions. Even in major metropolitan areas academic libraries may provide opportunities for homeschool students to learn about research in higher education, preparing them to further their studies later in life. For these reasons, academic libraries can supplement what is available through local public libraries.

Because academic libraries do not always recognize their usefulness in supporting the whole educational needs of their region, it can be difficult to see how we fit into this role. To demonstrate how this works at A&M–Central Texas, we will describe some of the services and collections we provide below.

Collections

Though the collections at academic libraries may not seem like a natural fit for homeschool families, there are two aspects of our collections that lend themselves to use by this community group. The first is that we tend to collect more heavily in nonfiction than our public counterparts. The second is that we often build children's collections that are tailored to student teachers, since they are primarily created to support our teacher training programs. As a result, they often include resources that would be more common in a school library, and in many ways mirror what children would have access to at a school. This includes nonfiction instructional materials, retrospective collections of children's and young adult fiction, and other niche collections that may not circulate heavily with the public, but are of value to teachers planning curriculum.

Homeschool parents often do not have the resources to build library collections at home with the breadth and depth that our academic collections can provide, and public libraries do not focus their collections on teacher training the way many academic libraries do. This breadth and depth is a hallmark of academic collections. As a result, for homeschool parents interested in giving their kids a strong background in research and academic exploration, the academic library is an essential resource. Moreover, academic libraries can provide resources for parents to use in home curriculum instruction that might not be collected at public libraries, but are available at libraries with a focus on teacher education. This even includes K–12 textbooks, though it should be noted that they often have restrictions on who can check them out, and may be limited to education students, especially in the case of teachers' editions. We have found that many homeschool parents use our library because it saves them time and money—we have items that they would otherwise have to purchase or for which they would have to search. Often, the items will only be used once or for a brief period of time while they complete a specific unit, and having them available for checkout is extremely valuable.

The utility of our book collections is not limited to our children's and young adult resources. We also have a full research collection related to education, which is not available at most public libraries. This includes resources to help homeschool parents learn how to plan their curriculum, as well as those with ideas for activities and assignments that can help round out the education their children receive. Most parents who homeschool have no formal training in education, and many do not have an advanced degree. Having access to these resources can help homeschool parents enrich their education practice at little cost using the same high quality resources that teachers-in-training use.

This is especially important for subject areas in which a homeschool parent may feel unsure. For instance, science or math, where pedagogical practice can be vitally important to ensuring mastery, and where there are many different ways to teach the same content. Our collections allow parents to explore each of these approaches to determine which will work best in their unique context.

Though many homeschool parents are not affiliated with a university, they can often still check out available items through resource sharing agreements between libraries. In the case of A&M–Central Texas, we participate in two resource sharing agreements that allow members of the community to check out our collections. One is a statewide agreement in which many libraries participate. The second is a local agreement with the public library system in the town where we are located, which is not a participant in the statewide agreement. These agreements are beneficial for homeschool families because they open the door to a wide variety of library resources, so that these parents can determine which library is most useful in their given context. Homeschoolers in our community use these agreements to check out educational resources, such as books, media, and educational manipulatives.

Educational Resources

Like book collections, the library also has educational resources that are targeted toward providing a base of support for our teachers in training. This is a collection of hands-on educational materials, such as puzzles, puppets, board games, Snap Circuits®, K'NEX™, and bingo that address the core curriculum in grades K–6. Many of these resources are kits that allow scientific experimentation, or mathematical tools that help children visualize abstract concepts. We initially purchased these resources using funding from the U.S. Institute of Museum and Library Services through a grant to the Texas State Library and Archives Commission, and we have been looking for opportunities to engage the community using these resources in new ways. Like with our book collections, we have heard from homeschool parents that they often purchase these items and use them for only a brief period of time. There is a popular homeschool fair in our community where parents try to re-sell manipulatives after they have completed the units where they were used. By offering these for checkout to this community, we can save them this effort, especially since we have resources at different levels, allowing parents to age up curriculum as their children advance.

Further, the variety of resources that we have—with thousands of items in our collection—far surpasses what a homeschool parent might be able to purchase. This variety allows parents to try different kinds of resources with their children to determine which ones work best at meeting their education goals and needs. When you can only purchase one item that may or may not be exactly what you need, you do not have the luxury of exploring the possibilities. With a ready collection of many resources, the potential to explore and experiment exists, allowing for a much more effective educational experience.

Though some public libraries have similar collections of educational resources, they are more common at academic libraries that support education departments. As an example, in our community, there is one public library with a notable collection of these resources, but this collection focuses on the pre-school level, rather than K–12, the assumption being that older students will have access to them in their classrooms at school. Again, in this case, our collections complement one another. For homeschool families, it is important to stress how public and academic libraries can work together to offer a whole variety of resources that one library alone is unlikely to be able to provide. These resources are important because they engage kids in learning concepts in new ways. For instance, we have a cash register that can be used to teach concepts in math. Kids respond to it and learn from it because it makes abstract concepts concrete.

Makerspace

Along with educational assets, our academic library also has resources commonly found in makerspaces. Makerspaces are popular in all types of libraries right now; they allow people to make something new using unique and creative equipment and resources. Makerspace equipment can be expensive, like 3D printers, production-quality photography equipment, and sewing machines; or relatively inexpensive, like scrap materials.

Homeschool groups can sign up to use our makerspace tools for projects of their own design, or for guided sessions designed by our librarians. These programs can either involve creating a specific item, or designing something unique that shows students how to use specialized equipment, such as a silhouette or sewing machine. Activities might include creating an image that can be iron-transferred to an article of clothing, or programming the 3D printer to make a small figure. This access is important, because homeschool parents who want their children to use these tools may not be able to afford the quality of equipment that is available in many school systems. Some public libraries offer these types of resources, though in our economically depressed city this is not the case. As a result, we are the only local library that has this equipment available to the public. This is likely true in many rural areas, and in towns with few financial means. As a result, in these communities the academic library can be a vital resource for homeschool parents. Again, these tools are primarily available to spur creativity and innovation for our students, but they are also a convenient resource for homeschool families.

Programming

In addition to our resources, we also provide some programming for K–12 students, which is available to both the independent school districts and our homeschool families. This includes a menu of potential "pop-up" programming and summer programs related to both STEM topics and literacy. Though this programming was largely designed to help our local school districts supplement classroom instruction with enrichment activities, it can also help enrich homeschool instruction, especially for the homeschool groups that commonly form in our area to help socialize homeschool kids and expand the homeschool experience.

The first type of programming, which we call "pop-up" programming, is one-to-two-hour interactive instruction sessions with curriculum designed by our faculty. These use educational resources to explore a topic somewhat outside of the standard curriculum for a subject area. For instance, we have programming that teaches students how to write a free-form poem with imagery, or how to test electrical concepts with Snap Circuits®

and other electrical equipment. Our criteria for these programs are that they must include hands-on activities, and that they must be able to travel, so that we can offer them on campus or in another location. Our menu includes information about the curriculum of the program, how long it takes, how many students we can accommodate at one time, what grade levels the program is best suited for, and information about whether or not there is a cost associated with the program—generally, there is no cost. These programs are compiled under the umbrella of "Warrior Kids" (http://tamuct.libguides.com/warriorkids).

Like our educational resource collection, our menu of "pop-up" educational programs grew out of our grant through TSLAC and IMLS. We were provided funding to pay our faculty members a small stipend to create the curriculum that our librarians present. This menu aids us in advertising field trip opportunities to children's groups in our region, including school and homeschool groups. Because our region has few educational enrichment options, these programs act as a way for students to supplement what they learn in the classroom with additional content created by professors. Homeschool groups are free to meet at the library or an outside location to participate in this programming, which often provides them with the chance to use resources and activities that might not otherwise be available outside of a school setting.

We also offer summer programs that can help enrich the educational experience of homeschool students. Parents often look for things for their children to do during the summer months, and homeschool parents are no exception. They have more reasons to find alternative educational activities since they are year-round teachers of their children. Summer activities add variety to their own daily schedule, as well as to their own teaching style. Ideally, these activities give all of our students a unique learning opportunity that they may not be able to get elsewhere. We have a variety of programs for a wide range of age groups. These include STEM camps and literacy programs. Each program offers hands-on activities. Our STEM camps focus on hands-on scientific experiments that encourage students to engage with and learn about the scientific process through a variety of activities and long-term projects. Our literacy camps help foster reading comprehension and development through intensive sessions with teachers in training. Both of these programs offer an opportunity for homeschool parents to provide new learning experiences for their children, and are open to the public.

The STEM camp began as a camp for girls, but has been changed to two camps where one is girls only and one is co-educational. The curriculum includes STEM-related activities focused on a central topic. The first STEM camp looked at STEM topics related to three countries—France, India, and China. The students worked in groups to research the culture and STEM-related issues facing each country. One of such issues was clean water. They thought of ways to filter the water and created a science project to reflect their ideas. At the end of the program, these projects were judged and awarded prizes. Girls met and worked with other girls from the community, learned about research and science projects outside of their normal educational environment, and engaged with new and different teachers who brought their own enthusiasm and knowledge to the program. Similar to the STEM camp, the reading enrichment program allowed participating children to work with teachers in training at the university to improve their reading comprehension skills by focusing on literacy. This program featured guided readings, where a group of students would read the same text and discuss it. The students who participated appeared to be much more excited about reading when they finished the program.

Tutoring

Our free K–5 tutoring covers reading and math with the goal of improving comprehension with hands-on active learning activities. The tutoring is offered through the federal work-study program, with our education students as the tutors. Students participate in tutoring once a week at scheduled times. This is especially valuable for homeschool parents looking for help in a particular subject area. The parents are given suggestions on what they can work on further with their children, along with items in the collection that could aid them in their studies.

This program is advertised by word of mouth, in our library, and on our webpage. Since many of our adult students are parents, this method of advertising works well. We also send information out to homeschool contacts, public libraries, and local school districts, asking to pass on the information to those who need this service. We ask the parents to describe the area where their child needs the most help. If possible, we ask the child to bring an example of a worksheet or classwork that shows the problem they are having. Since this is a tightly focused tutoring program, it is better for our tutors to know what the concern is from the beginning. Our tutors are already involved in teaching classes and are visiting classrooms in the area. This is an opportunity for them to learn firsthand how to work with children of different needs and abilities before they get into a classroom; to implement the techniques they have learned in the classroom; and to determine the aspect of education for which they are best suited.

Facilities

Finally, the library offers facilities designed for younger patrons, which are open for use by homeschool families. The facilities where we keep our children's resources resemble a public library more than your typical academic library, thanks to a child-friendly atmosphere, which provides a welcoming place for homeschoolers to explore our collections. Our children's area has children-sized furniture, low stacks, and is decorated with stuffed animals. One of these is a large bookworm that serves as an approachable face to both children and adults. Notably, we operate in a part of town where there is no public library nearby, but close to many new housing developments. This situates us well to fill a need in our community and to assist the families closest to our campus.

In addition to our general access facilities, we also have small and large meeting rooms that are available to the public. This provides places where homeschool families can get together and share resources in a spot devoted to education. This is especially useful in the winter months, when other recreational or outdoor meeting places may not be available for use due to cold weather.

Conclusion

The most important factor for all of these services, and the factor that allows us to offer them, is that we already own most of the resources necessary to be successful. We have purchased these items through grants and in support of our education programs. Opening these resources to homeschool families is just one extra step, but one that makes a big impact on the homeschool community in our region. Many academic libraries are in a similar position. They have the resources, but they need to package them and make them accessible.

To this end, our biggest challenge is promoting that these resources are available. For people outside of higher education, academic libraries can be intimidating and may not seem like a natural fit for the goals of a homeschool parent. We have had to do a lot of leg work just to get the word out to these families. This is especially true because we advertise many of our programs through the local school districts, making it difficult to reach homeschool families. We have found that advertising to homeschool co-ops, on local community message boards, and by word of mouth have been of most use to us in getting the word out to our homeschool families. Notably, after a few years of offering these services, we are really starting to witness how valuable they are when the families who need them become aware of them.

The biggest gain we have gotten from these activities is that we now play a central role in promoting the University across the community. Since we are a regional institution, many of the child-aged homeschool students we work with may eventually become our students as they progress in their studies. Our work helps to get the University's name into the community and to strengthen existing ties. It also provides our community with an understanding of how vitally important the University is, even if they are not currently enrolled. All of these benefits are recognized by our administration, and help us further the overarching goal of the library to be a regional resource.

Ultimately, though public libraries may always be seen as a more natural ally of the homeschool community, academic libraries also have a lot to offer. Informal educational settings are critical for any student, and acclimating homeschool students to an academic library before they ever start a college class can give them a leg up later in their academic career. At A&M–Central Texas, we recognize this value, and view ourselves as a library for the entire region, not just our students, faculty, and staff.

WORKS CITED

Edwards, J.B., Unger, K.R., and Robinson, M.S. 2013. *Transforming Libraries, Building Communities: The Community-Centered Library*. Lanham: Scarecrow Press.

Mills, S., and Kraftl, P. 2014. *Informal Education, Childhood and Youth: Geographies, Histories, Practices*. Basingstoke: Palgrave Macmillan.

Prothero, A. 2016. "Growing Number of Military Families Opt for Homeschool." *PBS News Hour*. Retrieved from https://www.pbs.org/newshour/education/growing-number-of-military-families-opt-for-homeschool.

Partnering with the Past

Special Collections Libraries for Homeschoolers

Nancy Richey

Technology and changing attitudes have caused a continuing surge in the popularity of homeschooling. These students, their parents, and instructors are part of a growing population who are coming to Special Collections libraries and bringing "their children in to get a firsthand look at history (Jones 2004, 88–105)." Recent statistics show that the number of children homeschooled is increasing by 3 percent to 8 percent a year (Weller 2017). The number of these students, ages 5–17, is estimated at approximately 3.5 million. Though the majority are white students, their diversity is growing and includes "atheists, Christians, and Mormons; conservatives, libertarians, and liberals; low-, middle-, and high-income families; Black, Hispanic, and white; parents with Ph.D.'s, GEDs, and no high-school diplomas. One study shows that 32 percent of homeschooled students are Black, Asian, Hispanic, and others, i.e., not White/non–Hispanic" (Ray 2018).

Public libraries have always offered much-needed support for the homeschooling community and these non-traditional students through the provision of books, periodicals, and encyclopedias. Some of these libraries have also offered study spaces and such resources as science lab equipment, math, language arts and social studies kits, music and art appreciation materials, as well as early literacy toys. In addition, teachers and parents of homeschoolers are looking for more inquiry-based learning activities and cooperative learning opportunities to supplement and enrich the homeschool experience. They are turning to the exceptional and distinctive holdings of Special Collections libraries and finding that these can be ideal partners in the learning process. Students and instructors quickly discover that the collections comprise materials unduplicated elsewhere and include items treasured because of their rarity. This also means that the items have an intrinsic reliability and "speak for themselves" without added interpretation.

Special Collections libraries are depositories for endless research, study and exploration of primary resource materials, and homeschoolers can benefit greatly from one-on-one assistance of an experienced librarian or archivist as they actively engage in studying the past. Moreover, because Special Collections librarians and staff are skilled in critical thinking, they have developed a "thorough understanding of the nature of records … and know how to 'analyz[e] the credibility of data from individual records'" (Devine 2001, 10). They can instruct students to look at all materials objectively noting that most creators may filter facts through their own worldview. Their bibliographical and well-honed research skills, as well as familiarity with the holdings, are also of great value to the homeschooler. As a reminder, students will benefit from a quick definition of a primary resource and studying a primary resources checklist.

- Who created the material?
- What does it say about a past event?
- When was it created?
- Where does the information come from?
- How does it add to our knowledge of the past?

Homeschoolers and their teachers who are accustomed to visiting public libraries may have to be prepared for a first visit to a Special Collections library. Library staff should do the following:

- Highlight that access to special collections involves more stringent security measures, for example, sign-in registration with valid identification; they will be asked to lock up their belongings and bring in only a pencil, notebook, and laptop.
- Note that many Special Collections have limited weekday hours and no weekend or major holiday access.
- Present polices about cell phone use as cameras and for calls; cover electronic scanners devices and their use.
- Explain to students that methods of describing and housing the collections and the techniques for accessing them will be different from those of general library collections, and that "browsing the shelves" may be limited.
- Inform students that not everything has a finding aid online, there may be collections that still use paper-based "analog" finding aids and catalogs
- Train students to properly use Special Collections materials; explain that they must be handled carefully which may involve the use of gloves and special devices such as book cradles.

Special Collections staff should be aware that increased outreach and instruction will call for more training on security, use, and preservation for the materials. Reiterate that we must exhibit a welcoming attitude and assist each student to the limits of time, staff, and expertise. However, we must also have clear and realistic policies in place about the research assistance we can offer homeschoolers in person, by mail or e-mail and clearly state any charges.

Furthermore, of particular concern in a Special Collections library are materials and images that are culturally sensitive, i.e., photographs of African- or Native Americans that present stereotypes or violence. These must be presented with an explanation and proviso, but they can also be an excellent teachable moment about history. Our libraries and archives should already have "sound archival policies and practices that take into consideration the needs and concerns of the different stakeholders of our particular cultural heritage/property collections…. [These policies should] show respect and understanding and a willingness to empathize with those users that have an emotional and cultural connection with the collections under our responsibility" (Ramos 2013).

An example of an excellent statement to share with students is at Cornell University Library's Digital Collections site: "The collection includes some historical images that reveal racist, disturbing, or otherwise negative representations or stereotypes of the people depicted. These images have been included as part of the historical record and should not be interpreted to mean that Cornell University or its staff endorse or approve of the negative representations or stereotypes presented (Cornell University n.d.)."

After presenting these caveats, homeschoolers can then be introduced to many surprising materials at their local Special Collections library. For example, these may include:

- cuneiform tablets
- manuscripts, letters, diaries
- prints and lithographs
- press and artist's books
- photographs
- maps and posters
- original rare books
- wills and other court documents
- slavery records
- State and House Journals
- broadsides and announcements
- advice and textbooks
- blueprints and scrapbooks
- fashion plates and patterns
- political ephemera

Additionally, some Special Collections libraries with education departments offer interactive exhibits, workshops and camps on art, sculpture, and crafts. Traveling kits with hands-on materials for the students that they can check out and take home may also be available. For example, one such traveling kit, the "Traveling Lincoln," is currently offered by our library for area homeschoolers. This popular kit includes *Lesson Plans and Teacher Resource Guides CD* with activities, digitized primary source material and printable worksheets; laminated reproduction primary documents and historic images; artifacts for hands-on history; music from the time period including Civil War bands, ballads and patriotic songs; and age-appropriate books. Among other themes for these traveling education kits there are the *Civil War, Native Americans,* and *Black History*.

Many Special Collections libraries' staff are also faculty members who teach introductory classes for research and present guest lectures about using primary resources in the classroom. They would welcome the addition of age-appropriate homeschoolers and their instructors, as this creates a richer research experience. Special Collections staff can teach homeschooled students that by using primary sources, they can form their own opinions about historical events. Using evidence from the past, in this way, creates a fresh interpretation of history and adds to the development and dissemination of new knowledge.

A few ideas for using images, oral histories, rare books, and genealogical materials in lesson planning are listed below. With images, the lesson plan can focus on the power and persuasion of a visual resource. Let the student know that images are "are a subtle dance, a conversation, an intimacy" unlike any other resource (Thein 2017). Educators recognize that "engagement with images promotes students' abilities to bolster their skills at analyzing and encourages students to consider the significance [of the image] within the larger context of U.S. history" (Marcus, Stoddard and Woodward 2016, 5). Photographs covering many historical themes are usually available with subjects such as early schools and education, industrialization and farming, transportation, Prohibition, the changing roles of women, and the Civil Rights movement.A student can choose one photograph or a series of photographs, and by applying the concepts of exploring, examining and explaining, create a storyline of what is happening in the photograph or visual resource. For an image, have the student study the resource closely for a few minutes and first give an oral description of the photograph. Ask what may be its time period, the sights, sounds and even smells that are invoked as one studies the image. Creating a comparison paper by what they see in the photograph and in their own lifetime will enable them to learn about the effects of progress and change in a historical context. Furthermore, this exercise creates an appreciation for the time in which they live. Discuss the questions whose answers are considered the basics for gathering information: who, what, when, where, why, and how. Other sample questions when examining a photograph are:

- What grabs your attention immediately?
- What persons or objects are shown?
- Does the photograph look staged or arranged?
- What is the physical setting?
- What, if any, words or signs do you see?
- What is happening and to whom?
- When do you think the image was made?

Primary sources from Special Collections are foundational for the study of many disciplines. Connecting and layering disciplines such as history and geography supports exploration of multiple perspectives and contributes to a multi-faceted appreciation of complex topics. A lesson plan using maps and letters is an effective way to combine these two sources. Maps are more than directions or listings of physical attributes but are "visual records of knowledge valued by people in an area and they point to belief systems as well as boundaries. The effective use of maps can illustrate concepts that may otherwise be difficult for students to understand, such as settlement patterns, trade routes, economic growth and development" (Eastern Illinois University n.d.). Combining period maps with letters, journals, census records and diary entries fleshes out the story being told. The Battey Family Letters in the Manuscripts Division of the Department of Special Collections at WKU are the letters of brothers Peter, Alfred and George Battey. They are writing to a sister and a brother James, during their Civil War service in the Union Army. From the "Colo Barracks" in Bowling Green, Kentucky, Peter describes his duties as a teamster, criticizes the length of the war, and relays news of the killing of John Hunt Morgan (in Greeneville, Tennessee). Writing on September 9, 1864, he tells this historically important news, reading, in part: "We have some pretty grand news from the army. They have killed Old Morgan and took all of his staff and killed 50 of his men and took 200 prisoners and the rest scattered all thru the woods for life. Farmer Gillman is the man that killed him … three cheers for him … [Sherman] has got Atlanta. They got a lot of prisoners … killed was estimated at eighteen thousand killed and taken prisoners. That is a pretty good haul…." Alfred writes from hospital in New Orleans, Louisiana where he is recovering from wounds. George writes from Bowling Green, where he and Peter continue on duty after the war. The brothers were English-born but refer to their home in Ohio.

Diaries, letters and personal journals are some of the most interesting resources for a student. The student enters the writer's life on a level not possible in secondary materials. She or he can study the person's motivation for writing, opinions, worldview, and character. The student can ask, what this individual would think of today's events and conditions. The use of oral histories by a student also creates an immediate connection to the past. The student can hear and sometimes see the person whose "eye-ear witness account" was recorded.

One oral history project in Kentucky focused on African American education in south central Kentucky, 1920–1960; it was conducted by Joseph Carl Ruff. He collected 26 interviews with African Americans "who were educated in and/or taught in south central Kentucky. Their first-hand accounts provide a unique perspective on the evolution of the education of African Americans in the region. Each interview reflects the determination of people to overcome the obstacles created by a flawed doctrine, 'separate but equal,' to achieve success, and for many of the interviewees, to become community leaders as teachers and school administrators" (Pass the Word 1993).

By continuing with the theme of "exploring, examining and explaining" and asking such questions as those listed below, the students can become active participants in the memories of people, communities, and past events. They can use other audio/analog collections of music and sheet music with lyrics, to compare today's music with the music styles and technology of the past. Additionally, oral history collections can be used to study one aspect of community life such as work, religion, family, or education and then the students can create a community or family oral history relevant to themselves.

Sample questions used in evaluating oral interviews are:

- What was the purpose of recording this?
- What can you tell about the person telling the story, and about that person's point of view?
- What is the significance of this oral history?
- Is it more personal or historical?
- How does encountering this story firsthand change its emotional impact?
- What can you learn from this oral history (Teacher's Guide n.d.)?

Students will also find local and regional genealogical collections at their special collections library whereby they may learn about their family's story and how their family's history, American, and world history are related. They may wish to trace their ancestry to a particular country and study those customs, language, dress, foods, and cultural traditions. They can use the resources that they locate to write a paper that will document how their family came to live in America or even their town. Using books that list local cemeteries may foster a trip to that cemetery to locate burial plots for their ancestors. This can also enable the students to study epidemic illnesses and the common causes of death in a certain time period. Furthermore, they may look at microfilm from their or their parent's birth date, or a hundred years or more ago when their great-grandparents were born.

Many exciting lessons can come from primary text materials as simple as a cookbook. Researching a recipe brings in elements of measurement, portion, and size. Students can taste a food in their home kitchen using a 200-year-old recipe and see how food preparation, consumption, and tastes have changed. In our collection, we have a cookbook, *Good Eats Will Bring Him Home Early with Smiling Countenance*. Such a title can be used to discuss gender roles and how they have changed.

Objects that many Special Collections libraries and museums have include uniforms, dresses, tools, and even weapons. These can be used to study fashion trends, invention, changes in the building process, and how wars are fought. With a piece of fine art, the student can research the artist, the date of the piece, and the medium, thus learning what the composition tells about the conditions of the time, symbolism, perspective, and world view.

Furthermore, using the librarian, archivist, or members of local historical societies, the homeschoolers may want to organize a tour of older homes in their community, and research the people who lived in these homes, when they were first built, their location, furnishings, and relation to the larger community.

Special Collections libraries, to parrot an old saying, are a goldmine or a "never failing [research] spring in the desert" for homeschooled students. Special Collections libraries, like museums, through their collections, "their physical space, artifacts, professional staff, special programs, online resources, ... create opportunities for students to deepen their understanding of specific content, and to develop historical thinking and critical literacy skills. They make 'studying history more vivid, engaging and relevant'" (Marcus, Stoddard and Woodward 2016, 5). In partnership with Special Collections librarians and staff, teachers and instructors of homeschooled students can equip learners with the highly valued skills of inquiry, critical thinking, and analysis that will provide a framework for lifelong learning. Positive effects for Special Collections and their outreach to homeschooling communities:

- highlight collections
- contribute to lifelong learning
- showcase librarians as authoritative arbiters of knowledge
- expand view of who we serve; maintain traditional constituencies and create new ones
- create valuable partnerships
- aid students in transition to higher education
- emphasize our role as an education portal and partner

As Special Collections librarians and information professionals, we must create relevant and sustainable programs to support and enhance the homeschool learning experience. This forces us to think innovatively about "research use beyond the obvious audiences. Who can use what for what purpose? When this question is inventively answered, our task then becomes to attract those people through the door of the department so we can get the 'stuff' into their hands" (Bahde 2011, 75). This author understands the complexities of limited funds and staff in many Special Collections. It is hard to open the doors to these primary resources in many ways and best practices must be followed. Dean and Professor, University of Tennessee Libraries, Steven Smith fittingly observed that "the suggestion that teaching from our collections is important to their survival may seem counterintuitive, for such activity will result in more exposure and more exposure could result in damage. We spend enormous amounts of time and money making sure that our collections are properly stored and carefully handled. We quite rightly resist any activity that poses a risk to them, including teaching. There is no disputing the fact that integrating rare materials into classroom assignments could result in a kind and frequency of handling that they would not likely be subject to if they are reserved exclusively for research. But in making this point, I am suggesting that in the interests of the overall institution (and even the larger culture) it may be worth increased exposure to certain individual items for a larger good" (Smith 2006, 31). Open access is a necessity, not only for homeschoolers but for every student. We must move beyond the mindset of protect and preserve, to promotion in Special Collections. As one Special Collections librarian noted: "We have got to market ourselves to the general public. We have got to show the connection between the [library] and their lives, or we're dead in the water" (Carlson 2005).

Additional Resources for Incorporating Primary Resource Materials into the Library and Homeschool Curriculum

- Teachers Page (https://www.loc.gov/education/): this wide-ranging web site is accessed at the Library of Congress web site and is designed to help educators use Library of Congress resources, and especially American Memory Digital collections. This site is the main place for K–12 educators to find information on how to use primary sources, to find lesson plans, primary source sets, and other classroom materials, and to learn about professional development opportunities from the Library. They spotlight materials for students and lifelong learners with history, literature and poetry, science with everyday mysteries and "Today in History."
- America's Story (http://www.americaslibrary.gov/): a colorful fun site for homeschoolers and their families. The site hopes to "put the story back in history and show you some things that you've never heard or seen before. The Library of Congress is the largest 'Special Library' in the world and is showcasing 'letters, diaries, records and tapes, films, sheet music, maps, prints, photographs and digital materials' at this wonderful site. The site offers a chance to 'meet amazing Americans, jump back in time, explore the states, join America at play and see, hear and sing America'" (America's Library 2018).
- Library of Congress Teaching with Primary Sources (http://www.loc.gov/teachers/tps/): another far-reaching web site that features creative programs and practical ways to teach with primary resources. They currently have twenty-one member institutions from nine states. It is an open door to the "Library of Congress's rich reservoir of digitized primary source materials to design challenging, high-quality instruction." These concepts and themes can also be applied to materials found in local special collections. They also offer free professional development resources for teachers. The *Teaching with Primary Sources Journal* (TPS) is an online publication created by the Library of Congress Educational Outreach Division and is a great help to the homeschool instructor. Each issue focuses on pedagogical approaches to teaching with primary sources in K–12 classrooms.

See also:

- History in the Raw: https: www.archives.gov/education/research/history-in-the-raw.html
- Teaching with Documents: https://www.archives.gov/education/lessons
- Using Primary Resources: http://www.loc.gov/teachers/usingprimarysources/
- Primary Resources: http://www.ala.org/rusa/sections/history/histcomm/instructionres/mil

- Quick How-To Guides: https://library.unr.edu/DIY/i-am-looking-for-primary-sources (a good definition page)

WORKS CITED

Bahde, Anne. 2011. "Taking the Show on the Road: Special Collections Instruction in the Campus Classroom." *RBM: A Journal of Rare Books, Manuscripts, and Cultural Heritage* 12, no. 2 (September): 75–88.

Carlson, Scott. 2005. "Special Effects." *Chronicle of Higher Education* 51, no. 41 (June): A23–A25.

Cornell University. 2016. "Cornell University Library Digital Collections: Lynching." Accessed October 1, 2017. https://digital.library.cornell.edu/catalog/ss:1508537.

Devine, Donn. 2001. "Defining Professionalism." *Professional Genealogy: A Manual for Researchers, Writers, Editors, Lecturers, and Librarians*. Baltimore, Genealogical Publishing Company.

Eastern Illinois University. n.d. "Childhood Lost: Child Labor During the Industrial Revolution, Teaching with Primary Resources." Accessed November 1, 2017. http://www.eiu.edu/eiutps/childhood_ps.php.

Jones, Barbara M. 2004. "Hidden Collections, Scholarly Barriers: Creating Access to Unprocessed Special Collection Materials in American's Research Libraries." *RBM: A Journal of Rare Books, Manuscripts, and Cultural Heritage* 5, no. 2 (September): 88–105.

Marcus, Alan S., Jeremy D. Stoddard and Walter W. Woodward. 2016. *Teaching History with Museums: Strategies for K–12 Social Studies*. London and New York: Routledge.

Pass The Word. "African American Education in South Central Kentucky." Accessed November 14, 2017. http://passtheword.ky.gov/collection/african-american-education-south-central-kentucky.

Ramos, Marisol. 2013. "Cultural Sensitivity in the Archives: Digitizing Controversial Materials, a Balancing Act." Storrs, Connecticut. University of Connecticut Library Presentation. http://opencommons.uconn.edu/cgi/viewcontent.cgi?article=1046&context=libr_pres.

Ray, Brian D. 2018. Research Facts on Homeschooling. Accessed January 1, 2018. https://www.nheri.org/research-facts-on-homeschooling/.

Smith, Steven Escar. 2006. "Treasure Room" to "School Room: Special Collections and Education." *RBM: A Journal of Rare Books, Manuscripts, and Cultural Heritage* 7, no. 1 (April): 31–39.

"Teacher's Guide Analyzing Oral Histories." Accessed September 14, 2017. http://www.loc.gov/teachers/using primarysources/resources/Analyzing_Oral_Histories.pdf.

Thein, Ming. 2017. "Photography and Psychology: It's All a Mind Game." Accessed November 1, 2017. https://www.huffingtonpost.com/ming-thein/photography-and-psychology-part-1_b_4380400.html.

Weller, Chris. 2017. "Americans Are Rejecting the 'Homeschool Myth'—and Experts Say the Misunderstood Education Might Be Better Than Public or Charter Schools." Business Insider, January 23, 2017. http://www.businessinsider.com/homeschooing-more-popular-than-ever-2017-1.

School Libraries
and Homeschooling

A Source for Socialization

RENE M. BURRESS, JENNA KAMMER
and BOBBIE BUSHMAN

"What about socialization?" is a dreaded question asked of homeschooling parents. When homeschooling was still a fringe movement, there may have been more legitimacy to this question. Today, socialization opportunities for homeschoolers are more prevalent in the community. Still, a homeschool parent's perspective about socialization is often different than that of the general public. Homeschooling parents often feel that traditional methods of socialization provided by public schools are unhealthy. The following survey of homeschooling parents indicates that the majority of parents homeschool due to various feelings of dissatisfaction with the public school system (McQuiggan and Megra 2017). Dissatisfaction with public schools may mean that fewer homeschoolers will be likely to consider the school library as a resource for socialization. However, school libraries offer a variety of programming, resources, and opportunities for socializing youth that could benefit a homeschooler.

Socialization, Homeschooling and Public Schools

Even though homeschoolers choose not to attend public school, they can still utilize the public school for socialization or academic enrichment opportunities. Families that live in equal access states can participate in public school programming (like sports, band, extracurricular clubs, afterschool programs, and special events). For example, some states will allow homeschoolers to play on the sports team of the public school within the district in which they reside (Moy 2015). This access extends to any public school activity, including allowing children to attend one or two classes at the school or online if desired. However, this policy is not without challenges. Bhatt (2014) points to the tension that exists in the public school related to homeschooled children using public school resources: while homeschool families pay property tax that funds schools, the school itself does not receive per-pupil funding for non-attendance. Because of this, Johnson (2013) describes the relationship between homeschoolers and the public schools as "complicated," explaining that some schools (or educators within the schools) will be more likely to cooperate with homeschoolers than others.

In today's homeschooling environment there are many social outlets for home-schoolers. Churches, co-ops, homeschool sports, dances, and proms, are all common places where homeschoolers can socialize. Although homeschooling families often hate the "socialization question," and many homeschoolers have found all the opportunities they need for socialization, others are still looking for them. Specifically, some groups may need extra avenues: new homeschoolers, teen homeschoolers, single child home-schoolers, and secular homeschoolers. New homeschoolers often don't have a social net-work in place yet, since they have just started homeschooling. Socialization is also increasingly important as homeschoolers age. By the teen years, many homeschooling parents have opted to place kids back in public school, with the most popular years for homeschooling being K–5 (National Center for Education Statistics 2012). Because of this, teen homeschoolers are often in the minority. Homeschoolers who have only one child will likely need more social experiences since the child doesn't get time with siblings. Secular homeschoolers may need extra socialization opportunities since they may not have the regular church involvement that their religious counterparts have. Additionally, some co-ops, classes, and groups in the homeschooling community require signing a statement of faith. This can make it difficult for secular homeschoolers to find a social group for their children. Although the public library can help with any homeschooler's socialization needs, an additional place that families may find a connection is their local school library.

In this essay, we present several ideas for socializing homeschool students in school libraries, with the assumption that the school librarian would extend access to these pro-grams for homeschoolers. Many homeschool families are aware of the many benefits that public libraries offer, but may not be as familiar with school library opportunities. In some communities, the school library is closer to home than the nearest public library. As taxpayers of the local school district, homeschooling families have access to the school library as they would other public school services. Participating in school library activities allows the homeschool child to socialize during specified time frames around the topic of literacy. School librarians are trained educators and are open to working with all stu-dents as part of their mission (AASL 2018). School librarians are also literacy leaders and engage students in all types of literacy activities to promote the love of reading (Moreillon 2018).

Listed below are many examples of programming that is common in school libraries. For all of these examples, the best way to get involved is to develop a relationship between local homeschoolers and a local school librarian. Once aware of the interest, the school librarian will be able to provide the homeschool family with opportunities and details such as curriculum and literacy content, times of events, and grade levels of participants.

Reader's Award Programs

In the United States, most states host yearly reader's awards or reader's choice pro-grams. These are different from the awards such as the Newbery or Caldecott because nominees are chosen by students and the winner is voted on by students. Maliszewski and Soleas (2018) found that students' involvement in reader's choice award programs built their love of reading and motivated them to read because the students could see that their voice had an impact. Homeschooling families can participate in these programs in a variety of ways. The easiest option is to get the reading lists for the current year. Have your child read the required number of books and then vote on their favorite. Another way is to become a reader/selector. Readers/selectors have an important job because they help select the books for the next award year. They often have read about 25 books over a period of a few months and rated them on a scale from 1 to 5. This process helps narrow down the books for the final list. Yet one more way to participate is to recommend books that you have read to be considered for the various awards. The school libraries in your area may have some curriculum activities related to reading the books that homeschool students may want to join. They also sometimes have voting parties that homeschool families might like to attend.

Story Times

Storytimes are available in public libraries, but school librarians provide storytime as well. A great way for a homeschool family to get involved in their public school activities would be to attend storytime at their local school library at the grade level(s) their children are suited to attend. Research supports the many benefits of children hearing stories read aloud including exposing children to new genres and extending their vocabulary and comprehension through discussion (Lowe 2016). Storytime at the school library often either connects to the state reader's award books or provides a curricular extension of what a specific grade-level is studying at the time. School librarians are knowledgeable of the school curriculum and this allows planning of appropriate stories and activities (Laretive 2017). Storytimes may be scheduled at the same time each week for specific grade levels, which would allow the busy homeschooling family to arrange a regular outing. For example, in McPherson, Kansas, school district, the district school librarian, Amanda Harrison provides a family story time for toddlers and preschoolers, with stories, finger plays, and sing-alongs. This activity is open to all families that live in the school district. Participating in school library storytime is a great way to naturally socialize with peers, check out a few books, and meet other students in their grade levels.

Author Visits

A great way to connect children and young adults with books is to meet real authors and illustrators. Former school librarian and author, Toni Buzzeo (2018) highlights several benefits of author visits, such as the understanding the process, being able to ask the author questions and making connections with real people who can serve as inspiring role models. While beneficial, these events can be very costly to arrange for homeschool groups or co-ops. School libraries often host such visits. The author/illustrator may speak at an elementary, middle, or high school. Families are encouraged to contact the school librarians in their area and ask for information about these visits. Many times schools will get ready for author visits by doing activities related to the author/genre. Authors and illustrators are willing to sign books, but sometimes those books must be ordered and prepaid before the event. To get details such as the schedule, curriculum activities, pre-purchase, and other pre-visit details, families will want to connect with the school librarian. School libraries will provide a great service to the homeschooling community by having this information ready for their local families.

Children's Literature Festivals

Another great way to meet authors and illustrators is to go on a field trip to children's literature festivals. Keep in mind the sometimes these festivals have a fee for attendance. One example of a festival is the annual Children's Literature Festival at the University of Central Missouri (Greife 2018). Every March, while the university campus is on spring break, the library hosts a three-day festival focused on children in grades 3 to 10. School librarians and teachers are encouraged to bring students to the university where over 20 authors and illustrators can meet them in classrooms throughout the campus. Students can meet up to five authors during a single day. When Rene Burress was a school librarian, she took students to the children's literature festival. The field trip fee was paid out of the school library budget for any student who read the required number of reader's award books for that year. If a family is willing to collaborate with the school librarian who is planning to attend the field trip, it is possible that the trip will be less expensive or paid for by the school.

Reading Promotion Programs

At both school and public libraries, there is a variety of reading promotion programs, such as, for example, summer reading programs that most public libraries host. School libraries also conduct incentive programs, reading challenges, and reading celebrations in which homeschool families may want to participate throughout the year. The purpose of these programs is to get students excited about reading and to motivate and encourage all students to read (Moreillon 2018). An example of this is a reading overnight program Rene Burress hosted when she was a school librarian. This program was designed for all students in the school who participated in the reading challenge throughout the school year (the challenge was to read 15 minutes each night at home and fill out a monthly log). Every month students who had submitted their reading logs received a treat from the Parent Teacher Organization. At the end of the academic year, the school library hosted an overnight party at the school that included dinner, bounce houses, hallway races, and other activities. There was a lot of fun and very little sleep! Getting involved in reading activities like these is a great way for homeschoolers to socialize with other students in the community. And if the parent wanted to volunteer to help out, school librarians would love the extra help.

Book Fairs

Many school libraries have book fairs that homeschool families attend. They often have activities related to book fairs that provide excellent socialization opportunities for homeschool children. As a school librarian, Rene Burress encouraged families to come to book fair-related events held before and after school. Over the years these included a special *Grandparents' Night, Muffins with Mom, Donuts with Dad* and other special times. Homeschooling families would have been welcome to attend these events! Having the schedule for activities such as these allows the homeschooling family to attend these special events and purchase books at the same time.

Afterschool Clubs

Both public and school libraries offer a variety of afterschool programs. Being involved in them allows homeschool families to socialize in a learning-focused environment. School library programs present many great options for homeschoolers. Witteveen (2017) shares several real-life examples of clubs that meet in school libraries including clubs focused on science, technology, engineering, and math (STEM) and literature. For example, Witteveen describes a middle school library advisory committee called SLACkers (Student Library Advisory Committee) where students meet to discuss library programming and books. Schnittka et al. (2016) studied an afterschool STEM club that took place in a middle school library. The school library provided a flexible learning environment and internet access the group needed to be successful.

Library Space

A public library is often referred to as a "third place"—a community anchor that the public can visit outside of work and home (for example, see Leckie and Buschman 2007). Johnson (2010) and Gray (2017) describe how the school library can also be a "third place" within the school that is not the classroom or playground. Gray (2017) also describes the school library as more of a "third space" (as opposed to "place") within the school where students can choose how they use it: to socialize, plan, relax or explore their own identity. School libraries are learning spaces where the librarian, student and teacher determine how and what should happen within that space. Diana Rendina (2017) explains how the school library space links the concepts of a learning space design and the "library as a third place" concept. She describes how the school library should have several types of spaces in it, including spaces for interaction, collaboration with technology, makerspaces, and spaces to work alone. A school library space might include a makerspace, media station, gaming area, tables or seating for groups, and reading areas. For a homeschooling family, this means that the school library can be an additional learning and social space for children to study, and to interact and engage with others.

School libraries routines include a variety of scheduling, from flexible (where students choose when to visit the library) to fixed (where classes are scheduled to visit the library regularly each week). That scheduling provides opportunities for homeschool students to either join in with regular classroom activities or to visit the library as an open library space to use existing resources. Additionally, homeschool groups are often in need of neutral locations to host events. Homes may not be big or centrally located. Churches sometimes charge fees and may only welcome certain homeschoolers. School libraries can provide the needed neutral space for homeschoolers to host social events where homeschoolers plan the parties and programs and the school library is simply provides a meeting room or other space.

Digital Resources

School libraries offer a variety of digital and print resources supporting social and emotional development of children that may be of interest to homeschooling families. Some of these resources include social networking and collaboration technology that public school students use to participate asynchronously in activities like reviewing content (i.e. online book reviews), rating materials or playing social games with others in the district. For example, Follett's Biblionasium in Destiny Discover™ has a student-to-student feature that allows students to "friend" others within the school network to share reading experiences. School libraries and educational technology departments may also purchase subscriptions that support the social and emotional growth of students within their school, but that might be useful to homeschoolers as well. For example, PenPal Schools has been purchased by some school libraries. PenPal Schools connects students globally and allows students to interact with other children in different parts of the country. Lastly, school librarians may curate or purchase tools specifically for the development of digital citizenship skills, which is one way for children to develop online socialization skills. Some of these tools include Interland, Cyberwise™, or BrainPOP® digital citizenship unit. Parents can speak with the school librarian to find out what technology and databases are available within their school district that may be useful for socialization, and determine if there is a way for homeschool students or parents to access these resources. Each school district may have different policies in place to allow access to these resources from home, or on school premises.

Homeschool Volunteers

Homeschoolers can be a huge source of reliable volunteers for public and school libraries. Homeschooled teens and their parents may be looking for volunteer opportunities to add to their middle and high school transcripts. Homeschooled children can volunteer during daytime hours when other children cannot. They can assist with a variety of things, but most integral to a library looking to expand homeschooling programming, homeschooled tweens and teens can help a youth librarian plan engaging programming. The homeschooled volunteer can market the program to friends and family, facilitate the program, plan dances, give insight into curriculum support, and consider creative ways the library can partner to meet extracurricular needs related to homeschooling like health and fitness, art, science labs, etc. This can be just the help librarians need if they had struggled to provide well-attended homeschool social programming in the past. This approach is supported by research about providing inclusive programming. In order to facilitate successful programming for underserved groups, librarians must include that target group in planning facilitating, promoting, and evaluating the program (Bushman 2018).

Conclusion

School libraries have many programs that can enrich a homeschooling curriculum and provide additional social opportunities with other homeschoolers, or other students in the public school. For example, an author visit at a public school will often happen during the school day, be age appropriate, and provide enrichment with peers that a homeschooler may not have at a public library. Or, the school library can provide spaces and resources for homeschoolers to use that are related to teaching and learning. There may also be opportunities to engage in volunteering at the school library that will provide a homeschooled teen a chance to work with younger children, or learn more about the library. In addition, school librarians are certified teachers that share the mission of the American Library Association. The school librarian could be a valuable resource for homeschoolers and their parent educators.

All of the ideas featured in this essay require the homeschooling parent and school librarian to collaborate and communicate. The partnership between a homeschool parent and school librarian can include sharing information or events or providing access to resources and district technology. Homeschoolers are a varied group and each family will have unique needs and interests. They are comprised of all races, ethnicities, religions, and motivations for homeschooling. This can make it difficult to meet their needs in any one area, such as socialization. However, a proactive librarian will be able to make the connections needed to begin facilitating programming to assist with homeschooling socialization.

WORKS CITED

American Association of School Librarians. 2018. *National School Library Standards for Learners, School Librarians, and School Libraries.* Chicago: ALA.

Bhatt, Rachana. 2014. "Home Is Where the School Is: The Impact of Homeschool Legislation on School Choice." *Journal of School Choice* 8 (2): 192–212.

Bilandzic, Mark, and Marcus Foth. 2013. "Libraries as Coworking Spaces: Understanding User Motivations and Perceived Barriers to Social Learning." *Library Hi Tech* 31 (2): 254–73.

Bushman, Bobbi. 2018. "Library Services and Early Literacy Approaches in Public Libraries for Deaf and Hard of Hearing Children." *The International Journal of Information, Diversity & Inclusion* 2 (1/2) https://publish.lib.umd.edu/IJIDI/issue/view/32.

Buzzeo, Toni. 2018. "Benefits of Author and Illustrator Visits." Accessed December 12. https://www.tonibuzzeo.com/SPEAKING_files/benefitsofauthorandillustratorvisits.pdf.

Gray, Martin. 2017. "School Libraries as the Third Place." *Access* (Online) 31 (4): 36–7.

Greife, Mike. 2018. "UCM Celebrates the 50th Annual Children's Literature Festival." University of Central Missouri, March 6. https://www.ucmo.edu/news/university-news/posts/2018-03-06-ucm-celebrates-the-50th-annual-childrens-literature-festival.php.

Johnson, Donna M. 2013. "Confrontation and Cooperation: The Complicated Relationship Between Homeschoolers and Public Schools." *Peabody Journal of Education* 88 (3): 298.

Johnson, Doug. 2010. "School Libraries as a "Third Place." *Library Media Connection* 29 (1).

Laretive, Josephine. 2017. "Creating a Community of Readers." *Access.* 31 (3): 16–23.

Leckie, Gloria J., and John Buschman. 2007. The Library as Place: History, Community, and Culture. Westport, CN: Libraries Unlimited.

Lowe, Kaye. 2016. *For the Love of Reading: Supporting Struggling Readers.* Australia: Primary English Teaching Association Australia.

Maliszewski, Diana P., and Eleftherios K. Soleas. 2018. "Reading Between the Lines: Motivation Lessons Learned from the Forest of Reading in Ontario." *School Libraries Worldwide* 24 (2): 46.

McQuiggan, Megan, and Mahi Megra. 2017. "Parent and Family Involvement in Education: Results from the National Household Education Surveys Program of 2016," U.S. Department of Education, https://nces.ed.gov/pubsearch/pubsinfo.asp?pubid=2017102.

Moreillon, Judi. 2018. "Reading Champions: A Leadership Opportunity for School Libraries." *Knowledge Quest* 47 (1): 52–60.

Moy, Cora. 2015. "Equal Access: A Proposal for Homeschooled Students and Athletics." *Northern Illinois University Law Review* 7: 29–55.

National Center for Education Statistics. 2012 "Number and Percentage of Homeschooled Students Ages 5 Through 17 with a Grade Equivalent of Kindergarten Through 12th Grade, by Selected Child, Parent, and Household Characteristics: 2003, 2007, and 2012." Institute of Education, https://nces.ed.gov/programs/digest/d13/tables/dt13_206.10.asp.

Rendina, Diana L. 2017. *Reimagining Library Spaces: Transform Your Space on Any Budget*. Portland: International Society for Technology in Education.

Schnittka, Christine G., Michael A. Evans, Samantha G.L. Won, and Tiffany A. Drape. 2016. "After-School Spaces: Looking for Learning in All the Right Places." *Research in Science Education*. 46 (3): 389–412.

Witteveen, April. 2017. "School Year Jump Starts." *School Library Journal* 63 (8).

PART V

Finding Resources

Funding for Library Services to Homeschoolers

CASEY CUSTER *and* REBECCA RICH-WULFMEYER

Typically underfunded, public libraries receive most of their financial support from one of four sources: as part of a government entity; as part of a library district; as a non-profit organization; or by a for-profit private business that operates that library. In addition to this base support, public libraries seek out supplemental funding to help them offer additional programs, collections, services, facilities, and other resources for audiences, including homeschoolers. There are many avenues for obtaining additional funding for libraries and their homeschool resources. To that end, it is wise to think of the library, the homeschool community, and the surrounding community as parts of a larger ecosystem of components that support each other.

With the growth of homeschooling and the ever-present need for more money in budgets, libraries can always use extra cash. If we narrow our focus specifically on home-schooling programs, it is obvious that libraries could use additional funding for special collections or supplements such as microscopes or other science equipment as a part of the library's "libratory" for homeschoolers. For example, Dawn Jardine, Director of the Red Hook Public Library, mentions that homeschoolers can find it difficult to teach science at home, so she sees it as an opportunity to help the homeschooling community by having a year-long homeschooling "libratory" science program. She emphasizes that bringing in homeschoolers with the equipment and programming also increases their circulation of books and other thematically related materials (Jardine 2017).

Fundraising experts take semester-long classes and annual training to learn about funding and develop skills. Their careers are spent on understanding how not-for-profit organizations such as libraries operate and how to get them more money. While we cannot turn you into a major rainmaker, this essay will introduce you to some types of funding and examples of projects of use to any type of library. We encourage you to consider possibilities and proactively seek the support you need.

Grants

Governmental agencies, non-profit organizations, and for-profit companies offer grants. There are four types of grants awarded: competitive (discretionary) funding, formula funding, continuation funding, and pass-through funding. With competitive funding grants, "proposal selection [is] based on the evaluation of a reviewer or team of reviewers. Funding is based on the merits of the application, and recipients are not predetermined." In formula funding, "grants are given to pre-determined recipients. Non-competitive awards are usually allocated to eligible entities according to population and/or other census criteria, and all applicants who meet the minimum requirements of the application process are entitled to receive money." With continuation funding, current grant award recipients are offered "the option of renewing grants for the following year. Some programs are restricted to existing grantees only, while others invite applications from current grantees and new applicants. Since priority is often given to continuing applicants, if you are a new applicant, you should consider entering into a partnership with a currently funded entity." And lastly, "pass-through grants are funds given by the federal government to the states for further distribution to local governments. Under this funding structure, states may disburse federal funds to eligible local jurisdictions through formula allocations or open competitions" (eCivis 2019).

Grants can provide those extra monies libraries need to support homeschoolers in their community, especially for homeschool-specific projects, collection development, and programs. Below is a list of some helpful and informative websites that will get you started. While they are not homeschool-specific, there is no reason why a year-long enhanced robotics program for homeschool kids could not fit the description of many individual grants listed on these pages. As librarians imagine or recognize a need for a specific program, collection items, equipment, or project for homeschoolers, they should search for a grant that might help satisfy that need.

- The Library Corporation: Provides a wonderful list of a wide variety of resources on business, state, federal, for- and non-profit levels. These websites, in turn, describe numerous grant opportunities [TLC 2017].
- Grants.gov: Librarians can search this site for government agencies providing grant opportunities. There are also features to learn about grants, granting agencies, and grant policies [Grants.gov 2019].
- American Library Association: Offers several grant opportunities, and while none are homeschool-specific, some could be used for homeschool purposes. For example, the BWI Collection Development Grant is geared towards a public librarian who works with the 12–18-year-old age group [ALA 2019].
- Scholastic: Lists grant opportunities. For example, a grant by the Rockwell Collins Charitable Corporation awards funds of $5,000 or more to nonprofit organizations providing programs to the youth in math, science and engineering or culture and the arts. While it is not homeschooling-specific, a homeschool program could easily fit this description [Scholastic 2019].
- THE Journal: Offers lists of grants pertaining to K–12 students. Of a particular interest is the Honda Power of Dreams Grant that is awarded to support youth education, specifically in the areas of science, technology, engineering, math, the environment, job training and literacy—all topics of interest to homeschoolers [THE Journal 2019].
- The Institute of Museum and Library Services (IMLS): "Advances, supports, and empowers America's museums, libraries, and related organizations through

grantmaking, research, and policy development." Annually, IMLS awards hundreds of grants to libraries and museums, many of which arrive at individual libraries as pass-through grants coming out of state libraries. Some IMLS grant projects "support the purposes and priorities outlined in the Library Services and Technology Act (LSTA)" [IMLS 2019].

- GrantWatch.com: Provides free and subscription-based information on "federal, state, local, foundation, and corporation grants with more than 20,149 current grants, funding opportunities, awards, contracts and archived grants (that will soon be available again)" [Grantwatch 2019].

Below are examples of some IMLS grants that had been awarded in the past: four to libraries and one to a museum. Some were created specifically for homeschoolers, while others were designed with conscious knowledge that homeschoolers would benefit. You will notice that all of these grants came as IMLS LSTA grants and they each relate to STEM (science, technology, engineering, and math) programming.

- Lincoln County Public Library System, North Carolina, received a $50,000 EZ Literacy and Lifelong Learning Grant from the State Library of North Carolina (funded as a pass-through grant from IMLS as supported by LSTA) for their robotics program. A portion of the grant was "used to implement the library's new homeschool connection initiative." They noticed that they have "a number of homeschool families come in because they don't necessarily have all of the resources that a school would have. Bringing in robotics equipment and things like that would be costly for every family to do but, by participating in our library programming, they're able to supplement the instruction that they're receiving at home" [Chapman 2018].
- The Haywood County Public Library, North Carolina, received a Strengthening Public and Academic Library Collections grant, from the State Library of North Carolina (funded as a pass-through grant from IMLS as supported by LSTA) for their Homeschool Collection. For the fiscal year 2011–12, they received $18,500 for an outreach collection including print and audio materials for children ages kindergarten through high school to enrich the lives of home-schooled children [Haywood County 2019].
- Fontana Regional Library, North Carolina, received a 2016–17 grant from the State Library of North Carolina (funded as a pass-through grant from IMLS as supported by LSTA). It was awarded for the library to "assist students to meet the NC Essential Standards in space and astronomy education by bringing programming to the schools and libraries featuring topics relating to space exploration and astronomy. We will purchase a portable planetarium and curriculum kits for teacher and homeschool use based on those education standards, as well as computers, interactive learning stations, and other tools of astronomical observation, encouraging lifelong STEM learning" [Library Development 2016].
- Beginning in fiscal year 2014, CTLS, Incorporated, Texas, received grant funding for three years from the Texas State Library and Archives Commission (funded as a pass-through grant from IMLS as supported by LSTA) to purchase materials and equipment to supply LEGO robotics equipment to libraries across Texas in their Bots and Books program. Some libraries used this equipment to

serve the homeschooling communities in their areas [Central Texas Library System 2016].

- The Children's Museum in Bloomsburg, Pennsylvania, created the Homeschool Hangout program. This program, which meets bi-monthly and runs concurrently with the school year, was funded in part through an IMLS grant. The museum identified underserved populations in their area and developed beneficial programs. Area homeschoolers were identified as an underserved community. Education Coordinator Ginny Weibel, Ph.D., said, "We found that, although there were many homeschool and cyber-school groups in the area, there was little to no interaction between the organizations. In fact, many individual families felt like they were 'on their own.' Additionally, we determined there was little educational support created specifically for the homeschooled community in our area" [Weibel 2016].

An important resource for libraries and other not-for-profit organizations wanting to understand worldwide philanthropy is Candid. Candid came into existence in February 2019 with the merge of the GuideStar and Foundation Center. Nonprofits, foundations, social enterprises, and individual donors can benefit from its combined data and knowledge. It offers a number of products and services including profiles of non-profit agencies, IRS 990 forms, training, GuideStar Pro, and the Foundation Directory. Some of Candid's projects and services are free, other have a cost.

The organization "connects people who want to change the world to the resources they need to do it. Candid's data tools on nonprofits, foundations, and grants are the most comprehensive in the world" (Candid 2019). Librarians can and do change the world. Through the Candid site, librarians can "research nonprofits, find funding—through 140,000 funders and 14 million grants, and verify [other granting] nonprofits" (Candid 2019).

Donations

For non-profit organizations, the goal of fundraising is to bring in revenue, but also "to build relationships, bring in foundation support, and attract new donors" (The Editors 2017). Cash donations can be easy and straight-forward. However, donors may want to give in other ways as well, offering in-kind donations, volunteer hours, or stock (MoneyMinder 2016). Through donations, libraries can also achieve goals they have set for developing and enhancing homeschooling collections, programs, and services.

In the past, cash donations would come in via check, credit card, or actual cash. In the 21st century, there are technology-based options as well. For example, PayPal's or other financial services' "Donate" buttons can be added to library or library foundation websites for patrons interested in making a donation. The Jervis Public Library in Rome, New York, includes a "Donate" button on a page of their website describing the ways to make donations, including checking out their wish list for a donation of goods (Jervis Public Library 2019). Libraries interested in having a try-before-you-buy curriculum set might add a set or two to a wish list to serve the homeschoolers in their community. Libraries can also run a successful crowdsourcing donation drive through a service such as Kickstarter or CrowdRise by GoFundMe®.

In-kind donations of goods and services can benefit a library greatly as it creates programs for its homeschooling community. For example, a certified yoga teacher in Austin, Texas, wanting to give back to the community and her local library, donated her time providing a six-week series of yoga classes for young children at the Yarborough Branch of Austin Public Library. These classes were offered at a time that served both homeschool and public school families. The donation of specific goods can be applied to either circulating or non-circulating resources. For example, homeschoolers with gently used or unused curricula may donate these materials (vet these materials through your library's collection development policy before adding them). Gameschooling is popular among home educators. Patrons may donate gently used board games they have outgrown or are not using to create a resource for the community. The staff at the same Yarborough Branch initially selected and purchased over 100 board games and puzzles creating a popular collection that could be used any time in the library and during their monthly Board with Books meet-up events. Several customers excited by and appreciative of this initiative donated many board games that their families had outgrown.

Partnerships

When the library develops partnerships with corporations, non-profits, professional clubs, museums, foundations, and chambers of commerce, not only does it get additional resources, but by becoming an integral part of the community it serves, it creates a stronger resource for this community. Dr. Ginny Weibel, the Education Coordinator and Science Instructor at The Children's Museum in Bloomsburg, Pennsylvania, says that "[they] actively seek out community partners and opportunities to share resources to maximize the impact of every funding dollar [they] attract to [their] area. It is [Weibel's] hope that the Institute of Museum and Library Services' supported Homeschool Program will act as a model for outreach and resource sharing for other museums with limited resources" (Weibel 2016). Even though she is speaking of her own museum's Homeschool Program, libraries can do the same by actively seeking community partners.

Here is a hypothetical example of a program utilizing the knowledge of others that would appeal greatly to homeschooling families. A library could plan a series of nature programs leading up to Earth Day. Different nature education and conservation entities and individuals (e.g., the botanical garden, children's nature and science center, Audubon society, students from college departments, beekeepers) could be invited to present and provide activities for the various age groups—toddlers to adults. By donating their services and knowledge, the organizations get the word out about their programs and ways to participate in future volunteer events. Homeschoolers benefit from the knowledge of the nature groups, immediately during these events at the library and in the future. The awareness of an organization often translates into action, both in service of time and possibly future donations for that organization. The library benefits because it gets help producing a high-quality program at a lower cost and builds social capital with its partners and the community.

In service to its community, the library's relationships with its patrons can extend to connections with their own affiliations and work relations. Librarians can also develop their own relationships with community partners such as nearby corporations, non-profits, and professional clubs. Knowing the local businesses can inspire programming for patrons, especially homeschoolers. These local professionals could be contacted to teach classes such as computer coding, financial literacy, yoga, or gardening. Especially for small libraries, developing relationships with the local business and industry creates and enhances community. The relationship is mutually beneficial; a professional offering a few free classes through the library also develops relationships with community members.

Some businesses can also be contacted to provide equipment such as laptop computers or art supplies. These could be gained in conjunction with a class taught or an informational event held. After seeing their impact on the community through the library, businesses would be more willing to donate cash for a homeschool need. Homeschooling families living day-to-day life in the community continue to develop these relationships, thus connecting to the businesses which supported them through the library.

Many times partnerships among libraries, businesses, and homeschoolers show the strength of the community; contributions from each partner strengthen the whole community. When individual partners are interconnected, a business partner may give more to additionally support each organization. For example, the library may partner with a local business that has interest in the homeschool student population and also supports a local museum. So the library, the business, the museum, and the homeschool community all come together to support each other.

Like any diligent parents, homeschooling parents want their children to become productive members of the community. Local businesses, chambers of commerce and workforce development whose missions are to develop and recruit a capable workforce can be great partners for libraries and homeschoolers. If Chick-fil-A is "so happy with its homeschool hires that it actively recruits them," then wouldn't a local owner/operator love to meet those students through homeschool programs at the library? (Somerville 2002).

As a resource for funding, programs and/or collections, partnerships make sense for libraries, for community businesses and organizations, and for homeschoolers.

Entrepreneurial Methods

In tough economic times, librarians are no strangers to using entrepreneurial methods to raise funds for their library and community. Tiffany B, a homeschooling mother in Austin, Texas, says that she could not possibly homeschool with the depth and breadth of knowledge and resources she is providing to her children without the use of the library (Tiffany B., Facebook message to Casey Custer, July 10, 2018). Homeschoolers, as diverse as they are, all use a lot of books. Of course, borrowed books from the library make up the largest number of the books used, but homeschoolers like to own (lots of) books as well.

It is rare that I (Casey) miss a library book sale, and as I live near three different library systems, I am often in luck. As a librarian and a homeschooling parent, I benefit myself and help the library. For one particular sale, I could not arrive early and when I got there, several members of one homeschool group I am a part of had snagged up most of the books already—you snooze, you lose! In all seriousness, homeschoolers can be fanatic about library sales, and it behooves the library to take advantage of that interest, both as a way of developing relationships with their homeschooling population by providing books for ownership but also to raise money, perhaps specifically for homeschool curriculum or collections.

In addition to the traditional used book sale, used curriculum sales can also benefit both homeschoolers and the libraries they frequent. One opportunity for the library to raise money is by selling curriculum they have acquired a while ago and that is now outdated by the library's standards and ready to be weeded. Another possibility is to partner with homeschoolers to host a curriculum sale where homeschoolers can come and shop each other's curriculum that they have finished using; yet another method would be to have homeschoolers donate their used curriculum to the library to either sell or keep in their collections.

Regular Budget

In the regular budget, libraries can advocate for more money for homeschool projects because homeschoolers are an important and large service population. In the American Library Association's resource *Making Budget Presentations*, the point is made that "[budgeting] is a cyclical process of listening to the community, working with decision-makers, telling compelling stories about your library—and bringing all these elements together in a budget presentation and then starting all over again" (ALA 2019). Knowing that homeschoolers are indeed a large part of library communities and telling compelling stories about their needs is one way to advocate for money allocation for their services in the regular budget. Homeschooling parents and students form a large constituent group that can also speak on behalf of the services they rely on from their public libraries.

Relationship Building: Libraries as a Part of the Homeschooling Ecosystem

Creating an ecosystem of community stakeholders where the library has formed important relationships with local businesses, local organizations, and the community of homeschoolers allows for additional funding and services that have not been added to the regular budget. Connecting first with the community of homeschoolers can sometimes be difficult but is necessary. Some homeschool communities are as diverse as the cities and towns libraries serve. Pulling them together to assess their needs and harness their advocacy for the creation of partnerships is mutually beneficial. Find contacts through email listservs, Facebook groups, and, of course, get to know the homeschoolers who frequent the library. Some Facebook groups include the wider community of homeschoolers for a specific area in town or even the whole town or city. Within the larger community, there can be several co-operatives, based on very specific needs, such as a chess, book, or cooking clubs; some co-ops provide academic classes; others are based on the various philosophies of educating at home, such as a field trip group, a Charlotte Mason group, or a Wild and Free group. Being able to connect with diverse homeschooling population provides many more opportunities to form partnerships with them and the larger community organizations and businesses that have similar goals and values.

Where do homeschool parents gather? Many homeschool groups have meet-ups for parents. When libraries provide space for these meet-ups, they also build relationships by getting to know homeschool parents and creating a partnership with them. This leads to understanding that homeschool parents are in a way business leaders themselves who can help form additional partnerships with the larger community and help raise funds for the programming, collections, and services wanted by the homeschoolers.

Conclusion

In the world of fundraising, there are many ways in which libraries can get revenue, services, goods, and other support to enhance programs, collections, and services geared towards homeschoolers. Grants, donations, partnerships, entrepreneurial methods, increases to the regular budget, and relationship building were discussed as ways of resource building. Libraries are an integral part of the whole community ecosystem. Library employees are passionate, intelligent, and hard-working. Like homeschoolers, they are creative and forward-thinking. Library workers can use these traits to find resources in a multitude of places to support homeschoolers in their communities.

WORKS CITED

ALA. 2019. "ALA Grants." Accessed May 2019. http://www.ala.org/awardsgrants/awards/browse/gnnt?show filter=no.
ALA. 2019. "Making Budget Presentations." Accessed May 2019. http://www.ala.org/advocacy/making-a-bud get-presentation.
Candid. 2019. "Foundation Center and GuideStar Are Candid." Accessed May 2019. https://candid.org/ ?utm_medium=email&utm_source=Org%20Global%20Email%20Blast%20DS&utm_campaign=FINAL +EMAIL_Candid.
Central Texas Library System. 2016. "Grant Resources—Bots and Books." Accessed May 2019. https://www. ctls.net/resources/bots-books-resources/.
Chapman, Matt. 2018. "Library Prepares 'homeschool Connection' Initiative Through LSTA Grand Funding." *Lincoln Times News*. Accessed May 2019. https://www.lincolntimesnews.com/news/library-prepares-homeschool-connection-initiative-through-lsta-grant-funding/article_ad433014-77af-11e8-a689-cbcdbc407718.html.
eCivis. 2019. "4 Types of Grant Funding." Accessed May 2019. https://cdn2.hubspot.net/hubfs/68523/docs/ Resource_Library_Slate/Four_Types_of_Grant_Funding.pdf?t=1478460699437.
The Editors. 2017. "What Is Fundraising?" *Nonprofit Quarterly*. Accessed May 2019. https://nonprofitquarterly. org/2017/07/01/what-is-fundraising-definition/.
Grants.gov. 2019. "Find. Apply. Succeed." Accessed May 2019. https://www.grants.gov/.
Grantspace. 2019. "Fundraising." Accessed May 2019. https://grantspace.org/topics/fundraising/.
Grantwatch. 2019. "Your #1 Grant Website." Accessed May 2019. https://www.grantwatch.com/about.php.
Jervis Public Library. 2019. "Where Discovery Begins." May 2019. http://www.jervislibrary.org/.
Haywood County, North Carolina. 2019. "Library to Use Grant Funds to Start New Homeschool Collection." Accessed May 2019. http://www.haywoodnc.net/index.php?option=com_content&view=article&id= 1141%3Anews-library-grant&catid=1%3Alatest-news&Itemid=19.
IMLS. 2019. "Federal Support for Libraries and Museums." Accessed May 2019. https://www.imls.gov/.
Jardine, Dawn. 2017. "Program Idea: Homeschool Libratory." *Webjunction*. Accessed May 2019. https://www. webjunction.org/news/webjunction/redhook-ny-homeschool-programs.html.
THE Journal. 2019. "K-12 Grant Opportunities and Ed Tech Event Listings." Accessed May 2019. https://the journal.com/grants.
Library Development: State Library of North Carolina. 2016. "2016–17 LSTA Grant Recipients." Accessed May 2019. https://statelibrarync.org/ldblog/2016/06/09/2016-17-lsta-grant-recipients-2/.
MoneyMinder. 2016. "The Differences Between Cash and In-Kind Donations." Accessed May 2019. https://moneyminder.com/blog/differences-between-cash-and-in-kind-donations/.
Somerville, Scott. (July/August 2002). "Can They Get a Job?" *HSLDA*. Accessed May 2019. https://nche.hslda.org/courtreport/V18N4/V18N401.asp.
Scholastic. 2019. "Activities & Programs: Library Grants." Accessed May 2019. http://www.scholastic.com/ librarians/programs/grants.htm.
TLC. 2017. "Library Grants and Funding." Accessed May 2019. https://tlcdelivers.com/library-grants/.
Weibel, Ginny. (2016). "The Benefits of Hanging Out with Homeschoolers." *Institute of Museum and Library Services*. Accessed May 2019. https://www.imls.gov/blog/2016/03/benefits-hanging-out-homeschoolers.

Camp Wonderopolis

An Intergenerational Program

Nadine Kramarz

The Place

Berwick is a rural borough of 10,477 individuals located in central Pennsylvania on the Susquehanna River. Seventeen percent of the population, or 1,781 individuals, fall between the ages of 5 and 18 (U.S. Census 2010). According to the Pennsylvania Department of Education, 33 children were registered as homeschoolers in the 2009/10 school year (the last verified numbers) in Berwick and 21,553 were identified across the state (Kids Count 2010), making homeschooled children less than 1 percent of the state and 2 percent of the Berwick population. That is a strong concentration of homeschooled children within a rural area.

There are 40.3 percent of children under the age of 18, or 4,223 individuals, who have spent the last year living below the poverty line (U.S. Census 2010). Conquering poverty is closely linked to academic achievement, so I knew that increasing literacy was my long-term goal to contribute to the solution of the area's poverty situation. This was a community ripe for experiential learning as a way to build literacy skills. I was the new director at McBride Memorial Library in Berwick. My background was in youth library services, and my mission was to turn McBride into a 21st century library. In order to accomplish this, I applied for the Camp Wonderopolis grant for their pilot year.

The Grant

The mission of the National Center for Families Learning (NCFL) is to "eradicate poverty through education solutions for families" (National Center for Families Learning 2018). As an organization, NCFL realized that poverty is an intergenerational problem that cannot be stopped without taking measures to teach the whole family. In 2016 they created a grant program with money from Better World Books so that six pilot public libraries could incorporate Camp Wonderopolis into their summer reading program. The idea was to bring Camp Wonderopolis (Camp Wonderopolis 2018), an online resource designed to encourage children's wonder in the world around them, to a physical and literacy-based location—the public library.

Camp Wonderopolis is a six-week virtual camp that offers families over 40 interactive learning modules with vocabulary words and videos to foster reading comprehension and hands-on activities to spark wonder. Camp was an offshoot from the 2010 NCFL site Wonderopolis (Camp Wonderopolis 2018) in order to provide quality learning experiences at a low cost. The Camp Wonderopolis framework of having intergenerational hands-on learning to build literacy skills increases learning by expanding the parts of the brain being used, keeping the participant focused on answering questions, and by creating a fun familial environment where parents, caregivers, and siblings learn together. This situation combines problem-solving processes (mental), with cause-and-effect actions (physical), and with social opportunities (social). McChesney and Wunar tackle the issue of summer reading programs in their book, *Summer Matters: Making All Learning Count*, and point to several studies that indicate the benefits of experiential, informal education and, in particular, the value of giving youth the agency to choose topics and experiences of interest to them as individuals. The research argues the importance of providing access to high-quality programming outside of school to low-income children who are at increased risk of suffering from summer slide (McChesney and Wunar 2017). Camp Wonderopolis meets this criteria. It appeals to all learners and enforces lessons learned by activating multiple parts of the brain. Combining two paradigms, intergenerational learning and hands-on learning, creates a powerful tool for expanding learning, literacy, and strengthening community bonds.

Development, Marketing, Audience

NCFL wanted to target families, particularly elementary-aged school children as well as their caregivers. Emily Kirkpatrick, Executive Director of the NCFL, states, "Families are hotspots for learning. The summer is the perfect time for families to leverage children's curiosity and help build a lifelong interest in learning" (Avetisian 2015). Camp Wonderopolis has a different edition each year with six tracks that relate to the core theme. Each of the selected libraries was required to submit a maker activity and book recommendations for different age groups for one of the tracks. The track my library chose was the Wonder Trail. It was a collaborative effort among the six libraries to design the workshops of the program. NCFL used the raw information provided by each library to create a comprehensive program with reading lists and hands-on learning activities. The guidelines established in the Program Kits recommended three books per age group (0–5, 6–12, 13–17, and adult) for a total of twelve books, and suggested a maker activity. The maker activity had to require all participants to communicate and contribute, have a STEM (Science, Technology, Engineering, and Math) focus, and be made of easy-to-acquire materials. I consulted my collection in order to make book recommendations. For the maker activity, I wanted something that required engineering; this was done because it would satisfy the STEM requirement, but also because building something that meets specific guidelines stimulates communication and negotiation, and the program can have a competitive element which drives participation. I selected an activity that required participants to build a paper structure that could support the weight of a tin can. NCFL did not choose my suggested maker activity and instead recommended that participants build their own obstacle course. I never received an explanation as to why. I used both activities in different programs and both were successful.

Prior to the start of Camp, all the libraries had to attend a development webinar that would review the materials being provided in the Camp Kits and suggestions on how to run the first session of Camp. Kits include a printed Family Guide, a deck of Wonder Cards, a Wonder Journal, supplies for fun activities, and other goodies to help families wonder and learn together. Program Kits were also available, providing online training, support materials, and ways to announce your location as an official physical "campsite." Camp Wonderopolis maintained its online presence and also held sessions at the six pilot libraries. It was recommended to make the first session longer in order to have time to pass out the goodies and to show parents how to sign up for the online component of the Camp. We encouraged families to participate in both face-to-face and online components.

Specific Sessions

For 2016, the core theme was "Flex Your Wonder" with six wonder tracks: Food Truck, Circuit, Trail, Stadium, Dash, and Pulse (Camp Wonderopolis 2016). The program consisted of six workshops with a recommended maker project and book tie-ins that were suggested by the grant-winning libraries. Each library had to present these six workshops during their summer reading program. In the following paragraph I will go into greater depth using the Wonder Pulse as a case study.

Wonder Food Truck session focused on food and diet as fuel for fitness. This was the first session offered at my library because food is always a great incentive for participation. We altered the recommended maker activity slightly making different scales instead of just the one suggested in the kit and used food instead of coins to weigh.

Wonder Circuit session focused on doing a series of activities together to work out multiple muscle groups, engage in cardio exercises, and feel the burn. We combined maker activities allowing participants create their own weights and then use them in an exercise circuit. We incorporated dance moves with shakers and water bottles to build muscle and get the heart pumping.

Wonder Trail session focused on exploration in the outside world. I love hiking and running, but they are hard to implement in a library setting. It was an interesting challenge to bring nature inside the library as a part of our homemade obstacle course. We used nature scents and also included sounds of birds singing and crickets chirping. Building their own obstacle course was so popular with our attendees that we included it in several different future sessions of Camp.

Wonder Pulse session focused on the human body and the activity included making a set of lungs. I will describe this session in more details further in the essay.

Wonder Dash session focused on the history of the Olympics. I found it to be a fun change of pace to include some history and discuss different events that still take place in the Olympics today. We altered the suggested maker activity so that instead of building a medal chart, our participants created their own medals using Play-Doh and stamps.

Wonder Stadium session focused on the physical space necessary to have the Olympics or professional sporting events. Engineering challenges are my favorite, so we used this session to build our own stadia out of LEGO bricks, which differed from the NCFL recommended activity of building basketball hoops.

The Wonder Pulse Program

The Wonder Pulse track deals with the human body and all the incredible things that it is able to accomplish because of how resources, specifically oxygen, are distributed through it. I wanted to start a conversation about what it means to be healthy; examine the body in motion as well as the body at rest. I did this program in a large community room. I started with the PowerPoint presentation, used tables for the experiment, and then utilized open floor space and materials to create an obstacle course with cones, hoops, and tunnels. The goal of this session was to help participants be more mindful of their body, understand how the breathing and blood flow (pulse) are interconnected, as well as provide information on health literacy.

I used word "defining" as a way to get the group communicating with each other and thinking about the topic. For this program, I asked them to define "healthy." This was a way to ease participants into communicating with the group and thinking about the idea at hand. Everyone had their own understanding of what it means to be healthy; the open forum encouraged contributions from all ages and experience levels. Participants were encouraged to shout out words, and I asked them to elaborate on what they meant or played devil's advocate. Once the group had a working definition, I provided a dictionary definition. Dictionary.com defines "healthy" as, "possessing or enjoying good health or a sound and vigorous mentality: a healthy body" (www.dictionary.com/browse/healthy?s=t 2012). Viewing the dictionary definition illustrated how the group's definition was based on their collective context. No group found the exact dictionary definition; the discrepancies provided an opportunity to introduce critical thinking skills illustrating the ways our context influenced our understanding of a word. Healthy to a teen is not the same as healthy to a grandparent. I used the opportunity to promote health literacy sites such as PubMed (https://www.ncbi.nlm.nih.gov/pubmed/) and MedlinePlus (https://medlineplus.gov/).

Next, I spoke about breathing, meditation, and stretching because these activities present an opportunity to practice mindfulness of the body. How does the body feel at rest? How does changing your breathing patterns affect your body? Can you feel your diaphragm expand and contract? Can you feel your pulse? Stretching is a wonderful activity to reduce discomfort from sitting too long and to prepare the body for movement. People can be shy about being physical in public. I find that leading by doing works best in those circumstances. I demonstrated how to do the 4–2–6 breathing method, where a breath is inhaled for four seconds, held for two, and released for six, as well as the stretches. I asked the participants to take their resting heart rate.

Once everyone had taken their resting heart rate, we segued into the maker activity. I had the group break up into familial units. The exercise was taken from Science Sparks (Vanstone 2012), a website that is dedicated to making science fun for all ages. The experiment replaced lungs and diaphragm with balloons and the torso with a clear plastic bottle that enabled the participants to visualize how manipulating the diaphragm caused the lungs to inflate.

At the conclusion of the program, participants made their own obstacle course and then ran it. Children love a challenge; this activity builds social communication and relationship skills and also provides a chance for physical activity and agility. As participants ran the obstacle course, their pulse quickened and their breathing increased, which provided an opportunity to apply what they have been learning in a practical context. Now they could experience the information in a visceral way which made the learning physical and enforced the lesson. The lung experiment gave them a way to see what their bodies were doing, feel their lungs expand, and know that their lungs fill their blood with oxygen.

Outcomes

As per the requirements of the grant, my library hosted six sessions of Camp that included a maker activity and had participation from all ages, and submitted two 300–500 word blog posts with pictures. At the end of year one, we had at least one family per session. We incorporated the intergenerational learning with science-based inquiry to build literacy skills by including a maker project. I had 5 percent of campers sign up to participate in the online program as well as "live" at the library. I wrote two blog posts and focused on the individual projects that we completed. I loved the program so much I incorporated Camp in our summer reading program in 2017 as well. We did not win a grant, but were able to use the maker activities and supporting resources that were available online (Camp Wonderopolis 2017). At the end of year two, we, again, hosted six sessions of Camp that included a cooperative maker activity as well as a take-home activity and engaged participants of various ages. The usual participation was at least 14 families per session with 35 percent of campers signing up for the online program. I found that sticking with the program was worthwhile even without the grant funding. We incorporated it into our 2018 summer reading program as well.

Challenges

The biggest challenge my library faced was that, since we were the pilot year, things did not run smoothly. Our first session of Camp took place before the development webinar was scheduled. We were able to participate in an early edition of the webinar, which was helpful, but that in that session we did not get the benefit of hearing the questions and observations of the other contributing librarians. We did not receive the Camp kits until July. The Camp kits included marketing materials such as a giant dry-erase poster where we could write the date of the next session of Camp and display it in a prominent location. It did make an impression when families walked into the children's library and saw a huge sign for Camp. It would have been great to have from the get-go.

Part of the first session was to explain Camp Wonderopolis, sign people up for the Camp website, and hand out goodies from the kit (book bags, a Camp journal, Frisbees, yo-yos, etc.). Since we had our first session prior to the official launch date set by NCFL, we were not able to sign initial attendees up or hand out any swag. We were not able to hand out anything until Camp was half over, which led to less free advertisement from children in their peer group. It was not easy to match the hours the library was open with parents' work obligations and other commitments, therefore it was a challenge to find a consistent schedule. These obstacles combined made it very difficult initially to reach a large audience and attract the numbers that we were hoping for.

Solutions

In our first year, we scheduled the Camp on the first Tuesday of the month from 6 p.m. to 7:30 p.m. and on the fourth Friday of the month from 1 p.m. to 3 p.m. Our Camp started before the official launch date and ended after the school year had begun. Future partnerships with grant winning libraries required only four workshops which made consistent scheduling easier to fit into the eight weeks of summer reading. This also solved the pre-camp development webinar problem. For the second summer, we adjusted the schedule to the second Monday of the month from 6 p.m. to 7 p.m. and the third Friday of the month from 12 p.m. to 1 p.m.; scheduling an hour of Camp and adjusting the dates and times allowed for more robust participation.

We did not get a grant the second year, so we did not receive a free Camp Kit. We did have leftover swag from the previous year that we utilized in later years. In subsequent years, families started the first session of Camp with the ability to sign up online; they could walk out of the first session sporting a Camp Wonderopolis bag or Frisbee; kids competed for Wonder Cards during each session. It helped to start in-house programs after the official Camp Wonderopolis online launch date.

We advertised on our website and social media, and continued to use the dry-erase board that we had received for the first year, but what really helped make the second year more successful was word of mouth. Sticking with the program helped immensely. Participants from the first year talked about the program when they got back to school, showed off their swag, and that generated a lot of interest. Word of mouth takes a while to spread, but it is the best way to advertise. Sticking with the program over multiple summers and re-utilizing resources allowed for continued growth in participation over multiple years.

In Conclusion

NCFL still offers a competitive partnership grant for public libraries to conduct Camp Wonderopolis in conjunction with their summer reading program. In 2018, three libraries received $3,000 each, as well as training, to host four workshops during the summer. Applications can be found online and are due in February. It is a wonderful experience and opportunity; however, even if your library does not apply or does not win the grant, Camp Wonderopolis resources are still available. In Camp Wonderopolis I had the ability to enhance my library's summer reading program, a trend that continues to this day. I also learned a valuable program paradigm that has impacted multiple programs and spawned its own year-long learning opportunities. NCFL now offers the Wonder Ground™, an online resource that supports educators. It has lesson plans and how-to guides for incorporating Wonderopolis into the classroom or library programs (Wonder Ground 2018).

Works Cited

Avetisian, Lisa. 2015. *Free, Online Camp Offers Summer Learning for Kids and Families.* Accessed July 12, 2018. http://www.familieslearning.org/public/uploads/press_releases/1434652125.g08t.Camp-Wonderopolis-2015.pdf.
Camp Wonderopolis. 2016. Accessed August 6. https://camp2016.wonderopolis.org/.
Camp Wonderopolis. 2017. Accessed August 6. https://camp2017.wonderopolis.org/.

Camp Wonderopolis. 2018. Accessed July 12. www.campwonderopolis.org.

Dictionary.com. 2012. Accessed July 12, 2018. http://www.dictionary.com/browse/healthy?s=t.

Kids Count Data Center. 2010. Accessed July 12, 2018. https://datacenter.kidscount.org/data/tables/2693-home-school—number-of-students-home-schooled-by-age-group#detailed/10/5509/true/824/214,389,390,391,182,215/9407.

McChesney, Elizabeth M., and Wunar, Bryan W. 2017. *Summer Matters: Making All Learning Count*. ProtoView. Academic OneFile (accessed July 20, 2018). http://link.galegroup.com/apps/doc/A497632687/GPS?u=23069_lcls&sid=GPS&xid=a36f2498.

National Center for Families Learning. 2018. Accessed July 12. http://www.familieslearning.org/.

U.S. Census. 2010. Accessed July 12, 2018. https://factfinder.census.gov/faces/nav/jsf/pages/community_facts.xhtml.

Vanstone, Emma. 2012. Accessed July 12, 2018. http://www.science-sparks.com/breathing-making-a-fake-lung/.

Wonder Ground. 2018. Accessed July 12, 2018. http://wg.wonderopolis.org/.

Wonder Pulse. 2016. Accessed July 12, 2018. https://camp2016.wonderopolis.org/track/wonder-pulse.

Wonderopolis. 2014. Accessed July 12, 2018. www.wonderopolis.org.

Preparing to Work
with Homeschooling Families

HOLLY S. HEBERT

Introduction

Working with homeschooling families is no different than any other special population group in the library. They are library users with individual needs and desires and cannot be lumped together as group. However, there are some commonalities that librarians across the United States find in helping the homeschooling families at their library. The essay will discuss the ways in which this librarian have learned to work with homeschooling families to provide needed and desired services, resources, and programs while cultivating a solid relationship between herself and the library. It will also provide background information on homeschooling families as well as specific resources and areas for professional development for librarians wishing to serve homeschoolers.

Connecting with Homeschooling Families

According to the National Center for Education Statistics (NCES), "Homeschooled students are school-age children (ages 5–17) in a grade equivalent to at least kindergarten and not higher than 12th grade who receive instruction at home instead of at a public or private school either all or most of the time" (NCES n.d.). With the rise of homeschooling across America since the early 1990s, when homeschooling became legal in all fifty states, it is highly likely that there are homeschooling families at every public library, whether or not they are recognized (Gaither 2017, 230). The numbers of homeschoolers vary from state to state and are difficult to nail down, but the latest numbers from NCES indicate that as of 2012, 3.4 percent of students are homeschooled in the United States (NCES 2017, 7). According to the 2012 study, seventy percent of homeschooling parents use the public library for sources to add to their curriculum (NCES 2017, 13). Many libraries have been actively engaging with homeschoolers for decades, although there are still some that have not. Before going any further, let's have a discussion about some reasons that may be preventing libraries from working more with homeschoolers. Some may not have enough staff or time in the day for extra programs; some may believe that homeschooling is weird and don't want to go out of their way to offer special services. Others might be worried that homeschooling families will be too demanding and will cause extra work for staff. It may be as simple as a lack of understanding of how to get started providing services for homeschoolers. At the same time, the continued rise in the number of homeschoolers in addition to greater awareness has led to increased attention to serving this population in libraries.

So, where to start? As with any special population in the library, when considering collections, services, and programs for homeschoolers, the first step for the librarian is to learn about the homeschooling population at their library and to get to know some of them. The homeschooling population at each library will be unique. Parents homeschool for many different reasons, including religious reasons, concerns about the quality of public schools, flexibility in their schedule, etc. There are also many different approaches to home education, including classic, Charlotte Mason, Montessori, eclectic, and unschooling. There will likely be any combination of these homeschooling families at any given library. Therefore, there is really no way to generalize homeschoolers at any particular library; the best approach is to get to know them personally. Sometimes, homeschooling families will self-identify when approaching library staff, or it may become evident as the reference interview is conducted. They are often eager to partner with the library to help them get the resources they need. However, if homeschooling patrons are not known, creating and offering a survey, or creating a special event to invite homeschooling families is a good place to start. Most likely librarians will already be aware of homeschooling families as they are active users and are in the library generally during the day, although their schedules may vary.

There is no way to understand users better than to talk to them! What do they use the library for? What would be especially helpful to them? Would they like a special tour of the library and an overview of resources that might be helpful?

Why Connect with Homeschooling Families?

The most obvious reason to connect with homeschoolers is that they are patrons in the library and deserve to have their resource needs met just like any other patrons. Also, as many libraries have found, homeschooling families are an asset to the library. They are generally heavy users of materials and programs. They check out lots of materials and show up to events thus increasing program numbers. As such, they can be strong advocates for the library. Each library is in need of those types of patrons, are they not? Abby Johnson, children's services/outreach manager at New Albany–Floyd County Public Library notes that homeschooling families have served on their Community Planning Committee, have volunteered with summer reading and programs, suggested titles, and alerted staff when items went missing. Overall, Johnson says, "Having homeschoolers in the library definitely makes our library more welcoming to all" (Johnson 2012, 86). When times are tough and budgets are being cut, it is important to have relationships established with users who can fight for library services. Since homeschoolers have flexible schedules, they are often able to volunteer at times when others can't. On occasion, they even become employees of the library who add valuable insight and skill in dealing with homeschooling families. Homeschoolers often are closely connected to the larger homeschooling community in the area, have a large network of friends who also homeschool, and can bring more people into the library. Lastly, homeschoolers want to work with librarians. They know that librarians are key people in their homeschooling journey and they want to connect!

Differences in Homeschooling Laws by State

After getting to know some homeschooling families, what should librarians do next? Since homeschooling is regulated by the education department in each state, the rules and relationships with public schools will be different, and librarians should acquaint themselves with the rules in their state. Some of the states with the strictest homeschooling laws are Massachusetts, New York, Pennsylvania, Rhode Island and Vermont, where homeschoolers must give notice to the school district, provide test scores and student progress; they also may have to provide hours in school, cover specific curriculum, and have home visits. States with the most leeway in homeschooling include Alaska, Connecticut, Idaho, Illinois, Iowa, Indiana, Michigan, Missouri, New Jersey, Oklahoma and Texas. In those states, according to the Home School Legal Defense Association (HSLDA), families are not required to give notice that they are homeschooling, but offer guidelines on years of compulsory education, curriculum, etc. The HSLDA is a major asset to the homeschooling community and has been involved in defending home education since 1983. Their website has a page for each state with the requirements for homeschooling (HSLDA 2019). The laws for homeschooling in each state are the final word, so librarians and home educators should consult the Department of Education in the state where they live. The laws can generally be found online by searching for "homeschooling" or "home education" on the state website which is usually a .gov site. For instance, the Pennsylvania Department of Education can be found online at https://www.education.pa.gov. Conducting a search on that site brings up the page *Home Education and Private Tutoring* which explains the law, lists the requirements, and links to forms that must be filled out.

Librarians should not be providing legal assistance, so any specific questions that are brought up about legalities should be referred to legal counsel. It's important for librarians to know where to find the laws and resources of their state in order to be able to provide reference to homeschooling families. Some families might be veterans at homeschooling, while others are at the initial point of considering homeschooling and don't know where to start. For beginners, after they consult resources at the Department of Education, the Home School Legal Defense Association (https://hslda.org) can provide assistance with getting started in homeschooling as well as legal counsel if problems arise.

Umbrellas, Co-Ops, Tutorials, Oh My!

There are state, regional, and local homeschooling organizations in every state. Some, such as "umbrella" or "cover" organizations are state-approved and have a formal structure. They can provide many benefits for families, even in states where they aren't required. Umbrella schools often have classes and field trips. They may issue report cards and diplomas, hold graduations, and offer standardized testing. They help homeschooling families comply with the state regulations as well as provide encouragement, community, and resources. These organizations can be a great point of contact for the local librarian as well. Reaching out to these organizations is a great way to learn about homeschooling in your community and to connect with homeschoolers.

Co-ops can vary from very informal groups of three to five families to more formal organizations. They generally share teaching responsibilities in that group. For instance, one parent might be proficient in Spanish and offer to teach a Spanish class to the other students in the co-op. The more formal co-ops often offer weekly classes in a variety of subjects, tutoring, field trips, and events for a fee. Students are required to register with the organization. In some areas of the country these groups are also called Tutorials.

The groups vary by area in what they are called and how they operate. It's best to do an online search for the specific area of interest to best determine what groups and services are available.

A point of clarification must be made here that homeschooling in this instance covers all types of schooling that is not done at a public or private school. This includes unschooling, distance and online learning, as well as hybrid learning, where students take advantage of certain services (such as special needs services) or activities like sports, theater, etc. Just as the reasons for homeschooling are varied, so are the ways in which homeschooling is utilized.

In states where umbrella schools are optional, librarians should reach out to catch those who aren't "under the umbrella" and may miss information that is distributed within these organizations. Librarians should make effort to ensure that everyone is welcome to homeschooling events and activities. Organizational "cliques" may easily form and make some patrons feel left out if they are not a part of the established, even if it is not formal, group. Librarians can do their part by watching for this and helping to integrate newcomers.

Listening to Your Homeschooling Families

After learning about homeschooling from various sources and getting to know your homeschooling families, there is no better place to learn about their needs and desires, except from them. "Librarians may think they know their users, but the demographics of any community will change over time. Those changing demographics will increase the number of nonusers if librarians don't recognize the need to change or expand their services and collections" (Gregory 2019, 14). Although informal exchanges are nice, it's a good idea to get more formal feedback, for example, needs assessments.

Surveys

Surveys can be done easily online with simple software and reach more patrons than one-on-one conversations. Care should be taken to construct a well-written survey. Web-Junction (https://www.webjunction.org) is a great source of free upcoming and archived webinars for librarians. For example, Colleen Eggett's webinar titled "Library Surveys for Success" can provide professional information on conducting surveys. Looking at similar surveys conducted elsewhere can provide ideas. Check with other librarians to see if they have surveys to share. Here are some questions from a survey conducted by Brenda Mills, a Branch Head at the Scotland Neck Memorial Library in North Carolina:

- Which resources could the Scotland Neck Memorial Library offer to help you homeschool?
- Which subject areas do you feel the Scotland Neck Memorial Library should target for additional resources?
- At this time, where do you obtain the majority of resources used for homeschooling?
- If anything, what prevents you from using the Scotland Neck Memorial Library?

The entire survey can be found online at https://www.surveymonkey.com/r/Q59QNYW (Brenda Mills, phone interview, March 28, 2019). Librarians at the Attleboro Public library also conducted an online survey which can be found online at https://www.surveymonkey.com/r/aplhomelearningresource. For more in-depth knowledge, librarians should dust off their research methods textbook and review the essay on creating and conducting surveys.

Focus Groups and Advisory Boards

Organizing a successful meeting of a focus group will take some effort and planning, but if done well, can be a great resource. Until you gain some experience in that, working with such groups will involve trial and error. Enthusiasm and attendance can ebb and flow, fizzle out and be renewed. Asking for input from patrons helps them feel included and valued. Find opportunities where they can provide input on an ongoing basis.

Focus groups are similar to interviews, but are done in groups instead of individually which can help foster discussion and ideas. *Five Steps of Outcome-Based Planning and Evaluations for Public Libraries* is a helpful book for librarians who want to utilize focus groups. In it, the authors state that "[i]deally, your focus group will consist of 6 to 10 people, who are willing to spend up to an hour talking about the program or service being evaluated. A good facilitator is required to keep the discussion on topic and ensure all participants are heard." Focus groups can be done faster than individually interviewing participants, but collecting and tabulating the data from them is more difficult (Gross, Mediavilla, and Walter 2016, 61). A focus group will generally last for one hour, start with introductions, and have a set of predetermined questions that the facilitator asks. A second researcher should be in the room to observe and help with the recording the answers.

Advisory boards or committees differ from focus groups in that while focus groups have set questions that are asked and discussed, advisory committees can discuss what they want. The North Vancouver Public Library has several Customer Advisory Committees (CAC). These committees can bring items to the attention of the library, which will then consider whether or not to make suggested changes. Michael Kerr puts it this way, "Unlike a focus group, which concentrates on issues posed by the library, the customer advisory committee is free to explore concerns that aren't yet on the library's radar" (Kerr 2012, 113).

Both focus groups and advisory boards can be an important part of engaging homeschooling families in libraries. Each library will have to determine the extent to which each is utilized.

The Changing Nature of Homeschooling Patrons

As with any user group, people, situations, and perception of what is popular change over time. Just because a survey of homeschoolers or a focus group was conducted in 2007 doesn't mean that the answers are still valid in the current year. Homeschoolers "age out" and move on. The makeup of the types of homeschoolers that use the library will transform over time, so the methods they use and resources they need may have to be adjusted as well. In addition to conceptual, population, and methodological shifts, there will be changes in personalities and group leaderships, so the relationships with this user group will need to be renewed and refreshed from time to time. Brenda Mills believes in revisiting the needs of homeschoolers in her library yearly if possible, as new families come in and others leave or age out. She has conducted several surveys in the nine years since she has been at that branch and plans on doing another one soon (Brenda Mills, personal phone interview, March 27, 2019).

Ongoing Feedback

As classes, activities and programs are held and collections developed, there should be opportunities for feedback from patrons. "Was the program helpful? Was it enjoyable? Are there other programs that you would like to see? How can we do better?" Collecting this feedback ensures that libraries have their finger on the pulse of their users and prevents patrons from leaving due to unmet needs or expectations.

Working with homeschooling families is a rewarding experience and serves a patron base that is found in nearly all libraries in the country. The more prepared libraries are to work with these families, the smoother the process and greater the outcomes will be. Once librarians make extra efforts to engage with homeschooling families, they will acquire active users of the library and big advocates of library services.

Resources

Homeschooling Conventions and Conferences

Much like libraries, homeschoolers also have statewide, regional, and national conferences. Librarians serving homeschool populations have found these conferences beneficial. There are presentations, curriculum examples, vendor exhibits, national speakers, and luncheons. Networking, encouragement, and hands-on learning are just a few examples of benefits of attending these conferences. The largest of these are the several regional conferences put on by Great Homeschool Conventions (https://greathomeschoolconventions.com). In 2019, they were held in Texas, South Carolina, Missouri, California, Ohio, New York, and Florida. There is also the Teach Them Diligently Conventions which are Christian-based events held mostly in the Southeastern United States. To find statewide conferences, check with the umbrella schools and the state organizations in each state.

Library Conferences

Presentations at state library conferences on serving homeschooling families are popular. An internet search found eight state conferences with presentations on this topic. Conferences are always a good way to learn and to connect with other librarians who have the same goals and can share experiences. For instance, when the Illinois Library Association (ILA) held their annual Youth Services Institute in March of 2019, there were multiple presentations on how to help homeschoolers (ILA 2019).

Network with Other Librarians

There is no lonelier place than to be a librarian feeling like they are alone on a project and have no one to be a sounding board for their ideas. Luckily, librarians, by and large, are a friendly bunch and are willing to share with each other. Find other librarians who are also working with homeschoolers in your city, or through a state or national library organization. Listservs like PUBLIB (https://www.webjunction.org/documents/webjunction/PubLib_Overview.html) and PUBYAC (https://lists.ischool.illinois.edu/lists/subscribe/pubyac) are useful, as are the newer message boards available through ALA Connect for members of the American Library Association (ALA), Young Adult Library Services Association (YALSA), and Public Library Association (PLA). In 2018, a Facebook Group Librarians Serving Homeschoolers (LSH) (https://www.facebook.com/groups/1616005898516578/) was started by Christina Giovannelli-Caputo, a librarian at the Arlington Heights Memorial Library in Illinois, in an effort to build a community of like-minded librarians. The group has grown to over 300 members where helpful hints, ideas, and encouragement are offered. Christina also started a local group of librarians called Librarians Serving Homeschool, which is sponsored by Reaching Across Illinois Library System (RAILS) (https://www.librarylearning.info/events/?eventID=27777). If there is no local group, start one!

Webinars

Webinars are helpful for those who can't attend sessions in person. The American Library Association has a webinar called *Making Your Library Work for Homeschoolers Workshop* presented by Suzanne Walker (https://www.alastore.ala.orgcontent/making-your-library-work-homeschoolers-workshop)

The Southwest Florida Network provided a webinar from 2017 called *Homeschool Families and Your Library* presented by Kelsey Bates who is a Teen Librarian at the Kansas City Public Library (https://www.youtube.com/watch?v=0i3m2De42o4).

LibraryLinkNJ has two free webinars available by Adrienne Furness who is the director of the Henrietta Public Library in New York. *Helping Homeschoolers in the Library* videos and notes can be found at http://librarylinknj.org/content/helping-homeschoolers-library.

Professional Journals

The National Home Education Research Institute (NHERI) (https://www.nheri.org) is the primary research organization for homeschoolers. Their journal, *Home School Researcher*, which is published quarterly, has been in existence since 1985. It covers all aspects of homeschooling research. Articles are peer reviewed by an editorial board.

Continuing Education Courses

Although the author could not identify full graduate courses on homeschooling in library science programs, there is currently a continuing education course called Services to Homeschoolers offered by the University of Wisconsin–Madison School of Information which is taught by Adrienne Furness. Additionally, librarians might be interested in courses on K–12 education for teachers and school media specialists (school librarians). Courses that lead to school library certification and/or teaching would certainly be helpful, especially in states where homeschoolers must follow state curriculum and standards.

Homeschooling Resources

There are several core books on homeschooling that librarians working with homeschoolers should be aware of for reference purposes and also to make sure they are available in the library. This is not an exhaustive list by any means, but is a good place to start.

Andreola, Karen. 1998. *A Charlotte Mason Companion: Personal Reflections on the Gentle Art of Learning.* London: Charlotte Mason Research & Supply Company.

Andreola, Karen and Robert E. Jones. 2002. *Pocketful of Pinecones: Nature Study with the Gentle Art of Learning: A Story for Mother Culture.* London: Charlotte Mason Research & Supply Company.

Bauer, Susan Wise and Jessie Wise. 2009. *The Well-Trained Mind: A Guide to Classical Education at Home, 3d ed.* New York: W.W. Norton & Company.

Bortins, Leigh A. 2010. *The Core: Teaching Your Child the Foundations of Classical Education.* New York: St. Martin's Griffin.

Carman, Rachael. 2008. *SoundBites from Heaven: What God Wants us to Hear When We Talk to Our Kids.* Colorado: Focus on the Family.

Clarkson, Clay and Sally Clarkson. 2011. *Educating the WholeHearted Child, 3d ed.* Indiana: Apologia Press.

Comstock, Anna Botsford. 2010. *Handbook of Nature Study.* UK: Yokai Publishing.

Gatto, John Taylor. 2010. *Weapons of Mass Instruction: A Schoolteacher's Journey Through the Dark World of Compulsory Schooling.* Canada: New Society Publishers.

Hawkins, Charity. 2012. *The Homeschool Experiment, a Novel.* Indiana: Familyman Ministries.

Macaulay, Susan Schaeffer. 2009. *For the Children's Sake: Foundations of Education for Home and School.* Illinois: Crossway.

Resources for Librarians Helping Homeschoolers

Several professional books have been written on the subject of homeschoolers and libraries and are good sources of reference.

Furness. A. 2008. *Helping Homeschoolers in the Library.* Chicago: American Library Association.

Lerch, M.T. and Welch, J. 2004. *Serving Homeschooled Teens and their Parents.* Westport, CT: Libraries Unlimited.

Scheps, S.G. 1998. *The Librarian's Guide to Homeschooling Resources.* Chicago: American Library Association.

Association for Library Service to Children has put out a pamphlet with a section that includes homeschoolers: http://www.ala.org/alsc/sites/ala.org.alsc/files/content/professional-tools/lsspcc-toolkit-2015.pdf

And the American Library Association maintains a webpage called Home Schooling Resources for librarians at http://www.ala.org/Template.cfm?Section=childrens&template=/ContentManagement/ContentDisplay.cfm&ContentID=90419.

Check your state or regional library associations for local sources.

WORKS CITED

Gaither, Milton. 2017. *Homeschool: An American History.* New York: Palgrave Macmillan.

Gregory, Vicki L. 2019. *"Collection Development and Management for 21st Century Library Collections."* 2nd ed. Chicago: American Library Association.

Gross, Melissa, Cindy Mediavilla, and Virginia A. Walter. 2016. *Five Steps of Outcome-Based Planning and Evaluation for Public Libraries.* Chicago: ALA Editions.

Home School Legal Defense Association. 2019. "Home School Laws in Your State." Accessed March 28, 2019. https://hslda.org/content/laws/.

Illinois Library Association. 2019. Youth Services Institute Program "CommUnity Building, March 21–22, 2019." https://www.ila.org/content/documents/iysi_2019_program.pdf.

Johnson, Abby. 2012. "Make Room for Homeschoolers." *American Libraries Magazine* 43 (5/6): 86.

Kerr, Michael. 2012. "Customer Advisory Committees: Giving a Voice to Library Users." *Feliciter* 58 no. 3: 113–115.

National Center for Education Statistics. 2017. *"Measuring the Homeschool Population."* Blog. Accessed March 28, 2019. https://nces.ed.gov/blogs/nces/post/measuring-the-homeschool-population.

National Center for Education Statistics. n.d. "Homeschooling." Accessed March 28, 2019. https://nces.ed.gov/fastfacts/display.asp?id=91.

Redford, Jeremy, Battle, Danielle, and Bielick, Stacey. April 2017. *Homeschooling in the United States: 2012.* (NCES 2016–096).

PART VI

Career Paths

Growing Up in the Library

Homeschooling a Future Librarian

JENNIFER C.L. SMATHERS *and* VIRGINIA M. LYLE

This is a story from both a teacher's and student's perspective of how a home-schooler's use of a public library led to an apprenticeship-type approach for a budding librarian. One of the authors, Virginia Lyle, homeschooled her five children. The other author, Virginia's eldest child, Jennifer Smathers, was homeschooled starting in 8th grade. After a year of volunteering in the elementary school library, Jennifer decided to follow a career as a children's librarian. The impact of time spent in libraries and with librarians on Jennifer's career and the ways the interest in libraries was woven into the homeschooling curriculum benefitting all her siblings are discussed in this essay.

The Teacher's Perspective (Virginia Lyle)

Some people have no idea what they want to do with their lives. Others have always known what they want to be when they grow up. My eldest, Jennifer, was the one who knew that she wanted to be a librarian. Since homeschooling allowed me to tailor our education plan to suit my children's interests, I was able to weave career interests into many subjects and allow additional time for field trips and apprentice-like experiences.

I had grown up in a family of readers. Mom read, Dad read, his parents read. When Grandma didn't have a garden trowel or a dish rag in her hands, she had a book. Dad used to read aloud to us. We would pile on him, clinging like cockle burrs to the over-stuffed chair as he used different voices to bring characters alive. It was my daily delight to follow Br'er Rabbit, Bartholomew Cubbins, Homer Price, but once I was expected to read for myself, I hit a wall.

Reading for myself, silently, was not fun. It was too much effort. Dick and Jane were dullards compared to Mike Mulligan and his Steam shovel. I began to measure books by their size. A thick book would be too much work for me. Things got so bad that I had to go to summer school for reading between fourth and fifth grades. Then in seventh grade, something unexpected happened. I got assigned to the advanced reading group. We used the *Readers' Digest* (collegiate edition which is no longer available) in place of a textbook. The articles were varied and brief enough to make reading exciting again. I rediscovered the joy of reading for entertainment.

When I had children, I read to them. I read aloud. I read a lot. We took frequent trips to the library for a never-ending supply of books. It was the cheapest, most entertaining way to build the lifetime love of reading. I knew instinctively that my children would need to have a love of a story—a taste for the treasure that books contain—in order to overcome difficulties such as I had encountered around fourth grade. Without the joy of reading good books, classroom instruction in the technical details of reading could become tedious for children.

By the time we had a house of our own and four children, I was looking for story time programs to help my sons develop skills they would need for school. Jennifer could sit for hours listening to me read or looking at books on her own, but the boys needed help sitting still, paying attention.

The Walworth Public Library was located in an old farmhouse. It was small, dark, depressingly cramped. So small, that parents were told to drop off their children and then come back after story time. When was I supposed to look for books for myself? The strict age segregation at library programs made it nearly impossible for me to give each child the story time experience. The library was only open a few hours a day, three days a week. Because the collection was so limited, each child was allowed to check out only one book per visit. I chafed at these restrictions.

Macedon, the next town over, had a far more robust schedule and a much more welcoming atmosphere. The children's collection was nearly one third of the total library collection. Best of all, there was a Mary Poppins–esque children's librarian. Rosalie Gabbert did a read-aloud story time and puppet shows. She allowed parents to browse the shelves while kids were participating in the program and also encouraged siblings of different ages to watch and listen.

We gave our allegiance to this newer, more welcoming library. Then we started homeschooling. The library became our source for a literature-based Language Arts curriculum. It became a social highlight of our week. Here we met like-minded adults to share book recommendations, other children to play with, even a rather strange old man who initially resented "noisy" children as he read through the encyclopedias. One day, as my children were telling the librarian about our field trip to Fort Ticonderoga, that gentleman joined in. Every time one of us said, "Ticonderoga" he would interject "A hundred and eleven." Eventually we understood the numeric value of the letters in "Ticonderoga" added up to 111. It was a breakthrough for all of us as we learned how to get along with different and sometimes unfriendly people.

I made homeschooling friends. We discovered authors we'd never met before. Each child was encouraged to apply for their own library card. You just had to be able to write your own name. That was the prime motivation for my dyslexic child to correctly print her name.

My family rule allowed each child to check out as many books as they cared to—so long as they could carry the books themselves. Overdue books were only a problem until I decided it was money well spent. Rosalie and I joked that the new wing of the library should be named after the Lyle family since we spent a lot of money on overdue fines. On a side note, speaking seriously of a new library wing, an expansion was clearly needed, and I joined the committee which brought it into reality a few years later.

Before long, Jennifer was helping check out books when the line at the circulation desk was too long. Every child loved the Gaylord Automatic Book Charging Machine. Its lovely "*Ka-Chunka*" noise as it stamped cards and clipped title cards is a fond memory for all my family. Thanks to the simplicity of the operation and the staff's willingness, well-behaved children were sometimes allowed to check out their own books.

Jennifer learned the shelving system in order to help with piles of returned books. She started tidying up the children's room toys and puzzles. We discovered Friends of the Library and their used book sales.

Between summer reading programs and volunteering, Jennifer sharpened her natural talent for connecting children with books that matched their interests. She produced a books-on-video project for her Senior Girl Scout Gold Award. As a family, we offered to help with summer reading programs. When asked for help with refreshments for the Canal Boat Sal presentation, we came up with "Bilge Water" (a mix of iced tea and lemonade) and "hard tack" (biscuits with gummy worm maggots). We provided the soup can cannon for the Great Piratical Rumbustification wherein we read and acted out Margaret Mahy's book of the same name.

Homeschooling is very flexible. New York State only required thirty to forty minutes worth of instruction in "library and information skills" [Part 100.4 (c) of the Commissioner's Regulations]. That was not enough for Jennifer. So we incorporated Jennifer's volunteer library work as an apprentice-like experience. By the time she reached the legal age for working part time, she was the most accomplished page this library had. She had to petition the Library Board to reconsider their policy of granting page jobs only to town residents. She formulated a convincing, logical argument and put it in a compelling letter (which I counted toward her English Language Arts requirement). At the age of 16, she became a full-fledged clerk. In a seamless progression she then became the closing staff member a few nights a week.

In the summer before she started college, Jennifer worked both at the town and the college libraries. Her dedication to exactness of detail (required in cataloging and shelving) made Jennifer a highly valued student worker. The work-study part of her financial aid was library-related all the way. Because we as a family supported Jennifer's library interest, her younger siblings picked up enough library prowess to work in their respective college libraries. All five of my children had work-study hours in libraries. You could say, they all grew up speaking Library.

The Future Librarian Perspective (Jennifer C.L. Smathers)

The worst consequence of growing up in the library may have been the boredom in the very first class of my Master's in Library Science program. Libraries 501 course was a painfully slow introduction meant for teachers who were looking to get permanent certification through a quick master's degree via library school. All those hours working at the Macedon Public Library led into working in Technical Services at my college library. Both work experiences had provided a much deeper understanding of libraries than that introductory class was going to present. I was fighting off boredom and astounded to hear a shaky voice from the back of the class that asked, "What are the stacks?" Through my years of graduate school, I ignored all suggestions of unpaid internships in a library. There wasn't much left for me to gain from such an unpaid position.

The best part of growing up in the library was the ability to engage in a practical apprenticeship in my chosen profession. While we had always been big users of the

Macedon Public Library, it wasn't until I became homeschooled that I was able to volunteer. When I was in public school, between the hours of a school day and time spent on extracurricular activities such as Girl Scouts, I was only available to volunteer at the Gananda K–12 school library during my 7th grade study hours. In 8th grade, with the benefits of condensed homeschooling hours I was able to spend more time volunteering. When my mom, Virginia, visited the library to find curricular support materials for my siblings, I liked to keep busy by exploring how a public library worked.

I learned the Dewey Decimal System, alphabetical filing, and book handling techniques while volunteering as a page. That included embracing the ultimate importance of properly filed books, even in the "dreaded red-dots" (local parlance for juvenile non-fiction). Red-dot spines were so skinny that the decimal numbers were not easy to read. My mother was invested in those red-dots for homeschooling materials. Having lost track of the numerous times I assisted finding a non-fiction book to support a younger sibling's education, I could see the advantages of proper order. When other pages heard me say that I'd take the time to do it right, as a matter of principle, they gladly stepped back, and the children's librarian named me the page in charge of that section. I soaked up everything about a small town public library. I skimmed books as I returned them to the shelves, slowly expanding my knowledge of all genres, so I would get better at conducting reference interviews and making book suggestions, even in a genre I did not personally read.

Librarians are often thought of as being in the book business, even as they've moved into new formats and maker spaces. At the Macedon Public Library, in the trenches, I learned that libraries were really about the people using them. The library was as beloved for being a spot to warm up after sledding (it had a great hill behind the parking lot) as it was for being a resource for students writing a high school paper. It was a place for that grumpy elderly man, who lived in the nearby group home, to come and be in a social environment while reading his way through the reference section's materials. Moms had an opportunity to chat with other adults during story time about the hazards of potty training or just about the weather. I honed my people skills by having to enforce library policies, even unpopular ones. I learned how to politely verbally nudge people out at closing time. It became clear that in this small town library, chatting about life was the best part of the library checkout experience. We had our own "frequent fliers," and also the opportunity to greet people brand new to town, brand new to the library.

Part of working with people is learning how to have a game face. There is no way to really teach that, you need practice. Since I was a homeschooled high-school student, the library positions I held allowed me that practice. Today I am told that I'm incredibly diplomatic and always seem to know what to say. Back then, I was learning. The library was attached to the town building, and often court sessions occurred at the same time as my shift. This never turned into a real issue for me, but I do remember how someone from my family tended to stick around for certain court nights just to keep an eye on me. By the time I was driving myself and in college, the need for extra level of security ceased to exist. I'll never forget the advice I received from Betty, a world-wary library clerk. "Do you know what this is?" Betty demanded one night while pointing at the typewriter. I scoffed internally, smiled, and said, "A typewriter." That wasn't the right answer. "A typewriter roller bar," she instructed, "it is a weapon, pop it out like this and you have a club to defend yourself with." That was my introduction to the stark realities of self-defense some librarians face.

Countless hours filing books, checkout cards, catalog cards, patron cards… all of that made me an alphabetizing wiz and gave me sneak peaks into the vast subjects available and the people interested in them. Customer service skills were developed when I was placing those dreaded overdue calls. While listening to sweet grandmotherly Rose use her "mean voice" with delinquent patrons, I gleaned the knack of polite insistence. Nothing like cold-calling with bad news to teach you how to remain calm while delivering less than pleasant information. It was a banner day when the library director first offered me the chance to make selections for the McNaughton rotating collection. The McNaughton collection was composed of books rented by the library for a period of time. It allowed the library to have extra copies of popular titles, or try new authors out without a long-term commitment through a firm purchase. Making temporary rental selections as a teenager was my introduction to real library collection management and acquisitions. Eventually I assisted with a few author and genre suggestions on firm purchases for the newly created young adult section. When I was encouraged to select worn out titles with low circulation to be withdrawn from the collection, I was actively contributing to the whole lifecycle of the library's collection development.

Public libraries deal with more than just readers of fiction; as a library clerk I also had reference responsibilities. While the Macedon library didn't have many phone-based reference questions, answering an occasional inquiry regarding a local business or library event built groundwork of reference skills that I still rely on. I studied ready reference materials, learned to use the *Reader's Guide to Periodical Literature*, navigated holdings of other libraries via a microfiche-based union catalog, and knew my way around the crisscross directory. I will never forget the day when I was home and answered the phone with a professional, "Macedon Public Library, how may I help you?" only to hear the person on the phone say, "No, *this* is the Macedon Public Library, we have a question for you…." Stories like these never age. The lessons I learned in my library internship in high school don't age either. Except, maybe, my skills fixing finicky microfiche printers that are now hardly ever used.

Confidence in my ability to work in libraries grew out of my work at the Macedon Public Library. One day staff were bemoaning the malfunctioning and completely useless microfilm reader/printer. I persuaded the library director that I wasn't afraid to take things apart and couldn't make it worse since it already wasn't functioning. Paying careful attention to how each piece was put together, I unscrewed piece after piece, took it apart, replaced the bulb, and removed a paper jam, which allowed me to resurrect the machine. I was also learning how to resurrect the love of reading in people who had finished the last book in a beloved series and were despondent. Talking a mother into trying out *Cam Jensen* for their child who had exhausted the *Encyclopedia Brown* series gave me such a boost when they were back the next week for more.

My professional growth continued during years at Nazareth College of Rochester's Lorette Wilmot Library. The librarians all knew that I planned to join their profession. They spent time mentoring me in various aspects of library work. I remember how during my first year I was told that I had better clean up my handwriting, or I'd never be a librarian. Now it sounds silly, but the cataloging workflow at the time involved manual editing on paper before logging in and using precious network time updating OCLC. If student workers couldn't read your handwriting, you would lose time fixing the resulting errors before you verified the record in the local save file and uploaded it to the local catalog. In addition to learning various aspects of technical services work, I began to understand the politics involved in operations of an academic library. I made the most of every opportunity the library offered and served on a several committees as the student representative.

One committee allowed me to give feedback on the creation of the honors students' study room as the college planned a massive library expansion and remodeling project. That summer I saw first-hand the sights and sounds of bulldozers, challenges of reallocating space and moving departments. As is often true of college, the life experience I gained from the mentorship of librarians was crucial to both my personal and professional growth.

In many ways, my work as a technical services student employee is directly responsible for my transition to academic libraries. While paying off my student loans was the driving force behind my career goal change from children's services to an academic librarian, the most compelling factors that allowed me to make the jump were my technical services experiences at college coupled with my people skills learned at the public library. I can truly say that without my homeschooling and immersive library experiences, I wouldn't be where I am today.

Encouraging the Next Generation

If you are a homeschooled student thinking about a career in librarianship and are able to volunteer or work in a library prior to college, do it. The dividends paid from learning the feel of library trenches, before you focus on the theoretical and ethical aspects of libraries in graduate school, are many and long lived. Try your hand at whatever activities are available. Assist with programing, work in circulation, shelve books, and immerse yourself in the collection. Challenge yourself to take on new tasks.

If you already are a librarian, give opportunities to a new volunteer or young page who expresses interest in the field. Seek out homeschool volunteers. They often have the time to help and may have the interest in a future library career. Ask homeschooled students to help plan events; get them involved in collection development; give them all the sneak peaks into the profession you can. Encourage them to ask questions, shadow others, and tear apart machinery that doesn't work when no one else knows how to fix it. You will grow the next generation of take-charge librarians.

Homeschoolers are both active users of library collections and a rich source of future librarians. Both homeschooling families and future librarians will reap benefits from an apprentice-like immersion in library services. As librarians we should continue to mentor homeschool students as volunteers and pages, cultivate their opportunities for real-life library job experiences, and model professional behavior as they are growing up in our libraries.

Introducing Homeschooling Students to the Librarian Profession and Personality Types

PAUL J. MCLAUGHLIN, JR.

Introduction

The librarian profession needs diversity in its membership to provide service to the variety of patrons who visit libraries and to have the array of skills needed for a library to succeed. Jaeger and Franklin (2017, 23–24) have encouraged the use of inclusive services and outreach programs that take advantage of the diversity inherent in the United States' population to stir interest in the librarianship profession. Homeschooling students come from a variety of cultural and social backgrounds and rely on public libraries to gain access to curriculum materials, educational programming, and technology. Librarians can use outreach programs to introduce homeschoolers to the variety of librarian positions available, the personality types found in librarianship, and to encourage homeschoolers to enter the library profession. This essay will describe personality types that may exist in librarianship and the need for librarians to know about them; it will also provide an example of an outreach workshop that is designed to stress the importance of having this knowledge for professional development.

Personality Types and Librarians

Personality Types and the Librarian Profession

Personality types are classifications of an individual's personality traits that describe how that individual behaves when interacting with others and their surroundings (Semeijn, Van der Heijden, and A. De Beuckelaer 2018, 1–3). The wide interest in librarian personality studies has been driven by librarians' self-curiosity and tendency to organize things by categories. Librarians have used personality type studies to analyze and discredit several negative stereotypes associated with their profession. In fiction and films, librarians are often portrayed as intelligent, middle-aged loners whose love of books and rules and lack of social skills isolate them from the rest of society (Jennings 2016, 97–98). Librarians have fought against such depictions because they do not display the true nature of the profession and present librarians as flawed, unsocial people. Librarians have also pushed back against the stereotypical image that they are stuck in the past with outdated books. Librarians are often at the front edge of technological adoption, and their knowledge of developments and trends allows them to help patrons become familiar with the newest technologies (Posner 2015, 2–4). Studies of librarian personalities have found that entertainment's stereotypical depictions do not reflect the true variety of librarians, their skills, and their personality types. While there is a tendency for librarians to appear overly professional and have reserved dispositions, they represent a diverse group with many personality types that are caring, open, and willing to share with coworkers and patrons (Sawal et al. 2016, 31–32).

Differing Personality Types in Various Librarian Positions

While librarians have a mixture of personality types, it has been shown that those with similar personality traits gravitate toward similar positions. Librarians with same personality traits often enter into positions in the same kinds of libraries whether they are academic, public, or specialized libraries. Librarians with outgoing personalities generally find satisfaction and success in positions that frequently interact with other individuals, such as reference services. Those who prefer solo projects usually enjoy and succeed in positions such as cataloging and technical services, where working with technology is essential (Dority 2016, 20–23). Librarians with either extroverted or introverted personalities can be leaders in their organizations, but there is a stronger tendency for extroverts to assume leadership roles. It is a good managerial strategy for libraries to have a mixture of personality types among their project leaders and administrators and to take advantage of their differing insights and strengths (Farrell 2017, 442–443).

The Need for Personality Type Training in the Library Profession

Employers' Rising Demands for Non-Traditional Skill Sets

Libraries must update their collections and adapt the services they provide to meet the needs of their patrons. It is now common for libraries to serve as more than repositories of information for a community. Many libraries have incorporated learning labs and makerspaces into their facilities to allow patrons to learn programs and use technologies they otherwise would not have access to (Koh and Abbas 2015, 119–122). Offering new resources and training for patrons has changed libraries and the proficiency requirements for librarians. While the traditional core competencies for librarians and information specialists are still valid, multidisciplinary soft skills are becoming more valued and demanded by employers (Bronstein 2015, 135–136). Soft skills are loosely defined as emotional intelligence and interpersonal skills that librarians use to assist patrons and work with other library staff and managers. Soft skills include, for example, the ability to leverage diversity, face to face and electronic communication expertise, decision making acumen, knowledge of and training in working with differing personality types, and social skills (Matteson, Anderson, and Boyden 2016, 75–78).

Librarians' Need for Personality Type Training

Career choices are driven by an individual's personality and internal motivations. Those interested in the librarian profession should seek positions with duties that align with their inherent traits and allow opportunities to be involved in projects they find interesting and valuable to themselves and their communities (Ho et al. 2018, 143–144). By learning about and knowing their own personality traits, librarians can bolster their self-image and gain information that will allow them find positions that offer satisfaction and success (Kalil 2016, 21–22). Librarians can also use their knowledge of personality types to better understand and adapt the librarianship profession beyond its traditional boundaries. For librarians involved in non-traditional functions, such as serving as an embedded librarian, being aware of their own personality type and the personality types in an organization can help them work with the dynamics of a group and provide the best service (Mlinar 2019, 55–58).

Library Leaders' Need for Personality Type Training

Library leaders need personality type training to understand their leadership style and gain insight into the variety of personalities that work in and visit their library. Library leaders can use personality type training to understand what drives different personalities and create outreach programing that engages library users in ways that fit their information-seeking motivations (Holley 2015, 600–602). Personality type training can also help library leaders make hiring determinations for positions based on an applicant's individual characteristics and the kinds of projects that the librarian would work on. Having knowledge of personality types can also help managers find effective ways to encourage library staff and to guide them to opportunities and training that would motivate them and allow them to grow (Williamson and Lorensbury 2016, 139–140).

Introducing Personality Types and Library Careers to Homeschooling Students

Librarians can use outreach workshops with homeschooling students to introduce them to different library positions and types of libraries. Linking examples of librarian's positions with individual student interests can broaden their knowledge of librarianship and encourage them to consider becoming librarians. Even if students decide not to pursue a career in the library field, attending the workshop will allow them to learn about personality types in general, their own Myers-Briggs personality type in particular, and ways this knowledge can help them in their career paths.

Knowing their personality type and receiving personality type training can help students succeed in several ways. It helps hone the processes they use to learn concepts, improve their career and educational decision making, and change the ways they interact with others (Moore, Dettlaff, and Dietz 2004, 340). Students who are aware of their personality type can use their knowledge to find learning strategies and tools that best fit their learning styles. It has become vital for students to know their personality types and learning styles as more digital and online learning tools are introduced into education.

This knowledge can help students determine which digital tools would be best for them so they can make the most out of the time they invest in studying (Tlili et al. 2016, 807–811). Students who know their personality type and how it can impact their choice of educational programs and professions have an easier time of deciding which universities and courses of study match their personality preferences and have better success in the paths they choose (Ismail, Basharirad, and Ismail 2017, 63–66). Students with personality type training usually solve group-based problem assignments more efficiently and work better with team members to accomplish goals (Main, Delcourt, and Treffinger 2017, 10).

Below is a sample outline of a workshop that librarians can use to introduce students to personality types and the librarian profession. The workshop is designed to take 60 minutes. It is framed as a non-graded activity, but can be adapted into a scored assignment if desired.

Who Are You and What Kind of Librarian Could You Be? Workshop

Resources Needed

- Instructor Librarian(s)
- Handouts and supporting materials for students
- Internet access—through a computer lab, laptops, or mobile devices
- 60 minutes

Goals for the Workshop

- Provide students with an introduction to personality types and personality testing.
- Teach students how knowledge of their personality type can help them discover library positions they may be interested in.
- Inform students how knowing about personality types can be useful in their personal and professional lives.

Objectives for Students

- Obtain knowledge of basic terminology and concepts of personality types
- Learn about possible librarian career paths
- Discover their individual personality type

Introduction (5 minutes)

During the session's opening, instructors introduce themselves, tell students what position they have in the library, and the letters of their own Myers-Briggs personality type. To start the session's conversation with the students, instructors ask students what they think personality types are and what they think each of the letters represent. Instructors then explain that each letter represents a personality trait that links with the other three letters and personality traits to form a personality type, which is a general description of how a person gets their energy and interacts with the people around them and the world.

Discussion of Personality Testing and Types (15 minutes)

Instructors tell students that there are a variety of ways of looking at individuals' personality characteristics and give examples of personality tests such as the Myers-Briggs Type Indicator, the Hexaco Personality Inventory, and the Enneagram personality test. Instructors then introduce the variety of ways that personality tests can be used, for example, in career development, counseling, and as aids to determining learning style preferences.

Instructors explain that they will focus on the Myers-Briggs personality test for the workshop because it has been linked with librarian personality studies and is one of the preferred tests used by career counselors. Instructors then describe the categories of the Myers-Briggs personality preferences and traits while using examples of differing library positions they believe would fit with the preferences and traits they are discussing. The following sample framework can be used for class discussions.

Extroversion and Introversion Traits and Preferences (Focus and Energy Gathering)

Extroversion and introversion describe how a person focuses on tasks and gains energy or motivation. Individuals who are extroverts prefer to work with others to accomplish tasks and like to share with others the knowledge they have in group settings. Those with introverted characteristics like to work on things alone and give the task they are working on their full attention. Introverts prefer to share with small groups or using indirect means such as writing to others about what they accomplished.

Extroverts (E)

- Gain energy and inspiration from others
- Remain interested in something if others are involved
- Focus on the world and those around them
- Librarians with Extrovert Preferences and Traits: Young Adult Librarians and Marketing and Outreach Librarians

Introverts (I)

- Gain energy and creativity while alone
- Retain interest if they are examining things or working solo
- Focus on internal impressions and thoughts
- Librarians with Introvert Preferences and Traits: Cataloging Librarians and Technical Services Librarians

Sensing and Intuition Traits and Preferences (Methods of Information Gathering)

The sensing and intuition traits describe how an individual takes in details and thinks about the world. Individuals with sensing tendencies take in details using the full array of senses and focus on what is around them. Those who have the intuitional trait focus on connections, ideas, and relationships between items or ideas and what is possible more than what is around them.

Sensing (S)

- Focus on what is available to them and enjoy established rules or steps
- Detail-oriented and use their senses to gain knowledge of the world
- Focused and patient with tasks
- Librarians with Sensing Preferences and Traits: Engineering Librarians and Biology or Medical Librarians

Intuition (N)

- Focus on future events and what could be
- Like abstract thinking and creating imaginative solutions or new approaches
- Come at tasks from a variety of directions and go with what feels right
- Librarians with Intuitive Preferences and Traits: Academic Librarians and Journalism Librarians

Thinking and Feeling
(Approaches to Reaching Conclusions)

The traits of thinking and feeling indicate how an individual comes to conclusions. Those who show thinking characteristics approach projects like a puzzle and use logic to break down what they are seeing or working with so that the most efficient solution can be reached. Individuals with feeling characteristics take their feelings and the feelings of others in consideration when examining a problem or working on a project so that the most people can be happy with an outcome.

Thinking (T)

- Focus on facts and logic
- Emphasize justice and fairness
- Detached and not prone to focus on feelings
- Librarians with Thinking Preferences and Traits: Research Librarians and Automation Librarians

Feeling (F)

- Concerned with personal values and maintaining happiness for themselves and others
- Show tendencies for compassion and forgiveness
- Consider others' emotions when thinking about solutions
- Librarians with Feeling Preferences and Traits: Children's Librarians and Public Librarians

Judging and Perceiving Traits
(Categorizing and Interacting with the World)

Judging and perceiving describe how a person interacts and organizes the world. Individuals with judging traits like to establish clear guidelines and have structure in their activities and surroundings. Those with perceiving traits are fluid in their routines and like to become involved in a project and then make necessary changes as things develop.

Judging (J)

- Like to have structure and clear ends to projects
- Plan out their actions before a project and remain organized
- Set goals and work to meet them
- Librarians with Judging Traits: Legal Librarians, Archivist Librarians

Perceiving (P)

- Flexible in their routines
- Gain context and information while working on a project
- Open to letting things happen and adapting as needed
- Librarians with Perceiving Traits: Interactive Media Librarians and Reference Librarians

After introducing the personality preferences and traits, it should be stressed to students that while there are positions that have a tendency to attract librarians with certain personality traits it does not mean those traits are required for someone to enter the position. It should also be pointed out that because an individual has a tendency to exhibit characteristics of one personality preference or trait it does not mean they cannot use a variety of approaches to what they are working on, much like having the ability to use either hand to open a door (Sides 2017, 4).

After learning about the Myers-Briggs personality preferences and traits, students are then introduced to the 16 personality types possible through the combinations of personality traits. To keep sessions under 60 minutes, a detailed examination of the various personality types may not be practical. Students will learn about their own personality types upon completion of the online Myers-Briggs assessment through the personality type descriptions at the end of the online assessments. If students ask for more information, offering handouts with detailed explanations is a practical solution. Instructors can point out that the main differentiation for personality types is based on the extroversion and introversion traits because of the substantial impact of ways a person interacts with others. Instructors can also tell students that librarians have been found to have a slightly higher tendency to be introverted when compared to the general population, but there are many extroverted librarians and there is a tendency for those in library leadership positions to be extroverts.

Preparing for and Taking the Myers-Briggs Assessment (30 minutes)

Before students take the Myers-Briggs assessment, instructors should ask them to write down the characteristics they think describe their personality. This prompts them to connect the theory they just learned to themselves and to think about their own personality characteristics. Their predictions will also be used as points of discussion during the review portion of the workshop.

Students should then be asked to take a version of the Myers-Briggs assessment online and to read the materials provided by the website about their personality traits and types. Sites such as 16personalities.com and humanmetrics.com allow users to take versions of the Myers-Briggs assessment without charge and without requesting test-takers to provide personal data. Online assessments take an average of 15 to 20 minutes to complete.

Discussion of Results and Possible Careers in Librarianship (10 minutes)

After completing the assessment and reviewing the personality type, instructors can prompt students to talk about their results and their thoughts by asking questions such as:

- Do the results of the test match up with the predictions you made?
- Are there any aspects of your personality type description you were surprised by?
- Are there any aspects of the personality trait description that you received that you do not agree with? If so, why do you think the trait is off the mark?
- Is there a personality trait you received that you are glad to see?
- Do you think people who know you would agree with the personality type you received?

Instructors can ask students what kinds of librarian positions they believe match their personality traits and whether they would find such positions appealing. Instructors should reiterate that personality traits and types preclude no one from pursuing a library position that interests them; that having a variety of personality types has been found to be an asset for libraries. Instructors can also point out that because of the changing dynamics within libraries, for example, the inclusion of makerspaces and learning labs, students may be able to enter new librarianship career paths that have not been developed yet.

Conclusion

To meet the need for diversity, librarians have used personality type studies and training to understand themselves and to strengthen the profession. To attract new professionals from a variety of backgrounds, librarians can reach out to homeschooling students through workshops introducing them to the librarianship and personality types. By discussing personality types and careers associated with them, librarians can introduce students to the types of libraries and the varied librarian positions. During workshops, students can learn about themselves and how knowing their personality type can help them in their careers and personal lives.

WORKS CITED

Bronstein, Jenny. 2015. "An Exploration of the Library and Information Science Professional Skills and Personal Competencies: An Israeli Perspective." *Library & Information Science Research* 37: 130–138. https://doi.org/10.1016/j.lisr.2015.02.003.

Dority, G. Kim. 2016. *Rethinking Information Work a Career Guide for Librarians and Other Information Professionals.* Denver: Libraries Unlimited.

Farrell, Maggie. 2017. "Leadership Reflections: Extrovert and Introvert Leaders." *Journal of Library Administration* 57: 436–443. https://doi.org/10.1080/01930826.2017.1300455.

Ho, Kevin K.W., Patrick Lo, Dickson K.W. Chiu, Elaine Wei San Kong, Joyce Chao-chen Chen, Qingshan Zhou, Yang Xu, and Soren Dalsguard. 2018. "Intrinsic V. Extrinsic Motivations of Masters of Library and Information Science Students: A Cross-cultural Comparative Study." *Journal of Librarian and Informational Science* 50(2): 141–156.

Holley, Robert P. 2015. "The Challenges of Teaching the Introductory LIS Management Course." *Journal of Library Administration* 55(7): 595–603. https://doi.org/10.1080/01930826.2015.1076316.

Ismail, Sarerusaenye, Babak Basharirad, and Shahrinaz Ismail. 2017. "Significant of MBTI Personality Model on Decision Making in University Program Selection." *2nd International Conferences on Information Technology, Information Systems and Electrical Engineering* 2017: 62–67. doi: 10.1109/ICITISEE.2017.828 5560.

Jaeger, Paul T., and Renee Franklin E. 2017. "The Virtuous Circle: Increasing Diversity in LIS Faculties to Create More Inclusive Library Services and Outreach." *Education Libraries* 30(1), 20–26. http://dx.doi.org/10.26443/el.v30i1.233.

Jennings, Eric. 2016. "The Librarian Stereotype: How Librarians Are Damaging Their Image and Profession." *College and Undergraduate Libraries* 23(1): 93–100. https://doi.org/10.1080/10691316.2016.1134241.

Kalil, Carolyn. 2016. "Following Your Inner Heroes to the Work You Love." *Career Planning and Adult Development Journal* 32(4):20–30.

Koh, Kyungwon, and June Abbas. 2015. "Competencies for Information Professionals in Learning Labsand Makerspaces." *Journal of Education for Library and Information Science* 56(2): 114–129. https://www.jstor.org/stable/10.2307/90015177.

Main, Laura F., Marcia A.B. Delcourt, and Donald J. Treffinger. 2017. "Effects of Group Training in Problem-Solving Style on Future Problem-Solving Performance." *The Journal of Creative Behavior*. 0(0): 1–12. https://doi.org/10.1002/jocb.176.

Matteson, Miriam, Lorien Anderson, and Cynthia Boyden. 2016. "Soft Skills: A Phrase in Search of Meaning." *portal: Libraries and the Academy*. 16(1): 77–88. doi: 10.1353/pla.2016.0009.

Mlinar, Courtney. 2019. *Embedded and Empowered a Practical Guide for Librarians*. New York: Rowman & Littlefield.

Moore, Linda S., Alan J. Dettlaff, and Tracy J. Dietz. 2004. "Field Notes: Using the Myers-Briggs Type Indicator in Field Education Supervision." *Journal of Social Work Education* 40(2): 337–349. https://www.jstor.org/stable/23044024.

Posner, Beth. 2015. "The Use of Psychological Defense Mechanisms—By Librarians and the Public—in Response to Traditional and Binary Librarian Stereotypes." In *The Psychology of Librarianship*, edited by H. Stephen Wright, Lynn Gullickson Spencer, and Leanne VandeCreek. Sacramento: Litwin Books.

Sawal, Mohd Zool Hilmie Mohamed, Nazni Noordin, Raja Alwi Raja Omar, Abd Latif Abdul Rahman, and Zaherawati Zakaria. "Librarians' Knowledge Sharing Behavior." In *Knowledge, Service, Tourism& Hospitality* edited by Ford Lumban Gaol, Fonny Hutagalung, Abd Razak Zakaria, and Zuwati Hasim, 27–33. New York: CRC Press.

Semeijn, J.H., B.I.J.M. Van der Heijden, and A. De Beuckelaer. 2018. "Personality Traits and Types in Relation to Career Success: An Empirical Comparison Using the Big Five." *Applied Psychology* 1–19 (2018). doi: 10.1111/apps.12174.

Sides, Charles H. 2017. *How to Write and Present Technical Information*. Santa Barbara: ABC-CLIO.

Tlili Ahmed, Fathi Essalini, Mohamed Jemni, Kinshak, and Nian-Shen Chen. 2016. "Role of Personality in Computer Based Learning." *Computers in Human Behavior* 64: 805–813. http://dx.doi.org/10.1016/j.chb.2016.07.043.

Williamson, Jeanine M. and John W. Lorensbury. 2016. "Distinctive 16 PF Personality Traits of Librarians." *Journal of Library Administration* 56(2): 124–143. doi:10.1080/01930826.2015.1105045.

Library Literati

*Information Literacy Classes
for Homeschoolers (and Others!)*

MARYANN MORI

Introduction

Review the educational requirements of most any state, and you will likely find references to technology literacy, information literacy, or more recently "digital literacy" as part of 21st Century Skills or core curriculum. In a traditional school environment, such training would undoubtedly be provided by a school librarian. In homeschool communities, the public librarian becomes the "school librarian" by default. As a former youth services librarian, I knew I had an educational role to fulfill in my community since it had a phenomenally large and active homeschool populace. I ended up fulfilling that role by providing information literacy classes that culminated into a 6-weeks course for elementary-aged students. This essay explains the development, implementation, and results of that course.

Reason

When I first realized the need for information literacy classes (not just among homeschool students, but among many students in public and parochial schools which were losing their school librarians), I was working in a large children's department of a public library. Having recently read about Jean Piaget, the Swiss-born scientist whose studies dealt with the way children develop knowledge, I targeted my classes for students ages 8–12—those in Piaget's "Concrete Operational Stage," which is "characterised by the development of organized and rational thinking" (McLeod 2018). One of the aspects of this stage is the fact that children have the "ability to perform multiple classification tasks, order objects in a logical sequence, and comprehend the principle of conservation" (Parenting Today n.d.). Loosely interpreted, these kids can understand Dewey classification! These students are also "capable of concrete problem-solving" (ibid.). They can create scenarios regarding research, develop search terms, and understand how to locate and use information.

Research

I began researching, gathering materials, planning, and doing a whole lot of organization in preparation for the information literacy instruction I planned to offer. As I contemplated the topic and the information I believed students needed to know, I realized I had more than just a single class; I had a set of classes! What I finally developed from all my research and planning was a 6-weeks course, suitable for my targeted age group, that covered a multitude of library skills in an educational yet entertaining way, and which could likewise be marketable and manageable.

Because such a lengthy multi-week course had never been offered at my library, I had to convince my supervisor that my idea was worth trying. My proposal was unusual since I wasn't proposing a typical one-off program or even a series of programs; I was proposing a course—something that would require preregistration and a promise to participate in all of the weeks' classes. Looking back, I'm not sure I would present the program in the exact same format now. However, at that time in my area (with its large homeschool community), I believed I could generate enough interest to get a group of dedicated students. The tech lab at my library had a maximum of 15 student desks, so that number became my target for enrollment. My supervisor somewhat pessimistically agreed that I could attempt the course, and so we began publicizing it as *Library Literati*—inviting students to become part of this elite group that would know "the ins & outs" of libraries and information. I didn't limit that publicity solely to homeschoolers because I believed the information would be beneficial to any student regardless of school enrollment. However, I did heartily promote the course to the homeschool community by submitting information about it to the local homeschool newsletter, sending email invitations to homeschool families I knew, and making sure homeschoolers in my library received a flyer about the course.

Imagine my delight and my supervisor's surprise when the 15 available student slots quickly filled, and were followed by enough interest and reservations on a waiting list that I was able to present the course three times! While not all of the registered students were homeschoolers, a majority of them were.

Since resources on this topic develop (and go out of print) at a fairly rapid pace, it is important that each librarian invest in some research in order to find appropriate resources. The important thing to remember is to select materials that are age appropriate, reproducible (assuming handouts will be used), and fun—all while clearly providing the topics determined to be covered in the course.

Using materials from numerous resources (both print and online), I compiled a notebook binder for each student I anticipated having in the course. The binders included selected activity sheets inserted in the order we would use them for the class. I did not allow students to take these binders home until the end of the entire course in order to ensure that each child would have the binder when needed for class.

As earlier stated, my enrollment cap was 15 students simply because that was the number of student computers available in my library's computer lab. I found that 15 seemed a good, manageable number, and I would not have wanted any more than that in these particular classes. Classes were conducted in one-hour periods.

Overview

Most of the classes were conducted in the storytime room of the children's department of my public library, with additional ones conducted in the library's computer lab. I realize that not all libraries have the same resources and spaces available, but I believe the general outline of this course can be replicated in varying degrees in smaller locations. Perhaps a smaller class size could work in a smaller library. Or perhaps the library could partner with another organization that has more space. Students might be able to bring their own devices if the library does not have many public computers available. Consider offering the classes during closed hours of the library in order to maximize space. The homeschooling community may have additional ideas for locations since they are adept at finding spots for their other educational opportunities. Brainstorm with some of the home educators for ideas of locations if the library facility is unsuitable.

Week-by-Week Overview, Class Topics and Examples

Week 1: Classification Concepts; Types of Materials in the Library; Introduction to Fiction vs. Nonfiction; Parts of a Book; Title, Author, Subject

This might seem like a lot of material to cover in 1 hour—particularly in the first class when introductions were also necessary. However, I wanted the classes to be fast-paced, and the variance of the concepts kept the students alert and interested. One of my first tasks was to help students understand the concept of classification and why it is important. When students first arrived in the class, I had name tags already made for them lying on a table in no particular order. (I'll explain why in a moment.) I began the class by dumping out a box of about ten different toys on a table. Items included electronic games, a teddy bear, a ball, a slinky, a yo-yo, a top, etc. During the class, I asked the students how we could group these toys into different categories. Answers ranged from texture (fabric, metal, wood, plastic) to color.

I next divided students into small groups and gave each group a paper bag with assorted candies inside. I had everything from LifeSavers to M&MS, from a Charm's Blow Pop (lollipop with bubble gum in the center) to favorite candy bars. Each bag held approximately a dozen different candies. Student groups were then asked to organize or "classify" these candies. After a few minutes, I asked each group how they had determined a classification system. Answers ranged from flavor (chocolate, fruity, nutty, etc.) to color of wrapper; from size (round vs. rectangular) to manufacturer (Mars vs. Hershey's). From this exercise, students learned that there are a lot of possibilities for arranging classification systems, and what one person thinks of as the "right" way to organize groups of items may not be what another person thinks of as the "correct" way. We also talked about the problem with items such as the Blow Pop. Is it bubble gum? Is it candy? It's both! In what group should it be put? I stated that "catalogers" (explained as "librarians who decide where to classify the books, movies, etc.") have the same kinds of considerations when a book comes with a movie and a CD or does not follow the presumed criteria of a typical library item.

I reminded the students that some of them had trouble locating their nametags when they arrived in the class. The reason for their confusion was that there had been no organized way I had put the nametags on the table. Thus, students learned firsthand that organization is important for finding things. Likewise, using, as well as understanding, a classification system is helpful and important for finding things. I explained that many public libraries (including all of them in the library system in my community) use the same kind of organization or classification system, so learning the system helps with navigation in most any library.

The class concluded with some lessons about the parts of a book such as title page, index, and table of contents, as well as an introduction to fiction vs. nonfiction. This portion included examining a cart of books that included historical fiction (based on fact, but a pretend story ... where should it be classified?), poetry, riddles, biographies, and plenty of popular fiction titles. Approximately 3–4 activity sheets were included with this class, which students completed individually during class time, and which we discussed collectively after completion. Aspects of title, author and subject were also included as an introduction to the ways the library classifies materials.

Candies that were used in the classifying exercise were dumped in a basket, and at the end of class, students were invited to choose two pieces to take home with them.

Week 2: Review of Fiction vs. Nonfiction; Cataloging and Shelving of Fiction Materials; Review of Title, Author, Subject; Overview of Dewey Decimal Classification®

This week's lesson began with a general review of fiction vs. nonfiction. I also explained how to "read" a library shelf (left to right, top to bottom, zigzag and around corners) and introduced students to the kinds of genre labels used at my library. We actually went into the stacks of the children's area to look at the way the books were arranged on the shelves and to spot the different genre labels and locations. We did a relay race to put books in alphabetical order and utilized accompanying activity sheets to reinforce the lessons.

Not underestimating students' abilities, I included in this week a discussion of Cutter's rules for a catalog—summarized as *finding, showing, choosing*. It was a good way to remind the students of why title, author and subject are preferred ways to identify library materials.

I then began telling the students about Melville Dewey and his ideas for classifying information. As I was speaking, "Mr. Dewey" suddenly appeared in the class! I had arranged for one of my colleagues to play the role of Dewey. He and I loosely followed a previously-prepared script—one that introduced students not only to Dewey as a person, but also to his classification system. The students loved it. This also proved a good collaboration effort since my colleague was in the library's IT department (not the children's department). Smaller libraries can consider recruiting a community or teen volunteer (someone who likes to "ham it up") to play the role of Dewey.

After Mr. Dewey left our class, I talked about the ten divisions of Dewey. Book topics and activity sheets reinforced the concept. I then used actual book examples to show that books on a topic might be located in various sections of Dewey, based upon the "aboutness" of the book. For example, books about Japan may be found in religion, fairy tales, culture/holidays, cooking, poetry, history, geography or biographies, depending on what focus they contain. Students realized how Dewey numbers classify a book based upon its content and not just its general topic.

Week 3: Arrangement of Dewey Numbers; Classes, Divisions, Sections; Putting Nonfiction Books in Order

This was the week that included heavier material for the students. However, students quickly picked up on the lessons. We did more in-depth study of Dewey classification, utilized some activity sheets, organized nonfiction numbers that I had written on a large flip chart (numbers that got progressively more complex), and played a relay game where two teams were given sets of identical nonfiction titles to put in order. Students were also given a treasure hunt of activities where they had to first match a nonfiction category with a Dewey number, then go into the stacks to find a book with that call number. By the end of this class period, students seemed quite comfortable with Dewey classification.

Week 4: Using the OPAC and Library's Databases

At the end of last week's class, I told the students that we would be learning about and using "the OPAC" in week four. "The OPAC" had such a mysterious sound to it that students seemed excited to return to class to learn what this secret thing was! I escorted the class to the library's computer lab and explained the OPAC (Online Public Access Catalog). We conducted some catalog searches by using title/subject/author access points, and we learned how to place holds.

While using the computers, I also introduced students to the library's kid-friendly databases. I used such a database to locate a biography of Melville Dewey, which the students appreciated. During this class time, instruction about keyword vs. subject searching was introduced, as were tips for better searching—including use of Boolean operators and truncation. Students were given an assignment to complete during the week that required use of the library's catalog and databases. Those who completed the assignment were promised a special prize. Note that advanced preparation for this week's class is vital, since the instructor needs to find search terms that will generate appropriate results during the sample searches.

Week 5: Review of Dewey Classification; Print Resources

Additional games and activities about the decimal system continued. This week also included some time devoted to looking at print reference sources. While they are not in use much anymore, I believed it was still important for students to see how resources such as an encyclopedias and dictionaries were arranged. Activity sheets encouraged students to explore physical atlases, almanacs, and encyclopedias. Having the physical examples of these materials helped these young students better understand the differences in the reference resources they find online. Additionally, many homeschool families have such print materials in their home libraries, so becoming more familiar with these resources has multiple benefits for students. Prizes (small library-related items donated by our Library Friends' group) were distributed to the students for completing the last week's assignment.

Week 6: Tour of TSD and Entire Library; Biblio-Baseball Game; Presentation of Certificates of Completion

Because my library was part of a multi-branch system, we had a designated large Technical Services Department (TSD) where all of our acquisitions, cataloging, and processing took place. It was located in a non-public area of the library. Allowing the *Library Literati* students access to this area of the library was viewed as a special privilege by the students (and indeed, it was a privilege!) Following the TSD visit, we toured the entire library, which was large enough that it took a bit of time. I realize such aspects won't be necessary or possible in many libraries, but a general overview and demonstration of "how we get books from the wish list to the shelf" could work in any size library.

A game of "Biblio-Baseball" served as a fun way to review everything that had been covered in the course. "Biblio-Baseball" is something I developed on my own—possibly from ideas I gleaned through the years from a variety of sources, including my own school days. It is a simple game where students are divided into two teams. Each team "bats" by answering a question drawn out of a hat by the student who is "up to bat." Students may confer with their team members to answer the question (which prevents any one student from being put on the spot and being uncomfortable with a possible wrong answer). If the answer is correct, the team is awarded a "run" (point). If the question is answered incorrectly, the team receives a "strike." The opposing team then has opportunity to answer the question, which is now worth two "runs" (points). Here are some sample questions:

- What do libraries call magazines? (Answer: periodicals)
- Which kind of search (subject or keyword) will usually give more results? (Answer: keyword)
- Which class of Dewey has books about sports? (Answer: 700s)

The first team to get three strikes is "out," and the other team becomes the winner. In one class, I had to determine a winner by the largest number of points since neither team received three strikes, and class time ended. All the students received a prize for playing the game, although the winning team got a bonus prize (again, provided by the Friends of the Library).

Students who had attended all six weeks of the course, which included most of them, received a certificate of completion displaying the student's name, the library's logo, and my "official" signature.

Results

Library Literati was a definite hit! As stated earlier, it ran three times, always with full enrollment. One of the homeschool parents whose two children completed the course sent the following email to me:

> The kids took [a standardized test] yesterday.... When we got home and talked about the test, they both talked about how easy the reference and information section was after Library Literati. They both commented they were asked questions about Dewey Decimal and already knew which numbers the topics they were asked were about. 'Thought you might like to hear that [Biever 2006].

Of course, I liked to hear that!

A colleague from another library branch observed Week Six of *Library Literati* and wrote in a program review for the system's youth services coordinator:

> Maryann was wrapping up six weeks of library study and I still learned some things I had forgotten (like what OPAC stands for). She involved all of the participants in several games. The kids were well versed in library lingo and really knew a lot about how to find items on the shelf and in the computer. They seemed to actually be enthused about it, which is amazing [Yontz 2006].

My experience in developing *Library Literati* not only helped the participants become better library users, but it also helped me gain a solid overview of information literacy instruction that I later used to develop classes for teens, college students, and even older adults. I continue to use these skills to this day. The program enabled me to develop a good relationship with homeschool families, and the course gave me opportunity to highlight my library and get kids enthused about using that library. It was a win-win-win situation: I was personally rewarded by preparing and presenting the course, the students gained useful information and skills, and the library was acknowledged as a place of value.

Modifications

Because it may not be possible for all libraries to present a multi-week course and/or because some librarians may choose to work with a different age group (e.g., teens), here are some suggested modifications of Library Literati.

- Develop a "Dewey Club" that is similar to other weekly kids' programs but which highlights a different Dewey number for each program. For instance, focus on 641 and have some cooking classes. Or focus on 736.7 and do a program about dogs.
- Create some passive programming that includes weekly scavenger hunts in the library and thereby encourages searching the shelves by alphabet and Dewey call numbers.
- Do a rotating display that highlights a different section of Dewey. Include not only books, but also some of the "things" associated with that particular number. For example, display sports equipment and highlight the "796" collection.
- Develop a weekly online scavenger hunt that encourages students to explore the library's databases. Consider offering prize drawings for students who complete the hunt.
- Offer a series of information literacy programs, but don't necessarily make them incremental. For instance, do a class on searching databases, one on learning Dewey, and one on website evaluation.
- Modify the age-appropriateness of class materials for older students. Go into more details about databases or teach more advanced website evaluation skills for older audiences.

- Offer to write a regular "Learning the Library" section for the local homeschool newsletter that highlights some of the *Library Literati* concepts.
- Do a presentation at a homeschool conference, perhaps explaining everything the library has to offer and highlighting the library's databases.
- Take the individual classes of *Library Literati* (or similar course) "on the road" to homeschool learning cooperatives or other school environments. Use the classes as an outreach program of the library.

Conclusion

Creating a library skills or information literacy instruction program takes a lot of time and effort. The results, however, are outstanding. And once the course/class is completed, it can be repeated, circulated among colleagues, or presented at other library locations, taken "on the road" to schools, or modified for use with other audiences. The effort put toward creating an information literacy instruction program will be worthwhile. Homeschool students—indeed, students from all types of schools—will use our libraries and the information we provide, and they can understand how to grasp the 21st-century skill of information literacy/digital literacy if we simply provide them with the training.

WORKS CITED

Biever, Mary. 2006. "Library Literati & More." E-mail message to Maryann Alldredge (Mori). June 1.

McLeod, Saul A. 2018. "Concrete Operational Stage." *SimplyPsychology*. Last modified January 14, 2018. Accessed June 5, 2019. https://www.simplypsychology.org/concrete-operational.html.

Parenting Today. N.d. "The Stages of Intellectual Development in Children and Teenagers." *Child Development Institute*. Accessed May 31, 2019. https://childdevelopmentinfo.com/child-development/piaget/#XK5_l-hKils.

Yontz, Tina. 2006. "library Literati." E-mail message to Maryann Alldredge (Mori). Mar 15.

PART VII

Points of View

We Are Book Rich

A Homeschooling Family's Use of Public Libraries

Jennifer C.L. Smathers *and* Jennifer M. Lyle

Homeschooling is certainly not for everyone, but libraries are. So, for the librarian without first-hand homeschooling experience, it is worthwhile to consider the perspectives of homeschoolers. The following essay aims to explore a homeschooling family's use of resources at the public library, through interviews with Jennifer Lyle, a mom and primary teacher for three boys, aged 4–8. From the hazards of late fees to the wonders of interlibrary loan, get a family-based perspective on services useful to elementary-aged homeschoolers. With practical suggestions for librarians serving homeschoolers as described by their librarian aunt, Jennifer Smathers, you too can encourage homeschooled children to marvel at how book rich they are.

Homeschool families' use of public libraries has changed the landscape of children's library services since the 1990s. As homeschooling gained popularity, libraries began to see some changes in the use of their resources and services. At least, that is what Jennifer Smathers observed during her career which has gone from homeschooled volunteer page to Interim Director of an academic library. The following are Jennifer Smathers' direct observations and an interview with Jennifer Lyle who is currently homeschooling her children.

Jennifer C.L. Smathers

During my time as a student and volunteer at the Macedon Public Library (New York State), I was happy to observe the progress towards recognition of the growing presence of the homeschool population at the library. I noticed that subject-themed kits which were once sent around county-wide systems to assist librarians with storytimes or teachers in public schools with their lessons were adapted to being used by homeschooled families. Storytime rules were relaxed to allow for multi-age children to be present, and parents appreciated when older kids helped keeping younger ones safe and cheerfully occupied. Librarians adjusted to receiving questions from curious students on educational topics during the school day, without an official school visit scheduled. Library staff stopped asking kids why they were not at school, and patrons learned that school-aged students at the library were not necessarily truants.

I've been privileged to watch, as a librarian, part of the next generation of my family being homeschooled. It is my hope that this essay will bring the perspective of a home-school family into the light of a better understood patron population. These families are often your most frequent library users, with their own specialized needs. A still-existing outdated and erroneous perception of a stereotypical homeschooler, with an uneducated parent homeschooling to avoid vaccines or merely to enforce strict religious codes, is not the reality you are likely to engage with. I have many homeschooling friends, from atheist polyamorous families to the more well-known evangelical faith-based home-schooling parents. Libraries are a critical part of the homeschool experience. With such a divergent set of backgrounds, how can a librarian help the most homeschoolers?

My brother and his family could be perceived as a stereotypical faith-based home-schooling family. However, both parents have college degrees, one parent works outside the home, and the children receive vaccines. The mother, Jennifer Lyle, plans and carries out much of the schooling, but not all. The family follows a curriculum that is literature-based and heavy with hands-on learning. They participate in homeschool support groups and supplement their home education with cooperative classes at a local church. They also participate in their town's recreational activities and are constantly visiting public libraries

To explore how this family is using the public library of today, I arranged to spend time with them in the Webster Public Library, the library they use the most. They met me as I came through the main doors. This allowed for a lovely procession to the children's room with boys hopping along carpet square stepping stones and over the bridge into a place they knew well. "It bothers them when I walk through the water" said Jennifer Lyle as we crossed blue carpet squares that looked like a creek and served as a visual boundary for the children's room.

The boys, ages 8, 7, and 4, hung up their coats and took off. The youngest was imme-diately drawn to the train table. The eldest had disappeared in the aisle where he could find non-fiction transportation books. I almost giggled out of joy observing the looks on their faces thinking, "This is why I became a librarian."

At the time we came into a children's room, there was no library staff present. A rather large gazebo-like desk was empty. The room was cheerful and vibrant, with trains and a puppet theatre in the main area, nearby restrooms, and colorful animals painted on the walls. I was surprised to see such high shelving. It wasn't a barrier to the 8 year old, but the 4 year old mostly browsed what looked like reshelving areas on the ends of stacks that were more accessible to him. The 7 year old was also less inclined to browse shelves, with one exception.

After I had talked my middle nephew into giving me a tour of the room, he led me directly to the comics and a shelf on which a particular series (Donald Duck) was placed. I then asked him for a tour, inquiring about the library's collections and how he used them. I was able to do this activity with each of the boys, with varying degrees of success. My oldest nephew had parked himself in the nonfiction Transportation section, declaring it to be his favorite place, so that he didn't need to go anywhere else. He proceeded to pick out numerous titles far beyond the four items he had been allotted by his mom for this trip. Later I watched the negotiations as he was reminded that some books must be left for other children who needed to learn about military vehicles; after that at least half of the set was returned to the shelves. My middle nephew gave me the most thorough tour, a result perhaps more due to his personality than any particular reaction to library resources or services. He showed me the picture books, comic books, videos, and a secret door (half-height) through to the multi-use room. He then directed me to the full sized-door further down the wall. Inside the multi-use room I observed several educational toys; this mostly empty space, I guessed, was used for storytimes and also had a small dress-up area. After later research, I learned it was called the Early Learning Center. The youngest nephew, with very few lower front-facing shelving areas to browse, was mostly interested in various toys, from the train to the large early education sets available in the adjoining room. Jennifer Lyle noted that it was great that such large early learning play sets were available at the library since the confines of a single-family dwelling did not lend themselves well to ownership of many large educational toy sets. For example, while the family had a play kitchen, it wasn't nearly as comprehensive as the one in the library.

Having gotten a good tour of our surroundings, I proceeded to ask questions trying to unravel how this family uses their library. They told me that they actually split their library time between two libraries. They used this one which is close to home, and another one closer to their church. With the latter, it was convenient to have a library trip with some of the kids while others were in co-op classes at the church. The ways that Jennifer Lyle and the boys described the different libraries was fascinating.

The factor that very much influenced parental use of the library was that the cost of fines was less at the library further away, the Penfield Public library. When dealing with the educational, curiosity, and entertainment needs of 3 children, even a small difference in the late fines could add up. One week of being down with colds could quickly add up to $20 worth of fines. In a single-income family, as many homeschooled families are, that can make a significant impact. The parent was highly interested in the fine-free approach that my academic library takes. Given that the true purpose of fines is to get the items back to the library, we do not charge late fees. Rather we only bill for the replacement cost of materials if they've been overdue for a certain length of time. Upon the return of those materials, all fees are waived. There is unequivocal support from the homeschooling parent for this sort of fine structure. The concept of not having to weigh financial penalties or limit books chosen by children for fear of fines was well received.

I was surprised at the amount of time that Jennifer Lyle said she spent on the library online portal. She made full use of online renewals, email alerts, and advance searching for books to support their chosen curriculum. When asked what the website could do to help her use the library, she said that the enhanced ability to make, sort, and save multiple lists would be of great benefit. She showed me one of the curriculum guides she was using this year. In the list of supporting materials for upcoming units she wrote down call numbers for both libraries she used. She said that the ability to set up lists based on study units showing the call numbers and shelf locations of the book at each library would be a great feature. Having worked with computers before she had children, she is aware that the capability of enhanced filtering and reporting on lists is possible in the online environment.

When talking about fines, she found automated messages sent from the library three days before an item is due helpful, but wished for a day-one overdue message to assist with fine avoidance. She explained that she wanted to have an email or text alert the first day that any item was overdue. The library is close enough to the house that the extra incentive to stop fines from accruing would be very welcome.

Given the amount of time Jennifer L. spent online, I asked her about announcements on the library websites about upcoming events. Jennifer M. Lyle responded that she didn't necessarily look for event publicity on the website because when she was online it was usually from home and directly on the county library system site. She knew that she could find event information on an individual library website but didn't routinely look for that online because she usually saw publicity in person at the library. "We are here all the time; we just see what they are having. I think we missed this year's Amerks (local pro-hockey team) reading program in Webster." The only time that she specifically looked for event information online was if they had missed a special program, like the Amerks Reading Power Play event, "I would look up on the website so we could travel to another library." She then showed me the whiteboard in the library's multi-use room that was advertising that week's events. She also showed me brochures on the gazebo desk with activities for the month. No special advertising was needed to reach this particular home-schooling family.

While chatting about the differences between their top two library choices, one distinction, that I wouldn't have thought of, came up. Their local library has very few face-out displays, very few themed displays of materials. The homeschool parent at the library with few displays doesn't have to be as worried about looking for inappropriate (for their family) materials on display that they would want to steer their children away from. This allows an extra level of freedom for students to explore. Of the other library, with more face-out displays, the parent said, "I have no problem with those displays. It is my job as a parent to decide what information I present to my children. My job is to be discerning about what is right for them, that's on me." This family has never had a clash with a librarian over book choices or censorship.

The choice of which library to use by homeschoolers also has a practical side. "How safe is it for me to get my three rambunctious boys into the library and back out to the car?" Because of this concern the parent made a decision to visit the large downtown public library mostly by herself. "That library has the best, largest collection. But when I think of navigating paid parking, while I have all three kids with me, I just don't want to take that chance. Maybe when they are a bit older we can try to do it."

This library system charges a fee for each interlibrary loan and hold request. Therefore, a frugal homeschooling family places such requests only in rare circumstances. They are often more likely to try and find a substitute item rather than pay a fee or purchase something needed for school. Only items that they anticipate will be read over and over again get purchased.

Speaking of purchasing, homeschooling families look for used book sales. Often homeschool groups have cooperative sales where they trade curriculum and other resources. When asked about library book sales this family responded that they have to be really careful not to go overboard and buy things that won't need repeated use. Then again, when their librarian aunt goes a bit crazy at used book sales, they grin in awe and wonder, look at their treasure and exclaim, "We are book rich!"

While books constitute the majority of their library material use, the family also takes advantage of audiobooks for long trips, non-fiction videos on DVD, and those handy subject-themed kits that align with their curriculum. It is a bonus, the homeschool mom noted, that kits contain several items, but only incur one overdue fine.

Librarian's (Jennifer C.L. Smathers) Questions Answered by a Homeschooling Mom (Jennifer M. Lyle)

Question: What do you do with library books that is different from the books you own?

Answer: I attempt to keep our library books on a dedicated shelf, although this can be an uphill battle. A firm rule in our house is that library books cannot be read in the car on the way home from the library (they have to stay in the bag), and they are never allowed to leave the house under any circumstances. If I am going to lose a library book, I like to know that it is lost in my house.

Any run-ins with library staff?

I'm not sure if this would count as a run in. This is literally the only negative experience that I have ever had in almost five years of homeschooling, so I almost hesitate to even mention it.

One frustration I have as an active user of the library is the process of checking the books back in. I regularly have 60–80 books out at a time, so I perhaps experience this more often than other patrons. I have probably had a dozen instances where books were not properly scanned back in when I returned them. In one instance, I dropped a book off at our nearest library where it was not scanned in, and then it was transferred to its home library, where it was still not scanned in, but was shelved. The library staff that I called to check on it looked for it, but could not find it on the shelf. I ultimately had to visit the book's home library and find it on the shelf myself: it was shelved on its side because it was an oversized book. Because of this, when I can't find a book, I generally check the library's shelf myself if I have exhausted other options. The last time I did this and brought a copy to the librarian to see if it might be the missing one, I was treated with great suspicion and scolded, as if I was smuggling in overdue library books to avoid fines. This was a frustrating experience, as I am happy to cough up my fines when I deserve them; I just want my books checked in when I return them.

How many library programs have you attended?

We have attended song and story times, craft nights, LEGO nights, special events such as the previous years' Amerks reading programs, homeschool events, and summer reading programs. We've also attended the Town Highway Department event featuring their heavy machinery when the library hosted it in its parking lot.

What programs appeal to you the most?

Our home library regularly displays the work of community artists. This can include photographs, drawings, paintings, mixed media, etc. These displays are set up on the way to the children's area, and they provide an excellent way for me to expose my children to a wide variety of art on a regular basis. What is unique about the exhibits is that we can expect to see many pieces with familiar subjects: the pier where my husband takes kids fishing, the bridge we like to visit to play "Pooh Sticks," or our favorite hiking trail. My kids connect with this art in a very personal way. They take great joy in being able to identify the place where a particular photo was taken. Other pieces of art have inspired my kids to research new topics. A painting of Venice exhibited just outside of the children's section sent my 7-year-old off to the children's librarian to help him find more information about why the streets were flooded.

I appreciate a structured summer reading program where my kids can meet reading goals and earn rewards based on their reading. As a homeschooling mom, I seek out opportunities for my kids to interact with other adults in this way.

I love the passes that can be checked out from our library. These offer free or discounted admission to community resources such as state parks, a wide variety of museums, and even the orchestra.

What programs would you like to see?:

I would like to see a "library skills" class aimed at elementary-aged homeschoolers. I would love to attend science or technology programs, especially programs that take advantage of materials or equipment that I don't have readily on hand.

Do you use ILL?

I use it on occasion when I really cannot find adequate materials for a given topic. I would use it a great deal more if the fees were not so high. I would even pay some type of annual fee—maybe $10 or $20—to be allowed to place unlimited holds from other libraries in the county system.

Do you limit the number of items your kids get? Why?

I don't have a firm limit, but I give them a number when we enter the library. I like to keep our total under about 70, and I usually have about 30–40 out for school or that I have selected for them based on quality/interests. I typically let them each select 4, and they generally each have about 10 books of their own choosing out at any given time since we visit frequently. If we start having more than 60–70 books at a time, I find it difficult to keep track of the books and ensure that they are being treated properly and returned on time.

How much other media content do you use from the library?

I love some of the history/science/technology DVDs that are available through our library. These are items that I would never use enough to justify owning, but they are valuable additions to our studies. I typically have at least two or three educational DVDs out at any given time. A few of these resources have eventually led to purchases if I find that I am using them all the time. The curriculum that I have used for the last few years includes all of the classical music that we are studying, but if it did not, I would be using the library's music collection to supplement as well.

Practical Ways for Librarians to Help Homeschoolers: From the Shared Perspective of Homeschooled Graduates Jennifer M. Lyle and Jennifer C.L. Smathers

1. Go fine free!
2. Remove other barriers to access such as fees, checkout limits, and anti-truancy policies.
3. Offer themed kits—they are a convenient way to supplement a school topic.
4. Find a local homeschool support group:
5. Promote your library meeting spaces as a resource available to local homeschool organizations.
6. Collaborate with local support groups to offer a Homeschool Hangout recurring event.

7. Offer times for library events during the school day; evenings are often blocked out for spending time with the working parent.

8. Bulk up your non-fiction section.

9. Increase direct student access with lower shelves and children's catalog search computers.

10. Add the ability for your users to keep multiple lists via their accounts in catalogs, integrated library systems, or library services platforms. The list feature could be used for items beyond materials they currently have out or on hold. This would help the homeschool parents prepare in advance for the next section of curriculum.

11. Allow for materials to be selected online pulled by library staff, checked out, and ready to go. Bonus points for a drive-thru window.

12. Create a homeschool resources book collection and an online subject guide to a variety of homeschool resources.

13. Educate yourself about homeschooling.

SAMPLE GUIDES FOR HOMESCHOOLERS TO LIBRARY RESOURCES

"Homeschool Families—Geneva Public Library." n.d. Accessed February 18, 2019a. https://gpld.org/home school-families-2669.

"Homeschool Hub | PPLD.Org." n.d. Accessed February 18, 2019a. https://ppld.org/homeschool-hub.

"Homeschool Resource Center | Johnsburg Public Library District." n.d. Accessed February 18, 2019a. http://www.johnsburglibrary.org/content/homeschool-resource-center.

"Homeschool Resources." n.d. Accessed February 18, 2019a. https://www.pendleton.lib.in.us/children/home school-resources.

"Homeschool Resources | Carol Stream Public Library." n.d. Accessed February 18, 2019. https://www.cslibrary. org/homeschool.

"Homeschoolers | Westerville Public Library." n.d. Accessed February 18, 2019.

INSPIRATION FOR LIBRARIANS SERVING HOMESCHOOLERS

Bruno, Tom. 2017. "Homeschool Resources That Extend the Curriculum and Build Community." *Medium* (blog). December 11, 2017. https://medium.com/everylibrary/homeschool-resources-that-extend-the-curriculum-and-build-community-1dba830c799b.

"Education Resources Center/Homeschooling | Middle Country Public Library." n.d. Accessed February 18, 2019. https://www.mcplibrary.org/children/education-resource-center/.

Faulconer, Jeanne. 2014. "Thirteen Ways to Help Your Library Help Homeschoolers." TheHomeSchoolMom. April 18, 2014. https://www.thehomeschoolmom.com/be-a-homeschool-library-liaison/.

"Homeschool." n.d. Arlington Public Library. Accessed February 18, 2019. https://www.arlingtonlibrary.org/youth/homeschool.

"How We Homeschool: Using the Library." 2015. *Learning Mama* (blog). November 30, 2015. https://www.learn ingmama.com/how-we-homeschool-using-the-library/.

"HSLDA | Library Fixes Discriminatory Policy." n.d. Accessed February 18, 2019. https://hslda.org/content/hs/state/ks/201306260.asp.

"Information Useful for Librarians | Johnsburg Public Library District." n.d. Accessed February 18, 2019. http://www.johnsburglibrary.org/content/information-useful-librarians-0.

Main, Debbie. 2016. "Homeschool Explorations." *Carnegie Library of Pittsburgh* (blog). July 11, 2016. https://www.carnegielibrary.org/homeschool-explorations/.

Marino, Nancy, Jeannie Collacott, and Glynis Wray. 2016. "MAKE ME Kits: Portable Kits Invite Unexpected Outcomes." *Children and Libraries* 14 (4): 16. https://doi.org/10.5860/cal.14n4.16.

Moorhead, Andrew. 2016. "Homeschool Hangout." *Campbell County Public Library* (blog). October 12, 2016. https://www.cc-pl.org/homeschool-hangout.

"Mount Prospect Public Library Homeschool Services." n.d. Accessed February 18, 2019. https://mppl.org/homeschool/.

Peet, Lisa. 2018. "The End of Fines?" *Library Journal* 143 (15): 21.

"Practical Homeschooling Magazine." n.d. Homeschool World. Accessed February 18, 2019. https://www.home school.com/groups/.

"Public Libraries Welcome Growing Homeschool Community." 2016. Programming Librarian. April 14, 2016. http://programminglibrarian.org/articles/public-libraries-welcome-growing-homeschool-community.

"Rochester Homeschool Mini-Con | Rochester (MN) Public Library." n.d. Accessed February 18, 2019. https://www.rplmn.org/my-rpl/kids/rochester-homeschool-mini-con.

Sangrey, Author Shelly. 2016. "10 Easy Ways to Use the Library in Your Homeschool." *There's No Place Like Home* (blog). July 18, 2016. https://redheadmom8.wordpress.com/2016/07/17/10-easy-ways-to-use-the-library-in-your-homeschool/.

FINDING LOCAL ORGANIZATIONS AND LAWS

"Homeschool Laws in Your State—HSLDA." n.d. Accessed February 18, 2019a. https://hslda.org/content/laws/.
"Homeschool Organizations." n.d. HSLDA. Accessed February 18, 2019. https://hslda.org/content/orgs/.
"NY Homeschool Support Website Links | How to Homeschool in New York." n.d. *NYS LEAH* (blog). Accessed February 18, 2019. https://www.leah.org/resources/homeschool-links/.
"SEA Homeschoolers—100% Secular Homeschool." n.d. SEA Homeschoolers. Accessed February 18, 2019. https://seahomeschoolers.com/.
"State Homeschooling Resources and Local Homeschooling Support Groups -." 2018. Homeschoolwww (blog). January 2, 2018. https://www.homeschool.com/supportgroups/.

SELECTED HOMESCHOOLING RESEARCH

Bosetti, Lynn, and Deani Van Pelt. 2017. "Provisions for Homeschooling in Canada: Parental Rights and the Role of the State." *Pro-Posições* 28 (2): 39–56. https://doi.org/10.1590/1980-6248-2016-0022.
Brewer, T. Jameson, and Christopher Lubienski. 2017. "Homeschooling in the United States: Examining the Rationales for Individualizing Education." *Pro-Posições* 28 (2): 21–38. https://doi.org/10.1590/1980-6248-2016-0040.
Gaither, Milton. 2016. *The Wiley Handbook of Home Education*. Wiley-Blackwell.
Gann, Courtney, and Dan Carpenter. 2018. "STEM Teaching and Learning Strategies of High School Parents with Homeschool Students." *Education and Urban Society* 50 (5): 461–82. https://doi.org/10.1177/0013124517713250.
Mazama, Ama. 2016. "African American Homeschooling Practices: Empirical Evidence." *Theory and Research in Education* 14 (1): 26–44. https://doi.org/10.1177/1477878515615734.
Neuman, Ari, and Oz Guterman. 2017. "Structured and Unstructured Homeschooling: A Proposal for Broadening the Taxonomy." *Cambridge Journal of Education* 47 (3): 355–71. https://doi.org/10.1080/0305764X.2016.1174190.
Romanowski, Michael H. 2006. "Revisiting the Common Myths About Homeschooling." *The Clearing House* 79 (3): 125–29.

A Library Trustee Perspective

Amy Koenig

I am a library trustee in my second of three potential three-year terms. I am also a homeschool parent. Understanding homeschooling is important to help trustees allocate budget dollars for library materials, collect appropriate resources for programming, and create policies. The public library is the school library for homeschooled students. It is the place for homeschoolers to find materials for school topics, check out books for pleasure reading, gather information for research papers, attend programs, and also visit for any other non-school-related purpose.

Homeschooling is not "one size fits all." If you know one homeschooling family, you know one homeschooling family; each family is different, therefore, boards should not make decisions on the basis of one family's experience. Families may choose to homeschool one student or all of their children. They may decide to homeschool for a semester or for the entire elementary, middle, and high school years. Homeschoolers may follow a strict curriculum with books, use an online school, or be "unschooled." Families may elect to homeschool because they have a struggling learner or because they have an exceptional student.

Homeschooling does not always mean that all academics are completed at home. School districts may allow students to attend just a few "brick-and-mortar" school classes per day without being enrolled full-time. There are hybrid schools where children attend classes a few days a week and complete the rest of their schoolwork at home. Many homeschool co-ops exist throughout the country where families learn together working cooperatively towards a common goal. One parent may teach science and another—art. Classes are often offered to homeschoolers on different subjects by different organizations, including libraries.

Do You Know Your Homeschool Population?

Homeschooling is legal in all fifty states, with laws that families should follow to legally homeschool. The laws vary greatly by state. Some have no strict guidelines; others require that a homeschooling family has their curriculum approved by the school district. Home School Legal Defense Association provides a great summary of each state's laws on its website https://hslda.org/content/hs/state/. Trustees should familiarize themselves with the basics of the laws in their state so they can better understand their library patrons. In the past decade, as homeschooling has become more acceptable and mainstream, homeschooled students have had more freedom to be out in public during the school day. The fear of truancy officers has lessened; the library is now viewed as a safe and fun place to be during school hours, for either schoolwork or general enrichment and leisure.

How do you find out about your homeschool population? How do homeschool families currently use the library and how would they want to use the library? Verbal communication with parents is the most direct method of gathering information. Library staff can easily start a conversation with a parent who has school-aged students in the library when school is in session. Even though homeschooling is legal everywhere in the United States, families may still be reluctant to provide information to the outsiders, especially to government organizations. School districts sometimes ask for too much information or attempt an illegal registration. Because of these occasional incidents of infringement on their rights, homeschooling families may shy away from answering questions. Observation and direct communication are still the best methods for gathering information about the number of homeschooling families that use your library. Asking a patron if they homeschool their children is acceptable, but make sure that your staff is prepared to answer a return question, such as, "Why do you want to know?" The homeschool families are generally very independent. They may have been criticized for their decision to homeschool by other family members or friends. At the time of your interaction with them, they may not feel like their school year is going great. Their child may not be working at grade level consistent with their age. For all of these reasons, a parent may not want to open up about their homeschooling choice to possibly another set of prying eyes or someone who may cast judgment on their family's decisions or their child. They may also think you are going to ask them to commit to something more in their busy schedule. How the question about their schooling choice is approached in tone, like in most life situations, can make a huge difference in the type of response. If the library is not open to the many flavors of homeschooling, you will easily put off your patrons. Casual communication is still a good way to get information but remember those who are reluctant to talk will not be represented in your sample data.

Ask about the age of children instead of school grade. Asking a child's grade in school seems like a very simple and straightforward question for those used to traditional school groupings. But in a homeschool setting, the student may be doing work at many different grade levels. You may hear that they are working on third grade math, but doing fifth grade science with their sibling, and that their reading isn't going so well, so their reading book is at a second grade level. Asking for ages will most likely give you a better idea if you are trying to understand how many students of what age utilize your library.

Should you take a survey in attempt to reach others that are not willing to talk? Many homeschooling families will be reluctant to provide detailed demographic or personal information. If you chose to create a survey, be very clear why you are asking the questions and how you plan to use the information that you gather. If you plan to publish the results in any way, be clear where the results will be published.

Should the library go out to homeschoolers to gather information? You may get a different representation when going to them instead of only communicating with those that spend time at the library. Even though homeschoolers can be fiercely independent, most are not isolationists. Every state has a state homeschool organization. Smaller groups are often organized in an area. Internet searches may easily reveal well-organized local groups. Homeschool groups originally formed to track and influence legislation for homeschooling. These groups still exist to follow any potential legal matters. Social media has changed how groups interact and are organized. Smaller groups exist in many different forms and may or may not be known by state organizations. Often groups will form based on similar interests or homeschooling style. Other groups will form for a specific purpose such as field trips. A library representative going to homeschoolers could be a speaker at a monthly support meeting, a presenter in a co-op class, or a field trip guide at the library.

Should you create a committee to gather information? Because collecting information is not a straightforward affair, with multiple methods involved, a committee is a good mechanism to create a strategy. Goals of the committee may be:

1. Determine what information you need to refine your Strategic Plan goals by learning how homeschoolers use the library or want to use the library.
2. Refine the purpose of collecting information.
3. Define the specific uses of the information collected.
4. Determine the pathway or multiple pathways of collecting information.
5. Report back to the homeschooling community.
6. Focus on learning about the homeschoolers in general to draw your own conclusions vs. focusing on what patrons want from the library.

Committee members should include at least one trustee, a library staff member who is interested in serving homeschool families, and a homeschool patron who has connections in the community.

A library board should be invested in meeting the varied needs of the community, which includes a growing homeschooling population. The board needs to ensure that their library has homeschoolers included in their library's strategic plan, with specific areas, such as collection development, programming, and library policies detailed among others. The plan should have concrete measurable goals and desirable outcomes to meet the needs of the homeschooling community. The board also needs to ensure that their library has a well-crafted mission statement that can be applied to all segments of their population, including their homeschooling families.

Collection Development

Review your collection development policy to ensure that it meets the needs of the homeschooling community. One example is the collection or preservation of classic literature and complete series of some classics. The definition of a classic may need to be adjusted to include "living books." Charlotte Mason was a British educator who devoted her life to improving the quality of children's education (Simply Charlotte Mason n.d.). The Charlotte Mason style of learning coined the term "living books." This term is used by many homeschool curriculum developers and homeschool vendors in classifying and recommending materials. According to the *Simply Charlotte Mason*, "Living books are usually written by one person who has a passion for the subject and writes in conversational or narrative style. The books pull you into the subject and involve your emotions, so it's easy to remember the events and facts. Living books make the subject 'come alive'" (Simply Charlotte Mason n.d.).

Homeschooling families choose the homeschooling lifestyle to spend more time with each other and may be looking for books that reflect that. According to Jan Bloom, author of *Who Should We Then Read?,* children's literature started to change in the '60s and '70s as a result of changes in our culture and the federalization of the school districts. Combined with culture changes, more people moving from smaller areas to cities, and more money for school districts, schools could buy a lot more books. Publishers took advantage of this opportunity and began publishing more new books. The tone of children's literature in the '70s changed with the introduction of the problem novel. In the 80s books moved to more scary stories, fantasy, and the supernatural. In contrast, earlier novels had the children having adventures and learning character from trusted adults (Jan Bloom, personal conversation with author, February 16, 2019). Evaluate your collection to make sure that a variety of reading interests, styles, and needs of homeschooling families are represented.

Information for Elementary and Middle School Research Papers

Your collection development planning needs to include research materials for elementary and middle school ages. A homeschool student may be tasked with writing a research paper by their curriculum or their parents. My experience has been that my local public library did not have sufficient resources to do research for these ages outside of using the internet. Getting information online may be more appropriate for teens and adults, but younger students are more successful in conducting research using resources that are created specifically for children instead of the "Googling" a topic or using Wikipedia. Do you have books on interesting nonfiction topics at different reading levels? Do you provide an online database geared towards children to do research? Are these tools known to all students including homeschoolers? The resources that you have may directly affect the topics that a student may write about. Promote materials that your library provides and bolster your collection or subscription resources to assist students in conducting research.

Nonfiction and Historical Fiction

Homeschoolers embraced learning history in an engaging way. Taking the lead from Charlotte Mason ideas, curriculum companies and blog writers have formed many programs and lists of great books to read about historical characters. Tarry Lindquist outlines reasons to teach with historical fiction highlighting how it gives a student a broader view of a time in history instead of just the facts (Lindquist 1995). Biographies can also inspire and make history come alive for young students. Does your collection include historical fiction and biographies of many different areas of history at a variety of reading levels? Do you have series available that parents can allow their children to choose without prescreening them? Lindquist offers several examples of historical fiction in her article cited above. Other examples of quality historical fiction series begin with *Magic Tree House* books for younger readers and later progress in reading levels. *Magic Tree House* books are early chapter books that introduce kids to many people and events in history. Another quality series is *Childhood of Famous Americans.* The *Landmark Books* series first published by Random House began enticing young readers in the 1950s and continue to do so today. Some *Landmarks* have been republished in paperback and are available for purchase new (Spear 2016). *We Were There* is another outstanding historical fiction series where "[each] book in the series is a fictional retelling of an historical event, featuring one or more children as primary characters" (Wikipedia 2019). *Signature Books*, published by Grosset and Dunlap are "easy to read and provide lively, entertaining, and factual stories about famous people. Though written simply enough for young readers, they make interesting reading for boys and girls well into their teens"(Reshelving Alexandria 2019). *The Julian Messner Shelf of Biographies* is a more advanced yet still a children's level biography series. According to the dust jacket of *Road to Alaska: The Story of Alaska Military Highway,* "The editors of Julian Messner, Inc. found that there was a great desire … for really authoritative biographies of characters of interest for this generation.… All of the books are by well-known authors who have had a special interest in and an enthusiasm for the particular character which has inspired them to recreate his life and meaning" (Reshelving Alexandria 2019).

These are just a few examples; many other quality series and historical children's books are available as well. Homeschoolers will be looking for well written and engaging historical fiction and biographies because they have been exposed to them through their curriculum and other homeschool resources.

Curriculum Supplements

Another angle to consider for the library's collection development are curriculum supplements or frequently used books in popular curricula.

My Father's World® built into their curriculum for kindergarten through eighth grade "Book Basket" time. According to Julie Hansell of *My Father's World*, "In the curriculum, the authors have recommended books to check out from the library that correspond to each week's topic. One of the tasks/part of the school day is for children to look at books in the book basket. *My Father's World*, curated a list of books to go with each topic and included a variety of reading levels for each topic" (Julie Hansell, e-mail message, February 18, 2019). Users of this curriculum will be coming to the library on a regular basis looking for books from this list.

AmblesideOnline is a free homeschool curriculum that uses Charlotte Mason's classically-based principles to prepare children for a life of rich relationships with everything around them: God, humanity, and the natural world. AO's detailed schedules, time-tested methods, and extensive teacher resources allow parents to focus effectively on the unique needs of each child (https://www.amblesideonline.org/). Though this curriculum does not specifically stress using the library, it does emphasize using books over textbooks. Also, since the plans are free, this program appeals to many thrifty homeschool families who would appreciate finding the recommended books in the library.

Five in a Row creates lessons and activities based on popular books. The idea behind this curriculum is that you read the same book for five days in a row followed by the lessons and activities. These would be ideal books to have in your library for use by those who have purchased the *Five in a Row* manuals. The books included in each manual can be found on their website, https://fiveinarow.com/.

Resource books, Books on Books (and books that these books recommend). Does your library have books that can recommend books? Here are some examples that might be of interest to homeschoolers:

- Bloom, Jan. 2001, 2008. *Who Should We Then Read? vol 1 and 2.* BooksBloom.
- Hunt, Gladys. 2002. *Honey for a Child's Heart.* Grand Rapids: Zondervan
- Wilson, Elizabeth. 2002. *Books Children Love: A Guide to the Best Children's Literature.* Wheaton: Crossway.

These are great books to have in your collection as well as have the actual books that many of these resources recommend.

Homeschooling Resource Books. Many books exist that discuss homeschooling in general. Does your library include these types of books? Are these books current? Trends in homeschooling and available resources have changed in the last decade, has your collection of books about homeschooling been updated as well? The relevancy of some older titles may be questionable and the access to the resources mentioned may also be a challenge.

Textbooks

Does your collection development policy address the acquisition of textbooks? At our library, the policy does not allow for library funds to be spent on anything classified as a textbook, especially if these books are only going to be used for a short period of time, such as one semester or one year. Some homeschool textbooks, however, may be appropriate for a library to include. One popular example of a non-consumable math textbook that is used for a short amount of time is the *Life of Fred Elementary Series* (Polka Dot Press, Reno, NV).

Programming

How do you want to allocate your programming budget? Do you want to consider homeschool-specific programming? Homeschoolers most likely participate in your quality library programming today even if you do not have programs specifically designated for them. If you are new to creating programming specifically for homeschooled patrons, knowing homeschool laws for your state will be helpful. For example, in a state that requires curriculum to be approved in advance, a weekly program that you announce in October may not be successful. The program may be excellent but it might not fit with the family's approved plans for the year. Even if a family's curriculum does not have to be approved, their plan and schedule may not easily be adjusted after the school year has started. Alternatively, some families may be looking for something to spice up their routine a few months into the year and need a new program. Knowing the laws of your state and your local families will be helpful in determining the appropriate subjects, formats, and timing of programming.

Consider the resources that your library already owns or expertise of your staff to create programming. Inventory any special talents, interests or knowledge of your staff and library board, and consider how that could be translated into a program. Would you allow a parent or other non-staff adult utilize your equipment to teach a class? For example, our library owns some iPads that are rarely used. You can increase your programming offerings if you train others to use equipment that may be underutilized.

Consider topics or subjects that are difficult for a family or student to do individually or require special equipment. For example, offer a program or a class introducing an art technique, science experiments, or computer labs with specific software.

Effective programming that fits homeschoolers' goals should be designed for a small age or grade range, about three years' worth. When choosing and marketing your programs, be clear on the targeted age range or specific expectations.

Examples of programming that may interest homeschooling families and their students:

1. Reading groups. A reading group may take on many different forms. Ask some retired teacher patrons to come listen to early readers to help with their fluency. Select a book, discuss it with a group, and do activities. Have the reading group create a presentation about some topic in the book.

2. A short series (3–8 weeks) on a topic such as music, or a specific science topic such as electricity. Ask a retired patron who has some expertise in an area to be the leader of this series.

3. Writing club. Have students share what they have written. Include challenges for the students for each week and then share the product of the challenge.

4. A guest speaker series. Invite community leaders, professionals, or other interesting people to speak to a group. Make sure to advertise to a specific age group and communicate this to your speakers.

5. Programs to prepare for competitions. National Geographic GeoBee, math competitions, spelling bees—all may be held outside of the library but students would like some assistance in preparing for these competitions.

As with any other segment of the population, it may take a while to get homeschoolers interested in attending your programming. Homeschoolers can be inconsistent about their attendance as many have a strong sense of independence. For example, a family may not come to a program that they have signed up for as a consequence of kids' bad behavior. Keep trying and talking with those who do come and those who do not. Like with most things in life, if you have a good thing happening, then they will come and invite their friends. If you want to start a new series of homeschooling activities, consider a kick-off party as a fun activity to introduce your new events.

Library Policies

Unattended Children

Policies need to be considered for different scenarios of a homeschooling family using the library. Our library has a policy for unattended children. This policy may be tricky to navigate for a family when there is a requirement for a parent to be present during the program. How do parents comply with the policy when they are required to be in the room with their younger child but can't leave an older child alone to look at books? I have a friend who never felt like she could attend story time with her children, because her seven-year-old was not welcome in the pre-school story time and also not allowed to browse books alone. Would an older sibling fulfill the need of a parent in some of these situations? Determine what is most important in your policies and allow for some flexibility for families. For example, if story time is in a different room or area than the picture books, allow the older siblings to be in the room if they are not disruptive. Or broaden the specification of an adult requirement to attend with the preschooler to a person 13 or older.

Special Circulation Privileges

Homeschool families who utilize the library a lot would like to have special policies for the number of items they can check out. A large family may reach the normal limit of check-outs quickly. Examine your homeschool population to determine if this policy could be abused, but if your total limit of check-outs is low, you may consider creating a special category for homeschool families and allow for different privileges. Families may also like to have special privileges for number of renewals or length of check-out period. Interlibrary loan (ILL) usage policies should be reviewed. Consider if the number of ILL requests allowed could be adjusted for homeschoolers. If the number of ILL requests is limited, what is the purpose of this limitation? If some patrons are not following the rules of the ILL process, consider imposing larger fines or reduction in access for those who abuse the privileges instead of limiting the usage for all. If the ILL process is too time consuming and you don't have the staff, consider looking at different resources that would provide the desired collection additions without additional staffing required.

Weeding

Many homeschoolers like old books. Most of my homeschool peers feel that older biographies are better written than current ones, and prefer those. If children's books are being considered for weeding because of low circulation, tell your homeschoolers about it. They may start checking them out more often or they might realize that it is time for the book to go away to allow for newer items. Purging children's books based solely on the publication date removes many quality books on great topics.

Are you weeding to "keep up with the times"? Homeschool families prefer to make their own judgment on what is and is not suitable for them when it comes to literature about family and gender roles. Try to have diverse angles in your collection. Most homeschool families will welcome traditional as well as non-traditional materials.

Meeting Room Usage

What is your meeting room usage policy? Does your policy encourage or discourage homeschool activities? Do you charge to use all or some sections of your facility? Do you have a designation on the types of activities that require a charge? How easy or difficult is the reservation process? Consider how your policy would apply in a few sample situations:

1. A group of homeschool families would like to have an invitation-only one-time event.

Our library would not allow this meeting because it was an invitation-only and not open to the public.

2. A homeschool mom would like to prepare a group of students for a geography bee in a meeting room once a week for 6 weeks. Our library would allow this activity at no charge, but only permit making the reservation no more than one month in advance. The activity would have to be open to the public.

3. A local homeschooling group would like to hold an evening information night at the library. If your library would normally charge for this type of activity in your meeting room, consider how this type of meeting could become a library program so no fee is required.

4. A group of homeschoolers would like to meet weekly for a group class for a semester. You would have to decide how this fits into your meeting room policy for many different aspects of the policy. Could you consider this a library program instead of an individual program?

Even if requests for using rooms are not a part of your formal meeting room policy, your staff should have a procedure on gathering information from groups prior to giving even a tentative acceptance or availability of the meeting space.

Marketing

How are you marketing your library? What is your board's involvement in the promotion of the services that your library offers? Is any of your marketing directed towards homeschoolers? Most libraries currently use social media and post photos, videos, and other information there (OCLC 2018). Does your library have a communication plan that includes the appropriate use of social media? According to the recent research conducted by OCLC, fewer than half of the surveyed libraries have a communication strategy; very few felt that their strategies were current. As a board, review your current marketing plans. Add marketing strategies to update your strategic plan, or create a strategic plan goal to develop marketing and communication plans. In these plans, consider how you will be reaching homeschoolers as one of your target audiences. Once you have a strategic plan, fund marketing plans through your budget including time allotment of personnel to carry out the marketing activities. Your homeschoolers in the area need to know about your great programming and resources that your library offers.

Fundraising

"Funding for libraries has always been difficult to obtain, but one of your main responsibilities as a trustee is to make sure that your library is as well funded as it can be" (Moore 2010, 86). As board members, if you have items in your strategic plan that are not funded, you have some responsibility to help locate the funding for those initiatives. Are homeschoolers a potential audience for a targeted fundraiser? If you have programs you want to implement for homeschoolers, a targeted fundraising effort with your homeschool community may be profitable. Homeschoolers are paying for their child's school instead of the government-provided school. So homeschooling families know that education and programs cost money. Often families are willing to support these types of programs where they see benefits to their family or the homeschool community.

Can the board influence the library administration/staff to focus on homeschooling by creating their own grant or research dollars? If the board would like the library to focus on developing programs for homeschooling, appropriate some grant money in the budget and accept proposals from the staff for use of the money. Give the grant to the proposal which the board feels provides the best plan to learn about your homeschool community and market existing programs or create new ones.

Evaluations

However you decide to engage homeschoolers, the process is not complete without evaluation. As part of your planning of events or modification of policies, determine a measurement statistic to evaluate any of your changes. Will you measure the attendance at programs? Will you measure the differences in usage of a resource based on a change in policy? Will you measure the increase in collection in a certain area? Will you collect an end-of-program written evaluation from participants? What do you want to know from the participants about their experience?

Once you know what you are measuring, will you expect the evaluation to be delivered to the board? Should the evaluations be given to the entire board or to a committee or subset of the board? As board members you need to help define your expectations on evaluations. Communicate your expectations on what is being measured, the time frame for the communication, and the communication mechanism. For example, if a new homeschool weekly program is started for a semester, request interim reports of monthly attendance. At the conclusion of the series, request total attendance numbers and a summary of the end-of-program evaluations. This information will help the board determine funding and personnel allocation for future homeschool programs.

Conclusion

For homeschool students the library is not only the public library for extracurricular reading and events, it is also their school library. For the homeschool parent, the library is a source of materials to assist in teaching their student as well as a place and resource for their non-homeschooling life. As trustees, you have the opportunity to attract this rich and diverse group in your community to use the resources and programming you already offer, and at the same time enhance your library. Homeschoolers want to use the library and want to be welcomed to the library. Understanding homeschooling is important to help trustees allocate budget dollars for library materials, collect appropriate resources for programming, and consider homeschoolers when creating policies. I hope that you are willing to foster learning among homeschoolers in your area and enrich their lives and their school.

Works Cited

Lindquist, Tarry. October 1995. "Why and How I Teach with Historical Fiction." Accessed March 16, 2019. https://www.scholastic.com/teachers/articles/teaching-content/why-and-how-i-teach-historical-fiction/.
Moore, Mary. 2010. *The Successful Library Trustee Handbook*. Chicago: American Library Association.
OCLC. 2018. *Public Libraries: Marketing and Communications Landscape*. Dublin, OH: OCLC.
Reshelving Alexandria. 2019. "Messner Shelf of Biographies" Accessed March 16, 2019. https://reshelvingalexandria.com/pub/series/messner-biographies.
"Signature Biographies" Accessed March 16, 2019. https://reshelvingalexandria.com/pub/series/signature-biographies.
Simply Charlotte Mason, n.d. "Who Is Charlotte Mason?" Accessed March 19, 2019. https://simplycharlottemason.com/what-is-the-charlotte-mason-method/who-was-charlotte-mason/.

Spear, David. October 17, 2016. "Generation Past" *Perspectives on History.* Accessed March 16, 2019. https://www.historians.org/publications-and-directories/perspectives-on-history/october-2016/generation-past-the-story-of-the-landmark-books.

Wikipedia. 2019. "National Association of University-Model Schools." Last modified January 26, 2019. https://en.wikipedia.org/wiki/National_Association_of_University-Model_Schools.

"We Were There" Last modified on February 27, 2019. https://en.wikipedia.org/wiki/We_Were_There.

PART VIII

Infinite Possibilities

Free Play Programming in Libraries and Communities

Antonio F. Buehler *and* Autumn E. Solomon

All work and no play makes Jack a dull boy, the proverb goes. But all work and no play makes Jill a higher achieving student in the eyes of many, including a large number of those who are making decisions for young people within our schools. However, play provides well-documented benefits in terms of intellectual development, language and literacy development, and social development (Saracho, and Spodek 2003, 21), and is "indispensable to the development of a healthy, well-functioning adult" (LaFreniere 2011, 467). By offering opportunities for Free Play and less structured programming libraries can be a child's safe place to explore, discover, and create in a way that they might not find in other learning institutions.

Libraries are in the unique position of being able to halt the societal decline in Free Play by remaking themselves as publicly accessible spaces that embrace and facilitate Free Play. While it would make sense to promote this as a service to the homeschooling community, especially because they are the ones who would tend to be most eager to embrace it, Free Play would benefit both homeschooled and traditionally schooled children.

Libraries can have impact beyond their own walls by helping homeschoolers build community through Free Play. As a central meeting point that provides not only the resources and programming traditionally associated with libraries, but also opportunities for Free Play, libraries will be able to connect homeschooled families who will then take Free Play back into their neighborhoods. That creates a second order effect of Free Play allowing non-patrons (often traditionally schooled students) to get the experience of Free Play.

Overview of Free Play

Free Play is not typically associated with directive or traditional schooling. In fact, "in school settings … many teachers define play as separate from [academic] work, or as a sequel to or reward for work" (Fromberg 2002, 113). Homeschooling families are less likely to make such a distinction, and for the more Self-Directed Education oriented homeschooling families (e.g., unschoolers) Free Play is often considered the basis for learning.

Not all play is Free Play. The play that many parents and educators promote is directed or structured play and often exists to serve the needs of adults. For example, many teacher-directed games in elementary schools are used to push academic learning objectives, while participation in sports leagues can often provide parents with a way to accomplish their unmet dreams vicariously through their children (Brummelman, 2013). The Free Play of children, on the other hand, is not for the adults—it is for the child. According to Peter Gray there are five elements of Free Play (Gray 2013, 141–153):

- Play is self-chosen and self-directed
- Play is motivated by means more than ends
- Play is guided by mental rules
- Play is imaginative
- Play is conducted in an alert, active, but non-stressed frame of mind

In short, Gray argues that Free Play is of the child's choosing, it is done for the sake of play itself, it has mental rules but those rules are self-chosen, it is in some way mentally removed from the real world, and it requires an active, alert mind that does not concern itself with a fear of failure (a state unlikely to be replicated in the classroom or sporting arena). Libraries and librarians have long known that many opportunities and sources allow for a learner to make their own discoveries, conclusions, and find the answers they need in a space that is free of judgment.

The Science of Free Play

As Joe L. Frost said "free, spontaneous play and outdoor playscapes, both natural and built, are essential for the fitness, health, and development of children and for their adaptation to their culture, society, and world. To the extent that children are deprived of this inherent need, their development is damaged…. Decades of research conclude that play promotes cognitive development, social development, language development, physical fitness and health, learning, and coping with trauma" (Frost 2010, 202).

Free Play is not only a more efficient way to develop and learn, it is a biological need. Many animals develop through play including all mammals and many birds, while some fish, reptiles, and even octopi have been observed at play. However, humans are the most dependent on play as a species, with the benefits having been noted by anthropologists, biologists, evolutionary psychologists, and sociologists alike.

Playfulness is more important in animals with more complex cognitive processes. Human brains are only about 40 percent formed at birth, meaning the need for post-birth cognitive development is already much greater in humans than other mammals that are born more developed and with far more instinctual survival habits intact (Abbott 2010, 33, 44). Considering that human society relies on collective learning, a growing and shared accumulation of knowledge whereby cultural change happens faster than genetic change, the cognitive development demands of humans are unmatched. Play may help explain how each successive generation is able to understand, manage, and add to the growing body of shared knowledge. What better place to have freedom to play than an institution of collective knowledge! Playing with ideas, art, computers, outdoor spaces, with community—these are all essential services a library can provide.

Anthropologists have observed that Free Play is central to the lives of young people in hunter-gatherer societies across multiple continents, indicating that play may be an inborn human need. It has been noted that even children in the worst of conditions sometimes need to engage in play. Indeed, even during the Holocaust play could not be eradicated as "children's yearning for play naturally burst forth even amidst the horror.… An instinctual, an almost atavistic impulse embedded in the human consciousness" (Eisen 1990, 60).

Free Play is also how humans come to understand the limits of their environment, develop a tolerance for risk, and learn how to interact and socialize with others. While development along these lines is important for all young people, non-homeschoolers often focus on the issue of socialization. And Free Play is perhaps the best answer to "but what about socialization?," the question nearly all homeschooling families have been asked.

Socialization has multiple connotations, and the way it is posed to homeschoolers typically revolves around the concern of how kids can learn to interact with each other if they are at home all day. While more orthodox homeschool families may want to limit outside influences on their children by limiting access to more mainstream children, most homeschooling families seek out opportunities for socialization. Traditional schools on the other hand are not always the best counterpoint to this concern with their practice of age segregation and limitations on socializing (e.g., no talking during class).

More relevant than how homeschool kids socialize with each other is how they get to interact with them. Free Play provides young people with the opportunity to "solve their own problems, control their impulses, modulate their emotions, see from others' perspectives, negotiate differences, and get along with others as equals" (Gray 2013, 175). The beauty of Free Play is that it is perhaps the most efficient way to develop social and emotional skills because it is sought out by children, and because it provides immediate feedback on the "causes, consequences and expressions of emotions" (Veiga, Neto, and Rieffe 2016, 51). Moreover, this learning is best done away from the monitoring of adults as adult interference in play often limits children's willingness to explore the boundaries of their own behavior (Gray 2013, 49).

From a schooling perspective, the benefits of Free Play on social and emotional learning can also produce long-term dividends in terms of higher education attainment. Many of the socialization skills that come from extensive Free Play would fall under the category of noncognitive skills such as adaptability, self-restraint, and motivation (Kirabo 2018). While content knowledge and test scores tend to get most of the attention, it is noncognitive skills, along with GPA, that are the best predictors of college success as measured by college completion (National Education Association, 2015).

Libraries to the Rescue

Given all the benefits of Free Play mentioned thus far, policy makers and educators should make Free Play a central component of primary and secondary education. Unfortunately, the opposite has happened, as Free Play has been in drastic decline for decades. The decline can be explained by a variety of factors to include parents' fear of abduction or other bodily harm, liability concerns on the part of institutions that used to tolerate children at play, an increase in schooling and enrichment activities intended to promote academic success, and a shortage of opportunities to engage in Free Play and peers to play with because of the aforementioned reasons (Veiga, Neto, and Rieffe 2016, 49).

Libraries are ideal Free Play spaces because of their approach to educating the public—they leave patrons alone. Libraries stand ready to provide resources and support, but they do not take on an authoritarian or paternalistic role with the patron; instead, they offer choice. In Free Play, patrons need resources and support, but they do not need directed play. Further, in reference to young people, libraries are freed from the demands placed on schools to push content according to age-based standards. Libraries have the luxury of making Free Play available to children without having to make tradeoffs on curriculum.

Three ways libraries can make Free Play available to students are by making their spaces available for Free Play, providing Free Play programming, and adapting the practices of the library to facilitate community building among homeschool families.

Case Study: Building a Free Play Program

The Self-Directed Learning movement, which has Free Play at its core, is an engaging and simple way to bring a community together. Play is an essential part of childhood, and libraries are a natural partner to offer programs that support discovery through open-ended, child-directed play. Westbank Libraries in Austin, Texas, created Free Play, a 3-hour weekly program that welcomes joyful noise and encourages parents to sit back while their kids explore and discover together. The ideas presented suggest application for working more playfully with adult communities and staff as well.

What Is Free Play at the Library?

"Free Play is free choice, free time, stress free, no expectations, no grades, no instruction. It arises spontaneously and when it has run its course, it fades. Its process is discovery, and its only standard of measurement is how much fun it is." This is the phrase Westbank Library Director, Mary Jo Finch, coined when she wrote a newsletter to library patrons describing Free Play. This description lets everyone know that Free Play is different from traditional programming, that it is educational but offers something different from schools. Free Play has a short set of goals to put the experience into the patrons' hands, asking them to:

- create their own games
- develop relationships with people of all ages
- pursue their own interests
- read just for fun
- enjoy unstructured time in a non-homework space

Staff and administration have consciously made minimal rules to allow children freedom to work out issues on their own without adult intervention. The simple rules are: stay safe, respect others, respect the space, have fun. With these rules in place, creating a welcoming atmosphere becomes the next step.

Hospitality plays a key role in making people feel welcome and comfortable at the library. Anticipating noise levels, offering snacks to hungry people, and answering questions about the program are part of the process of running Free Play. On the front door a sign reading "joyful noise" alerts all library patrons that there is programming that may spill into the main library. The level of noise is offset by playing instrumental music that modulates the sound and sets a subtle cue to caregivers and children that noise is part of the process of play. Staff and volunteers sit near the entrance to greet families and answer questions. They model a hands-off approach while enjoying conversation, games, and coffee with neighbors and friends. Kids who come to Free Play grow comfortable with their autonomy and develop ownership of the library as a place for them. Their parents support each other in the sometimes difficult process of sitting back and letting go.

When it comes to outfitting the space, start with what you have. Look in supply closets for materials that encourage open-ended interactions and discovery. Examples may include board games, LEGO®, blocks, cardboard tubes and boxes, art supplies, large butcher paper, parachutes, and other storytime items (scarves, wrist ribbons, etc.). Every time the room is set up, it looks different, but always has areas for building, games, reading, art, and indoor physical activity such as a balance beam. If you have an outdoor area, consider allowing the program to extend to that space, encouraging kids to discover chalk, toys, bubbles, buckets, shovels, hula hoops, and more.

Although it may be challenging, avoid setting expectations for how materials and spaces will be used during Free Play. It can be difficult for adults to avoid instructing a child on how to play a game, or to set rules. One of the great benefits of free play is to let kids figure out things for themselves. Over time, as more patrons begin attending a program, it will start to take a shape that will determine what rules, roles, needs, and supplies work best in each space.

Case Study: Incorporating Free Play into Existing Programs

At Westbank Library the experience gained from Free Play was folded into existing programs to create a more community focused and family friendly experience. What started to emerge was the community's need for flexibility on time, connection with neighbors, less emphasis on technology and grades, less structure, and more playfulness. Listed here are a few programs that incorporate these ideas.

Art Exploration

The simple idea behind this program is to let kids explore different mediums without an end product in mind. Each week the library offers a variety of paints, scratch paper, cyanotypes, oil pastels, felt, clay and other materials kids may not get the opportunity to interact with regularly. The experience is driven by texture, creation, play, and using multiple senses to create with no directions given. Occasionally there is a focus revolving around a concept such as, bird house creation, sand art, or more open-ended concepts such as water, dirt, or nature.

There is a place for traditional crafts in the library, but Westbank chose to scale these back to emphasize process over product and account for exploration versus following directions. The library also switched this and other programs to a drop-in time-frame to accommodate busy schedules, but mainly to allow kids to really immerse themselves in their own projects. Some patrons stay for fifteen minutes, some stay for two or three hours.

Arcade

After a few years of trying minimally successful video game nights for teens, lockins, and summer gaming programs, the library applied Free Play concepts to gaming. The result was the creation of an arcade for all ages. This includes different eras of consoles, LAN games, vintage arcade games—essentially different stations that appeal to parents, children, and teens. Attendance went from 12 to 14 at occasional programs to 30–50-plus monthly. What changed? Age restrictions were eliminated, drop-in timeframes were incorporated, but most importantly, Arcade added the element of choice. Choice to move from one game to another. Choice to stay and play or leave after twenty minutes. The first families on board were homeschool families in need of a relaxed setting where kids could play and adults could connect. Now it has expanded to include teen volunteers, two-year-old gamers, and forty-year-old parents reminiscing about their favorite childhood games. What is often something parents are trying to limit (screen time) the library embraced as a challenge to turn into an opportunity for social and emotional learning.

Discovery!

For a more structured drop-in program Westbank offers Discovery, which is an exploration based program that touches on general topics including science, technology, literature, art and more. There is an intention at the start of each Discovery, but there is no grade for how much fun or learning a kid is having when playing. Designed for curious kids this program encourages attendance each week to discover something new!

Case Study: Introducing a Free Play Program to Homeschoolers and to a Wider Community

Free Play programming has seen a large turnout of homeschool and unschool families looking for unconventional places to learn and opportunities to build a sense of community. To further support this population specific niche programs were created.

Homeschool Library

This program invites home school and unschool learners and families to gather at the library to connect, learn, and play. Librarians are available to introduce resources and discuss how the library can support each child's path to learning. The weekly setup includes art supplies, books, games, computers, crafts, music, and, of course, librarians. Participants are encouraged to share their needs and ideas with staff members to help the program evolve.

Music and Movement

Creative librarians are infusing storytimes with music and movement. These programs incorporate, dancing, singing, and reading. This provides an alternative to storytime that is less formal, less structured, and does not need an age restriction since it is appropriate for all. Kids explore different instruments, sounds, dance, yoga, and other movements in addition to listening to stories. They are encouraged to participate at the level they are comfortable with, and over time develop a better sense of proprioception through somatic learning. After the program, caregivers and children are invited to stay and play.

Education Book Club

To support these changes to children's programming, Westbank offers a monthly education book club for parents, teachers, and caregivers in conjunction with educational talks and screenings of documentaries. Parents may not always be able to attend, but there is a distribution list where ideas can be shared, and talks are recorded and archived.

Case Study: Making Free Play Integral to the Culture of the Library and the Day-to-Day Work of the Staff

Westbank Libraries have embraced self-directed education as part of a new strategic plan after seeing huge success in providing play-based, drop-in programs that support homeschool, unschool, and self-directed learners, as well as offering something unique to students in traditional school. The effects of Free Play shifted the entire direction and culture for library staff. Without staff who support these ideas, the programs would not get very far. To foster this attitude administration has designed a strategic plan that is more open-ended, allows for self-direction, encourages risk-taking, decision-making, mistakes, and self-assessment. Managers are encouraged to listen to where employees would like to grow their careers and focus their professional development time. To support these shifts the budget has a line item marked for innovation, which means a little money is set aside to try new ideas as they develop throughout the year.

Staff Training

One of the crucial elements of change was staff training. In preparation to shift library culture, staff had meetings dedicated to discussing ideas, sharing experiences, and connecting with the idea of play and self-directed learning as part of the library mission. Staff read and discussed Peter Gray's book *Free to Learn* creating a starting point to develop new programs and ways to work. Gray addresses the importance of play in the workplace by saying "Adults who have a great deal of freedom as to how and when to do their work commonly experience that work as play, even in fact, especially, when the work is difficult. In contrast, people who must follow others' directions with little creative input of their own, rarely experience their work as play" (Gray 2013, 142). Many of the changes made by Westbank are points Gray brought up in his book about people having creative input, self-reflection, and experiencing work as play.

First, it was crucial to put in self-assessment versus performance reviews. This is a conversation with prompts between a manager and employee that is driven by the employee versus the manager. It allows the employee to direct their own work. The goal is to have a two-way conversation that develops a mutually beneficial partnership for both library and employee. Second, it is important to view mistakes as opportunities so that members of staff feel comfortable making decisions, talking about ideas, and are able to relax. Third, the library hopes to foster connection in the workspace. Staff is encouraged to fully participate in programs and play—they are modeling what the library hopes to offer children.

Making the Changes

Feedback from families, whether they homeschool, unschool, or attend traditional school, is that they want more community. Community can alleviate loneliness and create opportunities for learning, sharing, and growing together. For this reason, the Library has started to host programs that focus on getting together for a simple reason.

Questions to Ask If You Want to Incorporate Free Play

- What do libraries already offer in regular programs that support Free Play?
- Why are there age restrictions on programs? Do they really need to be there?
- What are you saying no to? Why?
- Is there a way to embrace noise or designate a noisy versus quiet area of the library?
- What do staff members need to support changes?

It may feel like a big leap to trust kids and parents to come to Free Play programs with minimal rules, but parents and caregivers adapt quickly. It connects people in the neighborhood to each other, and librarians to the neighborhood. Many parents home-school because they do not want a traditional school experience, so the library offers programming that supports a vision for self-directed learning.

Change can be difficult and may be met with resistance at many levels, but the more you relax and laugh, the more parents and children will relax and laugh, which results in less stress for everyone. Try removing age barriers, incorporating more stay and play after storytime, host a neighborhood event to talk with homeschool families, and offer your community support through experience, discovery and play.

Works Cited

Abbott, John. 2010. *Overschooled but Undereducated: How the Crisis in Education Is Jeopardizing Our Adolescents.* London: Continuum.
Brummelman, Eddie, Sander Thomaes, Meike Slagt, Geertjan Overbeek, Bram Orobio De Castro, and Brad J. Bushman. 2013. "My Child Redeems My Broken Dreams: On Parents Transferring Their Unfulfilled Ambitions Onto Their Child." *PLoS ONE* 8, no. 6.
Eisen, George. 1990. *Children and Play in the Holocaust: Games Among the Shadows.* Amherst: University of Massachusetts Press.
Fromberg, Doris Pronin. 2002. *Play and Meaning in Early Childhood Education.* Boston: Allyn and Bacon.
Frost, Joe L. 2010. *A History of Children's Play and Play Environments: Toward a Contemporary Child-saving Movement.* Abingdon: Routledge.

Gray, Peter. 2013. *Free to Learn: Why Unleashing the Instinct to Play Will Make Our Children Happier, More Self-reliant, and Better Students for Life.* New York: Basic Books.

Greve, Werner, Tamara Thomsen, and Cornelia Dehio. 2014. "Does Playing Pay? the Fitness-Effect of Free Play During Childhood." *Evolutionary Psychology,* 12, no. 2.

Jackson, C. Kirabo. 2018. "What Do Test Scores Miss? the Importance of Teacher Effects on Non–Test Score Outcomes." *Journal of Political Economy* 126, no. 5: 2072–2107.

LaFreniere, Peter. 2011. "Evolutionary Functions of Social Play: Life Histories, Sex Differences, and Emotion Regulation." *American Journal of Play* 3, no. 4: 464–488.

National Education Association. 2015. "Indicators of Future Success: GPA and Noncognitive Skills." NEA Educational Policy and Practice Department. Washington, D.C.: National Education Association.

Saracho, Olivia, and Bernard Spodek. 2003. *"Contemporary Perspectives on Play in Early Childhood Education."* Charlotte: Information Age Publishing.

Veiga, Guida, Carlos Neto, and Carolien Rieffe. 2016. "Preschoolers' Free Play—Connections with Emotional and Social Functioning." *International Journal of Emotional Education* 8, no. 1:48–62.

Continuing Education Resources
for Librarians Serving Homeschoolers

Bobbie Bushman *and* Jenna Kammer

Who Are Your Homeschooling Patrons?

Homeschooling is a movement. As such, it is constantly changing and evolving. Homeschooling itself is on the rise (National Center for Education Statistics 2012, fig. 2). What used to be a fringe movement made up of mostly evangelicals, homeschooling has become a choice for families of all races, beliefs, incomes, and worldviews. Part of being informed about homeschoolers and their needs is learning more about the homeschooling population and becoming more aware of the diversity within the homeschooling community as well as the worldviews, homeschooling approaches, and leaders within homeschooling.

Many people associate homeschoolers with the conservative Christian movement, but that assumption is no longer correct. A librarian cannot assume that homeschoolers want Christian fiction, young Earth creationism, or any other worldview-specific information. Only 64 percent of homeschoolers listed providing religious instruction as an important reason for homeschooling (National Center for Education 2012, table 3). This means that throughout the last decade, secular homeschoolers, or those who homeschool for non-religious reasons, comprise the remaining 36 percent of homeschoolers. In the most recent NCES 2015–6 survey, findings indicated that the percentage of parents who homeschool for religious reasons is declining, while the majority of parents choose to homeschool because of concerns about the academic or public school system (McQuiggan and Megra 2017). This survey also indicated that the parents of homeschoolers are highly diverse, ranging in levels of education, income, race and spoken language. Homeschoolers are a diverse group of people from unique backgrounds, religions and political views.

The uniqueness of the homeschooling population is an opportunity for librarians to address homeschoolers as a special population within the library. Grover, Greer, and Agada (2010) describe how librarians can better serve diverse populations by getting to know the unique needs of specific communities or user groups through conversations and relationship development. Specifically, they suggest that librarians "get to know their clientele" by making efforts to solicit feedback from specific user groups to understand the information needs of that group. In addition, participating in community events or meetings is another way that librarians can understand more about the information needs of specific populations within their community. In this essay, we propose using this strategy with the homeschooling population and present several areas that can help librarians learn more about the homeschooling community.

Assessing the information needs of specific groups is one strategy that librarians can use to learn more about the homeschooling population in their community (Grover, Greer and Agada 2010). Once a group has been identified, Grover, Greer and Agada recommend that the librarian learn more about the types of meetings, sources of information and the implications for library services that are related to this group. This essay presents the foundation for assessing the information needs of homeschoolers within your library: we provide an overview of the approaches, worldviews and leadership of the homeschooling community, and perspectives on understanding the complexity of these attributes within the homeschooling population. In addition, specific, practical suggestions are presented to lead librarians through the process of learning more about the needs and desires of the homeschooling community.

Connecting with the Homeschool Community

As a community partner, the public library is often a hub for homeschoolers as it provides a meeting space for co-ops, programming and many useful resources for teaching and learning. Learning about specific homeschool approaches can help librarians understand more about this population. Connecting with these parents provides librarians with an opportunity to learn more about the community, while also developing relationships that can guide collection development, programming, and services.

Librarians can use surveys or qualitative methods to collect information about the homeschooling community in their area. In addition to talking to homeschooling families who visit the library, librarians can reach out to homeschooling groups through social media or email. Homeschooling groups or coops often have listservs or Facebook groups that the librarian can use to reach out to this population. Diaz (2016) describes how one public library surveyed their homeschooling groups to find out more about the needs of the homeschoolers in their area. The survey asked homeschooling families for their interest in curriculum materials and catalogs, math and science manipulatives, software, workshops and computer instruction. The results of the survey were analyzed and used to develop a "homeschooling resource center" that included science kits, curriculum resources to "try before you buy," games and software. Other public libraries offer programming specifically for homeschooling teens and tweens related to the needs of the group. One public library referenced themselves as "their [homeschoolers] school library" since the library space serves as a central meeting point for homeschooling groups, designs programming for them, and also provides current curriculum resources (para. 27). Diaz also describes how homeschooling families may spend up to $1000 on curriculum for their children and the library can offset these costs. Bruno (2017) also provides a guide for homeschooling parents on how to save money on homeschooling by using public library resources including its physical and digital resources (that often make exceptions to due dates and late fees for homeschoolers), makerspaces, community spaces, and programming (including programming specifically for homeschoolers).

The American Library Association maintains resources for librarians to learn more about working with homeschoolers, as well as provides programming for librarians on working with homeschoolers. In August of 2018, Suzanne Walker from the Indiana State Library offered a workshop titled, "Making Your Library Work for Homeschoolers" through ALA (ALA Member News 2018). ALA also hosts the "Homeschooling Resources for Librarians" page as a supplement to their "Resources for Children's Librarians and Educators" page (ALA 2019). In addition, *American Libraries* magazine has featured several articles on serving homeschoolers in the past (see Abby Johnson's column on youth in libraries). When attending an ALA or state library conference, a librarian can check for presentations related to working with homeschoolers or attend presentations by youth librarians who will often share how their practice involves working with homeschoolers. The ALA bookstore also has a book about helping homeschoolers in the library (ALA 2019).

Attending a homeschool conference (or presenting at one) is an excellent way for a librarian to learn more about the homeschooling community, the resources they use or need, or to make the homeschooling community aware of how the public library can offer homeschooling support. Not only will attending a homeschool conference help librarians understand the needs of homeschoolers better, they will be educating themselves on the wide offerings of homeschool curriculum and classes. Homeschool conventions can be labeled as Christian, Christian-based, inclusive, secular, or education-focused. Some of the major homeschooling conferences include the Great Home School Conventions (Christian-based) or the Secular Eclectic Academic Homeschool Convention (secular), and many state or regional conferences, like the Florida Homeschool Convention, the Washington Homeschool Organization, or the Wisconsin Parents Association. A librarian can attend the classes offered at these conferences for new homeschoolers and inquire about whether there is someone who'd like to lead such an event regularly at the public library. A librarian can also submit a proposal to give a presentation about library resources for homeschoolers or ask to host a library booth in the homeschool exhibit hall. Either option will be an excellent way for a librarian to showcase library resources for homeschoolers and connect with local homeschoolers. When connections are made at the homeschooling conference, a librarian would be utilizing those to gain information about potential programs, resources, volunteer opportunities that homeschoolers may wish to see offered at their local public library. Librarians can also collaborate with homeschool parents and co-op leaders to offer programs and resources for specific homeschooling groups such as a new parent homeschooling class, curriculum support for co-op classes, or other learning or social activities to support homeschoolers.

For librarians, the vendor hall of a homeschooling conference may also be a useful forum for learning more about what resources are trending for homeschoolers and provide opportunities to meet the major vendors that market to homeschoolers. Hosting a vendor booth on behalf of the public library and presenting are two additional ways to make the library's homeschooling resources known to homeschooling families in attendance. The vendor hall of a homeschooling conference will include authors of homeschool curriculum, publishers of print and electronic resources, new technologies (like virtual reality), and online providers. Talking with vendors will also help the librarian to make collection development decisions, or become more informed about the resources that are available. Gallagher (2018) describes how building healthy relationships with vendors can strengthen professional knowledge and working relationships that will have benefits for library users. Homeschooling parents often use the vendor hall for this exact opportunity: to scout new and relevant learning resources that will support their child's curriculum, as well as make connections should they decide to purchase the resources later (Sabol 2018).

Librarians can also connect with homeschoolers on social media. There is also a vast network of homeschool bloggers who provide ideas, resources, and insight into the practice of homeschooling. Homeschool bloggers can help orient librarians to which homeschool conferences are most relevant to them. For example, "This Crazy Homeschool Life" (Christian based) is a blog that maintains a list of homeschool conventions around the world and their affiliations (2018). Secular, Eclectic, Academic (SEA) Homeschoolers maintains a list of secular bloggers that are vetted through the organization (https://seahomeschoolers.com/blog/secular-bloggers/). To determine the affiliation of the blogger, librarians should examine the blog posts to determine if the blogger's philosophy is religious or secular.

Requirements for homeschoolers vary from state to state. While some states require parents to report their intention to homeschool, some do not. Some states will require that parents submit portfolios of student learning, while others have no oversight at all (Karinen 2016). Some states require yearly testing and others do not. The librarian can learn more about homeschool state laws and may want to have a ready reference guide available for those parents who ask about homeschooling. State homeschooling laws are unique and generally fall into one of four categories of legal oversight: no notice, low regulation, moderate regulation and high regulation (HSLDA). The Homeschooling Legal Defense Association represents the Christian faction of homeschoolers and is the major lobbying resource for homeschool policies, laws, and regulations, as well as advocacy resources related to homeschool law (Karinen 2016). Their website offers a variety of resources for those with an interest in homeschooling, including alerts, electronic newsletters and an issues/resources library (https://hslda.org/).

How Worldviews Influence Tools, Resources and Information

Homeschooling needs vary from family to family. No two homeschoolers are the same, and homeschoolers tend to be independent in their views and life choices, as evidenced by their decision to homeschool. Knowing a homeschoolers' worldview may provide insight into their homeschooling needs. Secular and religious homeschoolers, for example, are likely to make different choices around science information and curriculum. Religious homeschoolers may subscribe to a young Earth worldview or may teach evolution. Some religious homeschoolers may choose to keep religion and science or history education separate. Secular homeschoolers are more likely to seek science and history information including evolution. Librarians can ask about worldview when conducting readers' advisory interviews to best help homeschoolers select materials to support homeschooling curriculum.

Secular homeschoolers are people who are homeschooling for reasons other than religion. These homeschoolers may or may not identify as religious. For example, a homeschooler may identify their family as Christian but also as secular homeschoolers because they homeschool for academic rigor rather than homeschooling for religious reasons. Sometimes secular homeschooling is synonymous with inclusive homeschooling, with secular homeschoolers seeking inclusive, diverse, and/or scientific information, as opposed to requiring that all materials agree with their worldview.

While some homeschool curriculum will incorporate religious verses into all subjects, including math and English, it is science and history where homeschooling parents are most divided with regards to worldview. Parents must decide where the history timeline will begin and which topics science will cover, and this is usually consistent with religious vs. secular homeschoolers, with religious homeschoolers omitting evolution and choosing a history timeline that begins with creation and incorporates events from scripture. However, sometimes, science curriculum will take a third approach: the neutral worldview, which is neither Creationist nor Evolutionist. Evolution and references to creation will both be omitted in neutral worldview curriculum. Real Science-4-Kids is one example of a science curriculum provider with a neutral worldview. Examples of Christian publishers are Bob Jones, Abeka, Sonlight, Accelerated Christian Education, and My Father's World. Secular publishers include Calvert, Bookshark, Oak Meadow, and Moving Beyond the Page.

Key Figures in the Homeschooling Movement

Homeschoolers may be seeking information about their chosen method of homeschooling. While this may mean learning about different homeschooling approaches such as Classical, Unschooling, Waldorf, etc., it is also likely that homeschoolers will be seeking books and resources written by key figures in the homeschooling movement. John Holt, John Taylor, Gotto, Charlotte Mason, Raymond and Dorothy Moore, and Susan Wise Bauer are just a few key figures in the homeschooling movement. A good homeschooling library collection is going to feature books by such leaders in the homeschooling movement and will further build their collection based on input from their homeschooling patrons. Often certain subgroups of homeschoolers are more likely to use information from key figures. For example, the Moores are Seventh Day Adventist (SDA), and their homeschooling and child rearing philosophies are promoted by the SDA church. John Holt and John Taylor Gatto are leaders of unschooling and attachment parenting movements. Charlotte Mason is important for homeschoolers who follow a literature-based approach, whether using formal Christian literature-based curriculum like Ambleside Online, Sonlight, or My Father's World, formal secular curriculum like Bookshark or Build Your Library (Secular), or creating their own, or designing a personal literature-based curriculum using library books. Lastly, Susan Wise Bauer is the leader of the modern classical homeschooling approaches and has written curriculum such as the *Story of the World*.

Promoting Specialized Knowledge for Homeschoolers

Librarians are also able to support the specialized needs of homeschooled children. Homeschooled children are not limited to the public school curriculum and often seek out nontraditional learning experiences. This means that their parents organize many types of learning activities for them and will often encourage their children to learn a trade, a language or pursue other unique opportunity that aligns with the child's interest (Thomas 2018). Librarians can participate as partners with parents by providing events related to trades, apprenticeship information, resources for college or technical school, or access to online learning programs. Homeschoolers may prefer alternatives to the traditional college experience because homeschooled families are typically larger, thus making college for each child more expensive. Homeschoolers are used to educating themselves, so they have a clearer picture of what they want to do at an early age. Some homeschoolers may also have a worldview that discourages college life and prefers to see children start adult living at an earlier age (by getting married, gaining financial independence earlier, etc.). Whatever the reason, libraries can offer support by showcasing programing or resources around learning a trade, bring in guest speakers as part of a series, or otherwise offer programming to introduce homeschooled children to future careers that don't require a four-year degree.

Teens who attend public high school usually have an opportunity to attend a college day where colleges come and speak to them about college preparation, college life, and college applications. Homeschoolers, on the other hand, must locate these opportunities themselves and seek their own resources for college preparation materials such as ACT or SAT books or free online test practice. Since libraries provide many test preparation materials, curating them for homeschoolers, with or without collaboration from local colleges, can offer homeschoolers a similar college day opportunity. In addition, collaboration between the high school and public library may help librarians become aware of the college or career events at high school that benefit homeschoolers as well. Nelson and Dwyer (2015) discuss the value of public and school library collaboration for sharing information about the community and populations at each institution. In addition, school and public librarians can collaborate on professional development or grant writing opportunities, which can secure more resources that are relevant to traditional and homeschooled college-bound students.

The growth in online learning has been very beneficial for homeschoolers. Homeschooled students can receive high school or college credit by taking online classes and will often be able to take classes online that are not offered locally. For example, the Missouri Virtual High School offers an online Chinese language course to traditional and homeschooled students but does not teach it within the brick-and-mortar high school (Takata 2018). Hundreds of colleges, including schools like MIT, Harvard, and Stanford, offer open courseware courses, which are non-credit, free college courses (Open Education Database 2019). Homeschooled high schoolers can utilize these courses for high school credit. Librarians can provide a list of online learning resources to homeschooled students. Since homeschooled students often learn above grade level, access to K–12 online learning, as well as adult level online learning is essential.

Partnering with Local Homeschool Groups

Homeschool groups may learn certain subjects together on a regular basis, like a class, or may just take social or educational trips together to places like parks, libraries, and museums. Supporting cooperatively learned topics can be an effective way for libraries to build programming for homeschool groups. Designing a program or developing resources for an existing group provides a built-in audience for that programming or resource. Other homeschoolers will likely also utilize the service or program a librarian developed for that specific group.

One way to make contact with homeschoolers, is to be the first point of contact for them. Hosting a monthly new homeschoolers class or event is one way to accomplish this. With the help of a veteran homeschooler, a librarian can offer a presentation about homeschooling resources, homeschooling laws, an advice from a veteran homeschooler including tips for getting started, and a Q & A period. This new homeschooler meeting can be as formal or informal as a librarian dictates. It can be set up as a one-time class or can be more of a support group where new homeschoolers can come back with new questions and challenges.

Getting to know homeschooling patrons who visit the public library is probably the best way for librarians to locate homeschooling groups in their area. They can begin by asking homeschooling patrons about their needs for library programming (whether instructional or social). Librarians can ask to be connected with the leader of local home-school co-ops to collaborate building a strong homeschooling presence at the public library. Furthermore, librarians may want to facilitate programs specifically for that group, programs advertised for homeschoolers in general, or programs that are inclusive to all patrons.

If librarians are looking for homeschoolers outside of the library setting (they either aren't coming in or librarians can't connect with those who do), there are several ways to make initial contact and market programming to homeschoolers. Librarians can begin by searching online for homeschooling groups in their area and checking if there are several homeschooling co-op lists available. Homeschool Advocate groups such as the Homeschool Legal Defense Association (HSLDA) have a searchable database of home-school groups based on location. Facebook is another tool librarians can utilize to find homeschool groups by searching the city's name and the word homeschool. One thing to be aware of, though, is if the homeschool group account is set to be private, librarians will not be able to locate it with a search. Once librarians have become accepted members of the homeschool group they can pose questions to the group about needs, advertise programming, resources, and other library events as group rules allow. Librarians will also be able to use the group to learn more about what homeschoolers are doing, other groups they participate in, and where possible needs/gaps may be. This can be a great source of information for librarians about the needs of homeschoolers and ways to meet those needs through collection development, library resources, and programming.

When a librarian is creating homeschool programming, scheduling can be an obsta-cle to inclusiveness. Many homeschoolers have schedules busy with activities, group classes, co-ops, and lessons. Therefore, hosting the program on days and times that con-flict with the most popular homeschool activities may cause a low turnout. Likewise, a librarian should be mindful that homeschoolers often are able to attend programming in the daytime hours when other children are in school and afterschool activities. Sched-uling during daytime hours can be a way to utilize youth areas, collections, and staff that otherwise are largely unutilized in daytime hours.

Librarians can develop a homeschool resource center as a way to attract more home-schoolers, announce to the homeschooling community that the library is eager to serve them, or just to expand homeschooling service. Not only will a homeschool resource center serve as a reference area for staff to educate themselves about homeschooling practices, but it will also allow homeschoolers access important information (Faulconer 2014), while announcing to the community that your library focuses on serving home-schoolers. The Johnsburg Public Library District (Illinois) received $55,000 in 2001 to create a homeschool resource center. Other libraries have quickly followed suit, with homeschool resource centers being advertised on websites such as Pendleton, IN, St. Charles, IL, Manchester, CT, and Lakewood, OH (Homeschool Resources, Manchester 2018; Homeschool Resources, Pendleton 2018; Homeschool Services 2017). These are just a few of the libraries that advertise programs, services, and resources for homeschoolers on their websites.

Conclusion

Librarianship is a field that is constantly evolving. Homeschoolers constitute a group that is growing and changing. Librarians must continually learn about new technology, resources, and groups within their communities to best serve homeschoolers as well as other library users. Librarians can establish themselves as experts in certain areas so that communities think of the library first as a resource for homeschooling. To do this, librarians must stay abreast of the issues and topics that are important to homeschoolers. Knowledge of homeschooling resources, conferences, key figures in the homeschooling movement, local co-ops, training resources offered by ALA, and the needs of the local homeschooling community is essential for a librarian wanting to better serve homeschoolers. Librarians can assist homeschoolers by building collections, homeschool resource centers, and programming around the need of the local homeschooling community.

Works Cited

ALA Member News. 2018. "New Session: Making Your Library Work for Homeschoolers Workshop." http://www.ala.org/news/member-news/2018/06/new-session-making-your-library-work-homeschoolers-workshop.

American Library Association. 2019. "Homeschooling Resources for Librarians." http://www.ala.org/Template.cfm?Section=childrens&template=/ContentManagement/ContentDisplay.cfm&ContentID=90419.

Bruno, Tom. 2017. "Homeschool Resources That Extend the Curriculum and Build Community. EveryLibrary." https://medium.com/everylibrary/homeschool-resources-that-extend-the-curriculum-and-build-community-1dba830c799b.

Bushman, B. 2017. "Library Services and Early Literacy Approaches in Public Libraries for Deaf and Hard of Hearing Children." *The International Journal of Information, Diversity & Inclusion*, 2(1/2), ISSN 2574-3430, publish.lib.umd.edu/IJIDI/.

Diaz, Eleanor. 2016. "Public Libraries Welcome Growing Homeschool Community." *Programming Librarian.* http://programminglibrarian.org/articles/public-libraries-welcome-growing-homeschool-community.

Faulconer, J. 2014. "Thirteen Ways to Help Your Library Help Homeschoolers." *The Homeschool Mom.* April 18. https://www.thehomeschoolmom.com/be-a-homeschool-library-liaison/.

Gallagher, Erin. 2018. "What Collaboration Means to Me: Perspectives on Library/Vendor Collaboration." *Collaborative Librarianship* 10 (1): 7–12.

Grover, Robert, Roger C. Greer, and John Agada. 2010. *Assessing Information Needs: Managing Transformative Library Services.* ABC-CLIO.

Homeschool Resources 2018. *The Official Website of the Town of Manchester, Connecticut.* http://library1.townofmanchester.org/index.cfm/homeschooling-resources/.

Homeschool Resources. 2018. *Pendleton Community Library.* https://www.pendleton.lib.in.us/children/homeschool-resources.

Homeschool Services 2017. *St. Charles Public Library.* https://www.scpld.org/homeschool-services.

HSLDA. n.d. "Homeschooling Laws in Your State." Accessed Jan 7, 2019. https://hslda.org/content/laws/.

Johnson, Abby. 2012. "Make Room for Homeschoolers." Accessed Jan 5, 2018. https://americanlibrariesmagazine.org/2012/04/23/make-room-for-homeschoolers/.

Karinen, Jennifer. 2016. "Finding a Free Speech Right to Homeschool: An Emersonian Approach." *Georgetown Law Journal 105* (1): 191.

McQuiggan, Meghan, and Mahi Megra. 2017. "Parent and Family Involvement in Education: Results from the National Household Education Surveys Program of 2016. First Look. NCES 2017–102." *National Center for Education Statistics*. https://nces.ed.gov/pubs2017/2017102.pdf.

National Center for Education Statistics. 2012. "Homeschooling in the United States: 2012." *Institute of Education*. https://nces.ed.gov/pubs2016/2016096rev.pdf.

Nelson, J. T., & Dwyer, J. I. 2015. "What the Public Librarian Wishes the School Librarian Knew." *Children & Libraries, 13*(4), 26–27.

Open Education Database. 2019. "Explore Open Course: Choose from Over 10,000 Free Online Classes." https://oedb.org/open/.

Sabol, Joseph Michael. 2018. "Homeschool Parents' Perspective of the Learning Environment: A Multiple-Case Study of Homeschool Partnerships." ProQuest Dissertations Publishing.

Takata, Kristin. 2018. "Public Schools Would Have to Pay for Private Virtual Schools Under New Missouri Plan." St Louis Post Dispatch. https://www.stltoday.com/news/local/education/public-schools-would-have-to-pay-for-private-virtual-schools/article_ce678cd5-e7d5-5cdb-b579-65e9c39fedb5.html.

Thomas, Richard M., II. 2018. "Homeschool Students and Their Perception of Their College Success." ProQuest Dissertations Publishing.

Supplementing Education and Facilitating Relationships Through Role-Playing Games

Michael P. Buono

Homeschooling and Libraries

Role-playing games (RPGs) are valuable tools for customizing educational experiences for students. For professionals serving homeschool families, RPGs provide a framework for experiential learning that meets adolescents' developmental need for socialization and play. Role-playing games allow adolescents to fulfill developmental needs in a safe and acceptable way and also help forge friendships that last a lifetime.

When I started playing *Dungeons & Dragons* (*D&D*) at twelve years of age, I didn't know any of this. All I knew was what my friend told me, that I could play an elven thief, and I could steal treasure from an evil king. At that time, I was what people called a reluctant reader. Playing *D&D* opened my eyes to a new genre and to the many expansive worlds contained in books. Many of the books I read had tie-ins to games or they inspired the game scripts I wrote and which I facilitated for my friends. Before I graduated from high school, I had already written thousands of words of game planning documents, either preparing for games or playing them online.

Before we get into the details, there are some important questions that must be answered. What is the role you (a library professional) are meant to play? Is the library supplementing its formal education efforts with a more playful opportunity that focuses on specific topics? Are you helping the homeschoolers get more peer contact time? Did you notice that they come to the library to complete their studies, and you want to provide them with entertainment after the fact? How old are the homeschoolers you are serving? Who wants you to do this, the parents or the kids? How much time do you have with them and how often?

Why Choose Role-Playing Games?

Role-playing games are enjoying a comeback. New media companies such as Geek & Sundry, or Alpha, have debuted massively popular shows that are called "actual plays."

The entire show content consists of people playing a role-playing game. In *Titansgrave: The Ashes of Valkana* (https://geekandsundry.com/shows/titansgrave/), Will Wheaton runs a game for a group of voice actors using the system *Fantasy Age* by Green Ronin. In the landmark podcast/video series *Critical Role*, Matt Mercer leads a group of voice actors in a game using the system *Dungeons & Dragons Fifth Edition* by Wizards of the Coast. *Critical Role* is so popular that they have done several live shows in 2018 in large venues. The cost of the tickets can range from $60 to $250. *Critical Role* and *Titansgrave: The Ashes of Valkana* are professionally produced and lovingly crafted entertainment properties, but there are hundreds if not thousands of amateurly produced examples of what playing these games is like. This resurgence increased awareness of what the games actually are and how they are played.

What is a role-playing game? It is a game where players take on roles they create to tell a collective story of which they are not fully in control. In most role-playing games there is usually a "Dungeon Master" (DM), someone who "runs" the game and is responsible for the larger world. The other players take on the roles of individual characters in that world, and their actions are at the center of the story. The lack of control is usually represented by dice rolls that affect the outcome of actions taken both by the players and the Dungeon Master.

While capitalizing on their popularity is a sound enough reason on its own, there is real learning value to these games. In the world of education, a number of frameworks have recently captured widespread attention. Common Core and P21® are better known frameworks which have a lot in common. Both focus on the use of interdisciplinary content in core subjects to enhance students' understanding of the world. In the Common Core, the use of interdisciplinary content is woven into the standards for math, reading, and the anchor standards. Teachers are encouraged to interweave economic and political reading into English Language Arts (ELA) or mathematics. They can use fiction to illustrate points in social studies and science. Recently, the P21® framework and the organization behind it became part of Battelle for Kids, http://www.battelleforkids.org/. This is a new non-profit aimed at encouraging 21st century learning.

"The Future of Library Services for and with Teens: a Call to Action" is a report published by YALSA that outlines how we can fundamentally shift many of the things we already do to be more beneficial for teens. Its educational emphasis is on expanded literacies, similar to Common Core, but it focuses specifically on the role the library can play in the development of those literacies. Digital literacy is specifically called out in the YALSA report as a vital mission of libraries. Role-playing games are a great launching point for many endeavors that will help homeschoolers develop better digital literacy skills (Braun et al. 2013).

Some frameworks will eventually disappear, but they are important to review. Education is constantly evolving, and the implementation of the frameworks can vary widely between states. So why should we care? Because it's only by recognizing and incorporating educational frameworks as outlined by the state that we can properly advocate for and fund programming. You are much more likely to get money for supplies, a 3-D printer or money to pay a dungeon master if you can show how your program serves homeschoolers and meets state standards.

Tabletop role-playing games present a natural fusion of different academic disciplines. Fundamentally, a role-playing game involves adopting the role of a character that is part of a larger plot with randomness frequently represented by a dice roll. Game rule books often suggest fiction to inspire play. They offer blocks of text describing fictional economies, social issues, and politics in a manner similar to a textbook. The games rely heavily on probability, and the text presents ways players can alter probability to increase their chances of success. Teachers, schools, and the publishers of these games have begun investing time and money into adapting them for the classroom. Many game-based lesson plans are available online, but games are at their "funnest" when teachers and students create a personalized story together. Adolescents crave shared experiences, boundary-pushing experiences, and a sense of control. They tell stories to assert their identity and to build credibility among their peers. The educational use of role-playing games fundamentally changes the experience of young people in the learning environment, making it to be inherently about them rather than what is expected of them.

Considerations for Use with Homeschoolers

There are many reasons children are homeschooled. Parents can choose to have their children homeschooled for health, religious, or ethical reasons. They can choose to homeschool their children simply because they did not have a good experience in a formal school environment. Before using tabletop role-playing games with homeschoolers, it is vitally important that we understand what the boundaries the parents have for their child. Many games feature characters that wield "magic." This is not magic in the sense of a trick or illusion, but mighty arcane power. Other games might feature violence or uncomfortable political topics. There are many families that might not be comfortable with these features in their students' learning experience.

Before you bring up using tabletop role-playing games with the parents of your students, it is important to understand their sensitivities. This way when you frame the lesson to them, you can present it in a manner consistent with their values. In a group of kids with common values, this might mean designing a game around a work of literature (even a fantastical one) that all the parents find acceptable. For a Christian group, this could be a work by C.S. Lewis. For a group of students with mixed values, the game could focus on the works of Paulson as Roman did or the politics or economy of a fictional world (Roman 2018).

Another consideration is the homeschooling concept the parents have chosen to embrace and your involvement in this process. Before you bring up the idea of using a role-playing game as a part of the child's education, you should try to understand the style of their education. If they spend most of their time taking classes online, then maybe it would be better to run a game that involves a lot of social interaction. If they are in an environment that requires a lot of social interaction, then it might be better to do something focused on action. Even if you don't have a formal role in their education, you want to understand the need you are trying to meet. It will determine the style of the game you run.

The most important consideration is what is fun for the homeschoolers who come into your library. You are running the program for them. The best way to do this is to get to know them. It is a lot like reader's advisory. Many role-playing games are based on or inspired by media, especially books. Pull out the appeal terms for the kind of entertainment the home schoolers consume and try to find something that matches their interests.

Role-Playing Games as Education

Role-playing games are becoming increasingly popular as a part of formal education in the classroom. As teachers adapt them to their environment, lesson plans utilizing role playing are taking on a common format and theme. Some of the strategies they are using are important even if you are not planning on running the game as a formalized education experience.

The common approach to using games in a learning environment consists of four central aspects. Even if we are not participating in the homeschoolers' formal education, these are valuable to running a game more smoothly in our environments.

First, is game simplification. Role-playing games are large and complex. Some games are contained within dozens of published volumes with rules spread across all of them. Games need to be simplified for a traditional classroom environment, and it is recommended that the first games played as part of a homeschool environment be simplified as well (Cook, Gremo, and Morgan 2017; Roman 2018). A standard role-playing session can last from three to six hours. Teachers in traditional environments have much less time to run a game, and they have used RPGs effectively in the classroom. Librarians can typically spend up to two hours running a program, but that time is still short compared to the experience for most games.

The second core aspect of using games in learning is the integration of relevant materials into the game based on specific learning goals. This might seem like an obvious statement, but it is important to do this intentionally to maximize learning gains for students. For ELA, this could mean integrating a short story or story fragment into the game setup, like the site "Teaching with Dungeons and Dragons" does in their ready-made adventure for the survival classic "Hatchet" by Gary Paulson (https://teaching withdnd.com/). Sarah Roman integrates an early chapter from the book into the beginning of the adventure, and the setup she crafts can easily be used in an existing game student are playing or as a standalone (Roman 2018).

Even if you are running a game for pure entertainment, determining the specific thing you intend to accomplish in a session is important to being successful. It could be making use of a specific rule you had not introduced before or it could be the integration of some material you think would be fun. You can incorporate materials from media properties that the teens are drawn to. This builds engagement with program, and it is fairly simple. If they all seem to enjoy *Rick and Morty*, then they'll have more fun if you utilize time/space travel. Since you are not publishing this work, you can pull in the very characters they love without concern over copyright infringement.

The specific learning materials integrated do not need to be focused on abstract concepts. The gaming culture that surrounds tabletop role playing often incorporates the use of props into playing the game. Items such as miniatures to represent characters, maps, and terrain provide opportunities to incorporate 3-D modeling, 3-D design, traditional woodwork, or 3-D printing. This style of learning fits the mission of public libraries (Tanzi 2017).

Librarians can use role-playing games to encourage homeschoolers to experiment in their maker spaces. There are many 3-D printing projects from custom miniatures to terrain that homeschoolers can design. There is also a variety of three-dimensional paper crafts that homeschoolers can make to support their game (Tanzi, 2017). Maybe the most important aspect of the game is that you just have to get them started. Obviously, our personal labor hours are limited, and our libraries may not have the resources to have a librarian run a game every week. For this reason, I never had. However, I ran single session games a few times a year and every time I was able to get our teens interested enough to try and continue running the game themselves. Some of those teens are still playing the game with their friends years later.

The third aspect is whether it is a teacher- or student-led activity. In some cases, role-playing games can provide a great method for the teacher to model-learning. This can easily take the form of a teacher modeling creative writing, research, or communication skills. This is also an opportunity for students to take leadership. They can be assigned to design the game themselves, or the game can be designed to focus on solving a particular problem with minimum interjection from the teacher (Cook, Gremo and Morgan 2017).

One of the key elements of YALSA's "The Future of Library Services for and with Teens: A Call to Action" is the concept of "Librarian as Facilitator" of a teen-led program. Adolescents have been crafting and running their own stories set in fantastical settings for years. The major barrier to being able to play role-playing games for people of all ages is access to other interested people, space, and the materials. These are three elements libraries can easily provide for interested adolescents (Braun et al. 2013).

The fourth aspect of using a game for learning is the debriefing. Debriefing, or post-game review, is a part of many role-playing games, but it becomes more important in the educational setting. This is a time to review learning goals and concepts covered in the game, establish continued use of the game, and to give rewards. This is a good time to verify and reinforce student learning. It is also an opportunity to find out what worked for the students and what did not. If you are using a system of advancement like the one modeled by the one-shot based on *Hatchet*, then this is the time when you would also give out the rewards to students (Roman 2018).

In games that use this reflection period, such as the *Chronicles of Darkness*, the debriefing phase is when the game master discovers if the players are picking up on story elements and analyzes whether they accomplished their characters' goals. This reflection period is vital for keeping the events of the story fresh in the minds of the players; it also provides time for them to socialize over the events in the game.

What RPGs Should I Use?

As I stated earlier, always start by recognizing and respecting the choices of the parents and students. If magic, sorcery, or mythical creatures are not something they are comfortable with, then do not force the issue. Avoid games that feature those things as central parts of their rule set such as *Dungeons & Dragons* or *Dungeon World*.

Even if the values of their families do not present a particular boundary to the use of any game in the classroom, you may still want to use the freedom you have to tailor the game to the tastes of your students. If they enjoy anime or manga, then perhaps you would want to tailor the lessons to incorporate elements from that genre. It becomes even more interesting if they have a common media property or series that they all enjoy, such as when *Twilight* series by Stephenie Meyer had an almost ubiquitous popularity.

There are some games such as *Fiasco* which have very light rules and they do not rely on a single person to keep things going. This is a fun, social, and creative exercise in which you can participate as a player to get the homeschoolers started, but later they can run it without your assistance.

There are games about almost everything. There is the mystery-driven game *Gumshoe* by Robin Laws, and it is perfect if you want to frame the lesson as a mystery. There are a variety of "urban fantasy" games about mythological creatures in the modern age such as *Chronicles of Darkness* by Onyx Path and *Urban Shadows* by Magpie Games. There are games steeped in real world history such as *Sagas of the Icelanders* by Gregor Vuga. There are also game systems that provide you with the tools to create games all of your own such as *Fate Core* by Evil Hat Productions and *Savage Worlds* by Pinnacle Entertainment Group. There are even games officially licensed by media properties such as *Dragon Age, The Witcher* and *Supernatural*. Most of these games can be found on Amazon.com or Drivethrurpg.com, and there is a list on my website, www.michaelp-buono.com/lfg.

What Can Games Teach?

Anything. Really, they can be used to teach anything. They frequently are used in a variety of professional settings to teach adults how to handle specific topics. All those times you were asked to "pretend to be in a role" as part of a training is partially due to the rise of role-playing games in the late 1970s. *Fantasy Football*? You are just role playing as the coach of a football team, and you are using past player statistics to make a judgment about their future performance. Some *Fantasy Baseball* teams have budgets for player salaries. The use of simulation in learning is a well-developed and explored academic field.

Some disciplines will be easier to adapt than others. Skills, such as reading comprehension, basic financial literacy, and vocabulary are easier to teach using role-playing games. This might involve introducing role-playing elements into more traditional activities. You can use a cliffhanger of a book as an opportunity to have the students act out the next scene in small groups, or you can incorporate a fake bank account into your behavior controls.

Abstract concepts such as economic theory, consent, and cross-cultural skills are more difficult to teach. They will require more prep time, and might be better suited for students to learn through multiple interconnected lessons. They may also require you to create your own "house rules" for how the games will function. For example if you wish to simulate a wider economy in *Dungeons & Dragons*, it would be better if you could have the characters travel from city to city seeing how prices change for certain items rather than just telling them "the prices will be different."

Why Is Role Playing Such an Effective Learning Tool?

Role playing is an effective method of teaching for several reasons. One, it allows you to simulate complex theories, such as wider economies, in a controlled environment. Two, it is a form of experiential learning that some need. Three, it lends a sense of stakes to student decisions beyond grades. Stakes are really important for building an emotional connection to a topic. As beings, we always feel more connected to a topic when we know it impacts our life. Many of the topics covered in school may seem disconnected to students, and we can provide students with a sense of attachment to them through games (Cook, Gremo, and Morgan 2017; Roman 2018; TeachingwithD&D.com; Classcraft.com).

Take the example of using *Dungeons & Dragons* to teach economics. Let's say the characters have a long journey from a city to the underground labyrinth where the Minotaur lives. They have to pass through snow-covered mountains at a later point in the journey, and they can only carry so much. In which town do they buy the gear they need to survive? Do they carry heavy furs hundreds of miles on their carriage and slow down their trip? Do they buy them at the foot of the mountain for a premium? This might sound complicated, but the *Dungeons & Dragons Players Handbook* contains prices for a large number of items. The *Dungeon Master's Guide* also provides advice on currency and how to simulate an economy. It provides recommendations on the types of currency that could exist in the game, the price of items and how those prices might change based on location. If participants care about their characters, they will care about the answer.

Now let's look at the example of consent. In theory, it seems like a very simple concept. It's only ok when someone tells you it's ok. However, people have a hard time internalizing it. It is entirely possible to run a game where consent is a central part of the mechanic. In fact, there are many games where players co-create the world. In some games, both players have to agree before the story moves forward. In other games, one player gets to make a decision that changes the reality the other is operating in. The game is a safe environment to explore autonomy and consent away from sex. If handled correctly, it can still have emotional depth for the students when their character is forced by another player to jump into a river from a cliff. You can build dramatic encounters with a villain capable of mind control, and you can force players to attack their friends. You can hold conversations after a game about the use of the power in the game, and you can connect it directly to power abuse.

Finally, as a profession we've been very concerned by representation. The We Need Diverse Books movement while strong is still young. Old attitudes like "if you want to see it in a book, then you should write it yourself" still persist. With a role playing game, you can flip that old pushback on its head. You can allow a student the instant gratification of creating a character that represents them. At first, don't be surprised if it feeds some level of "power fantasy" for them. That's fine, it's developmentally appropriate. Just remember that even if you aren't having them write stories about their characters, they are crafting a narrative from the moment you start your game. They are creating a character that represents themselves. Vin Diesel connects the character Riddick in the *Chronicles of Riddick* back to his adolescence playing *Dungeons & Dragons*. He is working on a movie based on his actual *Dungeons & Dragons* character (Booker 2015).

Many of the lesson plans you find online will focus on adopting a role-playing game or elements of a role-playing game into single lessons. This works great in a school where teachers have administration with specific expectations. That method might not be the best way to utilize role-playing games to teach. Most, but not all games are designed around the idea of a "campaign" or "chronicle." In a campaign, a player takes on the role of a character for a series of interlocking stories that tell a whole narrative. Players spend more time with their characters and therefore they become more attached to them. This adds stakes to the game, because the player really cares about the outcome of the decision.

Even if your main goal is to occupy homeschoolers' time or provide them a social experience, there is value to approaching this as an educational opportunity. First, we are educational institutions. Regardless of the other missions we have taken on, literacy and education are at the core of what we are. Second, the lesson plan layouts are really easy to execute in a short amount of time for people new to role playing. The lesson plan format helps focus the person designing the session, and that increases player investment in short sessions. Even if you use a long narrative campaign over multiple sessions, if each session has a focus, it will help move the story along.

Where Do I Get Started?

If you are unfamiliar with role-playing games, then I would start by watching or listening to an episode or two of *Critical* Role (https://critrole.com/). *Dungeons & Dragons* is the oldest and most popular role-playing game on the market. Matt Mercer is the Dungeon Master of *Critical Role*, and his game is accessible, entertaining, and professionally produced. Just don't expect to be able to run a game like him off the bat.

If you are familiar with role-playing games, then I would start by checking out the *Fate Core System* book available in print and online (Balsera et al. 2013). It's a role-playing system that doesn't have a lot of rules, and it can be made to fit whatever setting you'd like. The game can be obtained directly from the publisher, Evil Hat Productions (https://www.evilhat.com), or through Drivethrurpg.com (Balsera et al. 2013). There is also a lot of fan-made material available for free online, such as one by a fan who created the entire Scooby Gang from *Scooby Doo* to be used with the Fate Core System. You can find the Scooby characters and more on the Evil Hat Productions Wiki (http://evilhat. wikidot.com/community-fate-core-extensions) Paired with the lesson plan format such as the examples on https://teachingwithdnd.com, it can be used effectively to run short/ focused games.

If your homeschoolers are asking you to specifically run *Dungeons & Dragons*, then I recommend for you to start with the basic rules. These are rules Wizards of the Coast (subsidiary of Hasbro, publisher of *Dungeons & Dragons*) created for people unfamiliar with the game to get started right away. You can find those rules on the *Dungeons & Dragons* website (http://dnd.wizards.com/), just search for Basic Rules. You may wish to run a campaign published by Wizards of the Coast, such as *The Curse of Strahd*, the *Temple of Elemental Evil* or *Waterdeep: Dragon Heist*. These campaigns are published as books and e-books, and they contain everything a Dungeon Master needs to run a game.

RPG publishing is a booming business. The major publishers such as Wizards of the Coast released the *Player's Handbook in Print*, PDF, as mixed-media enhanced e-books, as part of a subscription service that incorporates with an online play platform, and to third party applications that do something similar. There is also a large number of boutique publishers who are releasing games that might fit your needs much better than *Dungeons and Dragons*. For this reason, I can't send you to a single link or vendor that carries them all. Standard book distributors likely carry items from Wizards of the Coast, but you will have to go to other vendors like https://www.drivethrurpg.com/ or https://www.indiepressrevolution.com for smaller titles.

Before playing with students, I recommend trying it with your friends at least once. Role-playing games are a lot of fun, and there are new games getting published every month. Even if you aren't interested in *Dungeons & Dragons*, there is a game out there for you. Please feel free to reach out to me for advice and guidance. I have also collected a list of additional games and resources for you on www.michaelpbuono.com/lfg.

WORKS CITED

Backman, Antonio, Chayse Sundt, and Sarah Park Dahlen. 2018. "Asian American Teen Fiction: An Urban Public Library Analysis." *The Journal of Research on Libraries and Young Adults*, 9, 1 (July): 1–22.

Balsera, Leonard, Brian Engard, Jeremy Keller, Ryan Macklin, and Mike Olson. 2013. *Fate Core System*. Silver Spring, MD: Evil Hat Productions.

Booker, Logan. 2015. "Vin Diesel's Next Film Is Based on His Dungeons & Dragons Character." *Kotaku Australia*. Retrieved from: https://www.kotaku.com.au/2015/10/vin-diesels-next-film-is-based-on-his-dungeons-dragons-character/.

Braun, Linda W., Maureen L. Hartman, Sandra Hughes-Hassell, Kafi Kumasi, and Beth Yoke. 2013. *The Future of Library Services for and with Teens: A Call to Action*. Chicago: YALSA.

Cook, Mike P., Matthew Gremo, and Ryan Morgan. 2017. "Playing Around with Literature: Tabletop Role-Playing Games in Middle Grades ELA." *The National Council of Teachers of English* 25, no. 2: 62–69.

Copeland, Teresa, Brenda Henderson, Brian Mayer, and Scott Nicholson. 2013. "Three Different Paths for Tabletop Gaming in School Libraries." *Library Trends* 61 (4): 825–35. https://doi.org/10.1353/lib.2013.0018.

Neglia, Lou. 2018. "How I Use Dungeons and Dragons in the Classroom." *Classcraft*. https://www.classcraft.com/blog/features/how-use-dungeons-dragons-classroom/.

Roman, Sarah. 2018. "One-Shot: Hatchet by Gary Paulsen." *Teaching with Dungeons and Dragons*.

Tanzi, Nick 2017. "Got Game? Programming with RPGs." Presented November 2017 in Saratoga Springs, NY. https://www.slideshare.net/NickTanzi1/got-game-programming-with-rpgs.

About the Contributors

Antonio F. **Buehler** is the founder of Abrome, a K–12 Self-Directed Education learning community in Austin, Texas. He earned a BS in systems engineering from the United States Military Academy, and then served in the U.S. military as an Airborne Ranger qualified Engineer officer. He later received an MBA from Stanford University, which led to a career in finance. Seeking more meaning, he changed his focus to education becoming a middle and high school teacher. He received an EdM from Harvard University.

Michael P. **Buono** is an adjunct lecturer at CUNY Queens Graduate School of Library Science, speaker and a library leader in Suffolk County, New York. He received his MLS in 2012, and his master's in human resources management in 2015. His writing has appeared in *Young Adult Library Services*, *Library Services for Multicultural Patrons: Strategies to Encourage Library Use*, the *YALSA Blog* and *PMLIB.org*. You can read more about him on www.michaelpbuono.com, and you can follow him on twitter @MichaelBuono.

Rene M. **Burress** is an assistant professor and program coordinator of the Library Science and Information Services program at the University of Central Missouri (UCM). She earned a BS in early childhood education from Saint Louis University and MS in library science from UCM. She is a PhD candidate in School of Library and Information Management at Emporia State University. She teaches graduate courses in library science and her research interests include the impact of school librarians on student learning.

Heidi S. **Busch** is an assistant professor and the electronic resources librarian at Paul Meek Library, the University of Tennessee at Martin (UTM). She has worked at UTM for five years; her previous position was head of media services. She worked at Herman B. Wells Library at Indiana University–Bloomington as a serial control operator in Technical Services. She received her MLS from Indiana University–Bloomington in 2009 and also taught special education in Addison, Michigan, for 12 years.

Bobbie **Bushman** is an assistant professor at Emporia State University, where she provides library services to underserved populations, including children with disabilities, deaf and hard of hearing patrons, rural citizens in Uganda, incarcerated patrons, etc. In addition, she speaks at library conferences across the U.S. about how librarians can use research-based methods for creating inclusive programming, building library staff specializations, and diversifying the profession.

Cara **Chance** is the assistant manager at South Regional Library, part of the Lafayette (Louisiana) Public Library system. She received her MLIS from Louisiana State University in 1997 and her MEd from the University of Louisiana at Lafayette in 2007. She has been involved in education as a home educator and as a past faculty member of the University of Louisiana at Lafayette. She is exploring the pedagogy of making and is a core organizer of the Lafayette Mini-Maker Faire.

Meredith **Crawford** earned her MLIS from San Jose State University and was first professionally employed as an archivist before moving to the South. She is a children's librarian still learning the ropes, fingerplays, and latest tween technology gadgets at the Lafayette Public Library, Lafayette,

Louisiana. She is inspired by the families she serves, her fellow library staff members she collaborates with, and the greater community of professionals.

Casey **Custer** is a librarian and instructor at Cedar Cove Community School, where she teaches homeschooled students a love for learning through story time, reading workshops, nature walks, and STEM education. She serves as book club coordinator for her homeschool cooperative and contributes to *Wild + Free*, a magazine for homeschool moms. She lives in Dripping Springs, Texas.

Angiah **Davis** is the assistant branch manager/youth services manager at the Gladys S. Dennard Library at South Fulton with the Fulton County Library System in Atlanta. Her research interests include instructional design, library leadership and management, and professional development. Her memberships include the American Library Association, the Georgia Library Association, and the Black Caucus of the American Library Association. She obtained her MLIS degree from Florida State University and also holds a certificate in instructional design and technology.

Margaret **Dawson** has worked in academic and joint-use (academic and public) libraries. She has an MA in English from Sam Houston State University (Huntsville, Texas) and an MLS from Texas Woman's University (Denton, Texas). Since 2014 she has worked at Texas A&M University–Central Texas (Killeen, Texas) as an outreach and instruction librarian. She has developed programs for university students, their children, and the general public. She presented at the 2017 and 2018 Texas Library Association Conferences.

Amy **Dreger** has been working in children's library services since 2006. She serves as the children's librarian at the Beachwood Branch of the Cuyahoga County Public Library (Beachwood, Ohio). She obtained an MLIS from Drexel University (Philadelphia, Pennsylvania) in 2010. She has been leading a successful homeschool art program at her branch since 2014.

Aviva **Ebner**, PhD, has more than 30 years of experience, from teaching and library services to administration. She is the regional director for A3 Education Group, where she was honored as employee of the year, one of many awards she has earned during her career. She is a credentialed administrator and librarian, adjunct graduate school instructor, and author of more than a dozen books. She has also been an invited speaker at national education conferences on topics ranging from STEAM to media literacy.

Leah **Flippin** is a reference librarian at the Weatherford Public Library in Weatherford, Texas. She received her MLS from the University of North Texas in 2011. She has homeschooled her three children, including a son with autism. She develops programming and resources for the homeschool community residents of Weatherford and surrounding areas. Prior to her career in librarianship, she owned a local music business where she taught students of all ages and abilities.

Vera **Gubnitskaia** is an art fellow at Crealdé School, Winter Park, Florida, with library degrees from Moscow Institute of Culture (Russia) and Florida State University. She has worked in public and academic libraries in Russia and United States, and contributed chapters, coedited collections and created indexes for ALA, Bantam, McFarland, and Rowman & Littlefield. She has published book reviews in *Journal of International Women's Studies*, *Small Press Review*, and the *Florida Library Youth Program Newsletter*.

Barbara J. **Hampton** has been active in the field of gifted and talented education for 25 years, including as library director for Talcott Mountain Academy (Avon, Connecticut). She is an active member and past officer of the Connecticut Association for the Gifted. As an academic reference librarian at Sacred Heart University (Fairfield, Connecticut), she supported students and faculty studying current research and trends in education of gifted and talented students.

Holly S. **Hebert** earned her MLIS from Wayne State University in 2004 and her MSEd-OTL from California State University in 2010. She has worked in public and academic libraries and for a vendor. She is an assistant professor in the Master of Library Science program at Middle Tennessee State University.

Jenna **Kammer** is an assistant professor of library science and information services at the University of Central Missouri. She earned her master's of information resources and library science from the University of Arizona, her MSE in curriculum and instruction with an emphasis in educational technology from New Mexico State University, and a PhD from the University of Missouri. Her research interests are in information practices and sociocultural aspects of information use.

Amy **Koenig**, Library Trustee at the Rolla Public Library in Rolla, Missouri, is a homeschool parent. In addition to serving at the public library, she serves as a board member for the local homeschool athletic association and a local homeschool co-op. She holds an AAS in radiologic technology from Kaskaskia College and a BS in health science from Truman State University. She also owns a small consulting business focusing on radiology information systems.

Nadine **Kramarz** is a reference librarian, Lee County Library System, Fort Myers, Florida, with an MLIS from Drexel University in Philadelphia. She is a member of the American Library Association and was a part of the statewide Pennsylvania initiative, PA Forward, pilot group and earned McBride Memorial Library a Bronze Star as well as a pilot group for Camp Wonderopolis in Berwick, Pennsylvania. She received the 2017 Outstanding Citizen Award from the Columbia/Montour Women's Center for her programs that support their mission.

Jennifer M. **Lyle**, homeschooling mom, was homeschooled herself from ninth grade onward. She obtained a BS in math and computer science from Roberts Wesleyan College, and spent 11 years working in the technology field as a web developer/project manager before moving on to stay home with/homeschool her own children.

Virginia M. **Lyle**, homeschool teacher and primary caregiver for her parents, following the graduation of all her children, obtained a BA in English from Nazareth College of Rochester. Her memberships have included Team Mac, Sea Scouts (BSA), Girl Scouts, Friends of the Macedon Library, NYS LEAH, and Home School Legal Defense Association.

Bridgit **McCafferty** has served as the director of the university library at Texas A&M–Central Texas in Killeen, Texas, for five years. Prior to acting as the director, she coordinated the library's reference and instruction services. She has an MLS from Indiana University in Bloomington, in addition to an MA in literature from Texas A&M University in College Station, Texas. She co-authored *Literary Research and British Postmodernism* (Rowman & Littlefield, 2015).

Paul J. **McLaughlin**, Jr., obtained his Juris Doctorate from the Valparaiso School of Law and his MLIS from the University of Alabama. He has written on legal research pedagogy in the *Legal Reference Services Quarterly* and the impacts of social media on law school librarians and students in the *Reference Librarian*. He has also written on the subjects of international human rights in the *Journal of Medical Law and Ethics* and patient's rights in the *Journal of Legal Medicine*.

Maryann **Mori** has presented at several national library conferences and has been published in numerous titles including *Serving Teen Parents* (Libraries Unlimited, 2011), *Job Stress and the Librarian* (McFarland, 2013), and *Library Volunteers Welcome!* (McFarland, 2016). Formerly the teen specialist librarian for Evansville Vanderburgh Public Library (Indiana) and director of Waukee Public Library (Iowa), she is a consultant for the State Library of Iowa. Prior to becoming a librarian, she spent 15 years homeschooling her six children.

Dianne **Mueller** has served as a reference librarian and liaison to the College of Education at Texas A&M University–Central Texas in Killeen, Texas, for six years. Prior to becoming an academic librarian, she served as a librarian in middle school and high school in Illinois and Texas. She has an MLIS from Dominican University in River Forest, Illinois. She has co-presented at the Texas Library Association Conferences for the past two years.

Casey **O'Leary** is the director of Library Programs & Youth Services at the Mooresville Public Library, in Mooresville, Indiana. She has a bachelor's degree in elementary education, a master's in library science, and a school media specialist certification. She has facilitated homeschool programming at Mooresville Public Library for the last five years, as an instructor and then as a supervisor. She is a conference presenter, a reviewer for *School Library Journal*, and serves on the ALA–Children's Book Council Joint Committee.

Leslie **Paulovich** is an outreach librarian at Robinson Township Library in Pittsburgh, Pennsylvania. She obtained her MLS degree from Clarion University. She is a member of American Library Association, Public Library Association, and Pennsylvania Library Association. In 2017 and 2018 respectively, her library programs, Passport Pals and Zoo Keepers, both received a Best Practices Award for exceptional service to school-aged children, their families, and caregivers from the Pennsylvania Library Association.

Sarah **Polace** is the children's librarian at the Bay Village Branch of Cuyahoga County Public Library (Bay Village, Ohio). She has previously worked at the Parma-South and Maple Heights branches (Parma and Maple Heights, Ohio, respectively). She earned her MLIS from Kent State University in 2007. She has experience leading homeschool programs including book discussions, creative writing programs, and technology programs.

Nancy **Richey** is an associate professor and visual resources librarian for the Department of Library Special Collections, Western Kentucky University, Bowling Green. She has authored two local history books in the *Images of America* book series published by Arcadia Press and one about Kentucky musician, Mose Rager. She is responsible for collection development for the Kentucky Library for Genealogy and Local History, and for providing research assistance and library research instruction to individuals and classes.

Rebecca **Rich-Wulfmeyer** is a branch manager with the Austin Public Library, Texas. She has more than 30 years of experience in information and cultural heritage management working in libraries, archives, museums and records centers in Texas, Colorado, New Mexico, Arizona, and New York. She is an active member of the Austin-area homeschooling community, and she and her husband educate their son.

Cordelia **Riley** is a librarian with the Technical College System of Georgia. Her expertise is serving patrons who are affected by the digital divide and helping those who have learning differences. Her memberships include the Georgia Library Association, Dyslexia on the Southside of Atlanta, and Parents on the Move. As an alumna of both AmeriCorps and AmeriCorps VISTA, she assisted youth with disabilities and those who were academically at risk. She obtained her MLIS from Valdosta State University.

Sarah M. **Sieg**, a youth services librarian at Rolling Hills Library, St. Joseph, Missouri, obtained her MLIS from the University of North Carolina at Greensboro. She graduated *summa cum laude* from Liberty University with a BS in education and a BS in religion. She is a member of the Missouri Building Block Committee. She was homeschooled along with three younger brothers, two of whom have Down syndrome.

Carol **Smallwood** received an MLS from Western Michigan University and an MA in history from Eastern Michigan University. *Librarians as Community Partners: An Outreach Handbook* and *Bringing the Arts into the Library* are among her ALA anthologies. Her library experience includes school, public, academic, special, as well as administration, and library systems consultant. She has also been a public schools teacher.

Jennifer C.L. **Smathers**, the interim library director of Drake Memorial Library, the College at Brockport, was homeschooled through high school. She has an MLS from SUNY at Buffalo and is co-chair of the SUNY Metadata Standards and Policies Committee of the SUNY Libraries Consortium Library Services Platform Migration Project. In 2015 she received the SUNY Chancellor's Award for Excellence in Library Service.

Autumn E. **Solomon** has been cultivating a wealth of program, project, and management experience during the past 20 years through various roles at Seattle Public Schools, University of Southern

California, Los Angeles Public Library, and Washington Talking Book & Braille. She has also worked for private companies as an archivist, and as a project consultant designing library spaces. She is the associate director at Westbank Community Libraries in Austin, Texas, where she guides public services, human resources, and branch operations.

Ruth **Szpunar** has been a part-time instruction and reference librarian with rank of part-time associate professor at DePauw University for 13 years. She also took on an additional role as an information fluency coordinator for the Private Academic Library Network of Indiana (PALNI) in 2014. She received her MLS from Indiana University. She is a homeschool mom of two, has homeschooled for seven years and was also homeschooled herself.

Meghan **Villhauer** works at the Orange Branch of the Cuyahoga County Public Library in Pepper Pike, Ohio. She received an MLIS in 2011 from Kent State University, Kent, Ohio, and began teaching science and geography homeschool library programs in 2015. She co-authored an article entitled "Photographs and Fiction" for the August 2013 edition of *VOYA*.

Clarissa **West-White** is a reference librarian/instructor at Bethune-Cookman University in Daytona Beach, Florida. She has degrees in creative writing, curriculum and instruction, English education and information from Florida State University. She has experience as a middle and high school English teacher, program coordinator, adult literacy director, university department chair, and assistant professor and adjunct at a number of public and private universities in the state of Florida.

Amanda **Wilkerson** is the director of the Urban Teaching Initiatives Project at the University of Central Florida in the College of Community Innovation and Education. Additionally, she has written educational materials and coordinated forums on significant social, pedagogical, and educational equity matters. A prolific social justice advocate and scholar, she serves as guest editor and coeditor guest of a number of annuals. She has also served as the partnership committee chair for the Parramore Innovation Education District initiative.

Index